Lecture Notes in Computer Science 2370

Edited by G. Goos, J. Hartmanis, and J. van Leeuwen

Springer
Berlin
Heidelberg
New York
Barcelona
Hong Kong
London
Milan
Paris
Tokyo

Judith Bishop (Ed.)

Component Deployment

IFIP/ACM Working Conference, CD 2002
Berlin, Germany, June 20-21, 2002
Proceedings

 Springer

Series Editors

Gerhard Goos, Karlsruhe University, Germany
Juris Hartmanis, Cornell University, NY, USA
Jan van Leeuwen, Utrecht University, The Netherlands

Volume Editor

Judith Bishop
University of Pretoria, Department of Computer Science
0002 Pretoria, South Africa
E-mail: jbishop@cs.up.ac.za

Cataloging-in-Publication Data applied for

Die Deutsche Bibliothek - CIP-Einheitsaufnahme

Component deployment : IFIP/ACM working conference ; proceedings / CD 2002,
Berlin, Germany, June 20 - 21, 2002. Judith Bishop (ed.). - Berlin ;
Heidelberg ; New York ; Barcelona ; Hong Kong ; London ; Milan ; Paris ;
Tokyo : Springer, 2002
    (Lecture notes in computer science ; Vol. 2370)
    ISBN 3-540-43847-5

CR Subject Classification (1998): D.2, F.3, D.1, D.3, D.4

ISSN 0302-9743
ISBN 3-540-43847-5 Springer-Verlag Berlin Heidelberg New York

Springer-Verlag Berlin Heidelberg New York
a member of BertelsmannSpringer Science+Business Media GmbH

http://www.springer.de

© Springer-Verlag Berlin Heidelberg 2002
Printed in Germany

Typesetting: Camera-ready by author, data conversion by Steingräber Satztechnik GmbH, Heidelberg
Printed on acid-free paper   SPIN: 10870368   06/3142   5 4 3 2 1 0

Foreword

Deployment is the act of taking components and readying them for productive use. There may be steps following deployment, such as installation or management related functions, but all decisions about how to configure and compose/assemble a component are made at the deployment stage. This is therefore the one opportunity in the software lifecycle to bridge the gap between what the component developer couldn't know about the deployment environment and what the environment's developer couldn't know about the open set of deployable components.

It is not surprising that deployment as a dedicated step gains importance when addressing issues of system-wide qualities, such as coping with constrained resources or preparing for component adaptation and system evolution. Yet, component deployment is still a discipline in its infancy: it became mainstream practice only in the mid 1990s. Much of the best practice impulse originated in products like Microsoft's Transaction Server and its approach to attribute-based programming and later products like Enterprise JavaBeans and now the Corba Component Model. All these address the specific needs of enterprise application servers. However, the potential of the deployment concept goes far beyond this. Deployment can and should touch effectively all truly component-based solutions.

The proceedings of Component Deployment 2002 represent a good cross-section of the gamut of deployment issues. From customization to address resource constraints to reconfiguration of deployed systems and from architecture to design to languages, the avid reader will find some contribution.

Having said all this, it shouldn't go unnoticed that the conference venue is also "always worth a visit".

April 2002   Clemens Szyperski

Preface

The idea of holding a conference on Component Deployment was conceived in Berlin in June 2001. Within a few days, the nineteen people listed overleaf, all leaders in the field, had lent their enthusiastic support to the venture, and agreed to serve on the Programme Committee and executive. The conference was arranged to be co-located with ACM PLDI'02, which for the first time was being held outside the USA. It is fitting that a meeting on component deployment should follow one on programming language design and implementation, as the subjects complement each other extremely well.

In spite of the difficult times which might have discouraged potential authors from travelling to a conference, we received 43 submissions. Of these the majority were from France, Germany, and the United States, with others from Australia, Italy, Korea, Norway, South Africa, Spain, Switzerland, and the United Kingdom.

The members of the Program Committee took their refereeing task very seriously, and wanted to be sure that this very first conference on Component Deployment would set the scene for years to come. It was therefore resolved to have a physical meeting, and we gathered at University College, London on 17 January 2002. Eleven members were at the meeting and were joined for some lively debate and decision-making by three more on an international telephone conference call. Because of the two-day time limitation, we were initially looking for only 15 papers, but the quality and interest value of the submissions was so high, that we decided to select 13 and have 6 more as short papers, to be presented as posters. All the papers are included in these proceedings.

Bertrand Meyer from the Technical University in Zurich graciously agreed to give the keynote address on "From contracts to trusted components", a subject absolutely central to the theme of the conference.

The paper submissions and reviewing process were supported by the START system (http://www.softconf.com). I would like to thank Nigel Horspool for arranging for us to use the system, and for maintaining it at UVic. His support for the conference did not stop there, and he assisted in the organization in numerous ways, with advice and practical help, for which I am very grateful.

I wish to thank the Program Committee members for their selfless dedication and their excellent advice and friendly comments over the past year. Stephan Hermann, my co-chair, was an energetic and hard-working partner, with good insight into the scientific aspects of what we were trying to achieve, and was also a great help with the local organization. I'd like to thank Wolfgang Emmerich for hosting the PC meeting and his assistant Sally Longley for making all the arrangements. My two research assistants Basil Worrall and Kathrin Berg were a great help in advertising the conference and preparing the papers at various stages. I am very grateful to Stefan Jähnichen for offering the support of the Department of Computer Science at TU-Berlin as a command centre for the conference, and for obtaining the financial backing of our sponsors, Daimler-Chrysler and Microsoft. In terms of assistance, Jens Knoop, the Chair of PLDI, has been absolutely invaluable, and without him, we would not have been able to raise the conference to the profile it has managed to achieve.

Last, but by no means least, the most important person in the organisation of this conference has been Doris Fähndrich of TU-Berlin who has single handedly set up and maintained the website, organized all the local arrangements, finances, preparation of the advertising posters, proceedings, and registrations, always cheerfully, and extremely efficiently. Vielen Dank, Doris!

The conference takes place in Berlin, a city of great building projects over the past few years. As we reflect on the beauty, symmetry, and longevity of our surroundings, we can be inspired to develop software that will be as functional, long lasting, and indeed beautiful.

May 2002   Judith Bishop

Table of Contents

An Environment for Building Customizable Software Components

Anne-Françoise Le Meur, Charles Consel, and Benoît Escrig

INRIA/LaBRI, ENSEIRB,
1 avenue du Docteur Albert Schweitzer, 33402 Talence Cedex, France,
{lemeur,consel,escrig}@labri.fr, http://compose.labri.fr

Abstract. Customization often corresponds to a simple *functional cus-tomization*, restricting the functionalities of a component to some con-figuration values, without performing any code optimization. However, when resources are limited, as in embedded systems, customization needs to be pushed to *code customization*. This form of customization usually requires one to program low-level and intricate transformations.

This paper proposes a declarative approach to expressing customiza-tion properties of components. The declarations enable the developer to focus on *what* to customize in a component, as opposed to *how* to cus-tomize it. Customization transformations are automatically determined by compiling both the declarations and the component code; this process produces a *customizable component*. Such a component is then ready to be custom-fitted to any application.

Besides the declaration compiler, we have developed a graphical envi-ronment both to assist the component developer in the creation of a customizable component, and to enable a component user to tailor a component to a given application.

1   Introduction

Re-usability of software components is a key concern of most software architec-tures. An important dimension in re-usability is the ability to customize a com-ponent for a given context. In fact, some software architectures offer a mechanism to deal specifically with customization.

JavaBeans [15] provide such a mechanism. When developing a software com-ponent (*i.e.*, a bean), a programmer can explicitly declare some variables as being the parameters (sometimes named properties) of the component customization. The component's customization parameters represent a precise interface that enables it to be tailored to a target application. Unfortunately, JavaBeans is limited to *functional customization, i.e.,* it restricts the behavior of a compo-nent but does not perform any *code customization*. Code customization aims to exploit the customization values to produce a smaller and faster program by reducing its generality. Such a process is particularly needed in an area such as embedded systems.

Traditionally, the scope of code customization is limited to program frag-ments, not software components. Code customization is commonly programmed

J. Bishop (Ed.): CD 2002, LNCS 2370, pp. 1–14, 2002.

by low-level directives, such as `#ifdef` in the C language [6]. Programs, sprinkled with directives, are transformed by a preprocessor prior to compilation. The eCos configurable OS is a recent, large scale illustration of this approach [5]. Another well-known approach to code customization is the template mechanism of the C++ language. C++ templates were originally designed to support generic programming. But it was realized that this mechanism could also express complex computations to be performed at compile time. This capability has been used intensively to design efficient scientific libraries [14,18].

Relying on the programmer to code *how* to customize a program, as proposed by current approaches, poses a number of negative consequences for a software system: (i) The development process is more error prone because code customization requires the programmer to intertwine two levels of computation – normal computation and code generation; (ii) Testing and debugging are more difficult because tools rarely deal properly with programs that generate programs; (iii) Programs are less readable and more difficult to maintain because they are cluttered with directives.

Also, customizability is limited by the extent to which the programmer is willing to explicitly encode the necessary transformations. For example, in the C++ template approach, not only does the programmer have to implement the generic program but she also has to introduce all the needed versions that can be partially computed at compile time. This situation is illustrated the appendix.

In this paper, we describe the development and deployment of customizable components. Our approach is based on a declarative language to specify *what* can be customized in a component as opposed to *how* to customize it. This approach consists of three main steps shown in Figure 1. In step 1, the programmer groups customization declarations in a *module*, on the side, as the component code is being developed. The declarations define the customization parameters of a component. In step 2, once the components and their associated declaration modules are developed, they are compiled to create a customizable component. This compilation process carries out several analyses to determine *how* to customize the component and to verify that the customization process will be performed as declared. In step 3, a transformation engine takes as input both the customizable component and the user-provided customization values and automatically generates the customized component. Ultimately, the customized component is integrated in a complete application.

We have designed a declaration language in the context of the C language and implemented the corresponding compiler. We have also developed a graphical environment both to assist the component programmer in the process of making components customizable and to enable the component user to create customized components.

We illustrate our approach with the development of a customizable data encoder for Forward Error Correction (FEC) [8]. FEC prevents losses and errors by transmitting redundant information during digital communications (*e.g.*, modems and wireless communications). Because transmission errors are inevitable during data transfer, FEC is a critical operation: it enables maximal data

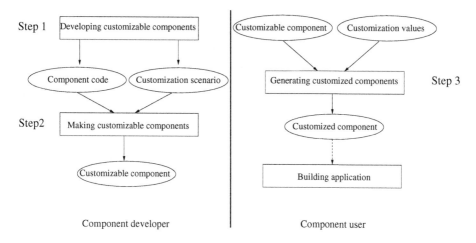

Fig. 1. Developing and deploying customizable components

transfer, using minimum bandwidth, while maintaining an acceptable quality of transmission. A FEC encoder can be customized according to four properties: the encoding method (*e.g.*, parity-bit, cyclic redundancy check), the size of the data block to be encoded, the required size of the resulting encoded data and the generator to produce the redundant data (*e.g.*, a vector, a matrix).

The rest of this paper is as follows. Section 2 details our approach and shows how our declaration language enables a developer to express the customization parameters of a component. Section 3 describes how customizable components are created. Section 4 explains the process of generating customized components. Section 5 compares the performance of customized encoders with both handwritten and generic encoders. Finally, Section 6 concludes and presents future work.

2   Developing Customizable Components

Typically, to make a component customizable, the programmer introduces parameters and some dispatching code to select appropriate behaviors and features. This parameterization also results in the definition of data structures or/and global variables.

Just as the component developer has to reason about the types of the data processed by the code, she should also reason about the customization properties of these data. That is, once the customization parameters have been determined, she should take particular care in how these parameters are used throughout the code.

The developer usually has in mind some *customization scenario* which could apply to a particular component. Indeed, when customizing a component, genericity can often be eliminated when the usage context of the component (*i.e.*, the set of the customization values) is given. To exploit this scenario, current strategies amount to programming *how* the component should be customized.

In contrast, we provide the developer with a high-level declarative language to specify *what* to customize.

2.1 Declaration Module

Following our approach, the programmer specifies customization scenarios in a *module* as a component is being developed. Because these declarations are later compiled and checked to ensure the desired customization, the programmer can write generic code without sacrificing efficiency. The customization scenario of a component defines the context in which the customization of this component is guaranteed. Since the customization aspects of a component are defined in a separate file, they do not clutter the code and can be easily modified. Furthermore, a declaration module allows an application developer to have a readable record of the customization capabilities of a component.

2.2 Intra-module Declarations

Declarations are associated with a given source program and describe the customization scenarios of specific program entities (global variables, parameterized procedures, data structures). These entities represent genericity in the component. Declarations are grouped into a module; they refer to program fragments that form a customizable software component. A program entity that is a customization parameter is said to *static*, otherwise it is *dynamic*.

Let us illustrate our approach with a component of our FEC software system. We consider the `multmat` component which multiplies a vector by a matrix. Intuitively, the vector corresponds to the data to encode, and the matrix to the generator of the redundant data. This matrix (both size and values) is a natural customization parameter because it can be noted that the matrix is fixed for a given encoder. The result of the multiplication should be stored in another vector. Pushing further the analysis, one may observe that more flexibility can be obtain by introducing an index to define where the calculated data are to be inserted in the result vector. Although, this index is not a parameter of the FEC component, it is a good candidate to be a customization parameter of the `multmat` component. The value of this parameter can be set by the callers of this component. Given these observations, the `multmat` component is implemented as follows.

```
void
multMat(int *v_in, int k, int n, int **matrix, int *v_out, int v_out_ind)
{
  int tmp, i, j;
  for(i = 0; i < n; i++)
    {
      tmp = 0;
      for(j = 0; j < k; j++)
        tmp ^= v_in[j] & matrix[j][i];
      v_out[v_out_ind + i] = tmp;
```

```
      }
}
```

Based on our analysis, a customization scenario thus declares the following parameters as static: the size of both the vector and the matrix, the matrix elements and the index in the output vector. Customizing `multMat` for some arbitrarily chosen values produces the following procedure.

```
void
multMat(int *v_in, int *v_out)
{
    v_out[0] = 0 ^ (v_in[0] & 1) ^ (v_in[1] & 0);
    v_out[1] = 0 ^ (v_in[0] & 0) ^ (v_in[1] & 1);
    v_out[2] = 0 ^ (v_in[0] & 0) ^ (v_in[1] & 1);
}
```

To achieve this kind of customization, the component developer writes the following module.

```
Module multmat {
    Defines {
        From multmat.c {
            BtmultMat :: intern multMat (D(int[]) v_in, S(int) k, S(int) n,
                                         S(int[][]) matrix, D(int[]) v_out,
                                         S(int) v_out_ind);
        }
    }
    Exports {BtmultMat;}
}
```

This declaration module, named `multmat`, is associated with the source file `multmat.c`. It defines a customization scenario, `BtmultMat`, which states that the procedure `multMat` can be customized if all its arguments but `v_in` and `v_out` are static (*i.e.*, noted `S`). This declaration includes the keyword `intern` which indicates that the source code of the procedure is available for transformation. Alternatively, a procedure can be `extern` if it is to be handled as a primitive, that is, it can be invoked when all its arguments are static, otherwise the call needs to be reconstructed.

2.3   Inter-module Declarations

Like any module system, our language for declaration modules provides *import* and *export* mechanisms. When writing a module, scenarios from another module may be imported. Similarly, exporting scenarios make them accessible to other modules.

Let us illustrate these mechanisms with the description of a component implementing a linear block coding (LBC) encoder with a systematic matrix. This component provides a procedure `systLBC` that takes two inputs, a vector and a matrix, and computes the encoded vector. This computation simply consists of both copying its input vector in the result vector and adding at the end of the vector the redundant data obtained through the multiplication of the input vector and the matrix. Intuitively, the customization scenario for the procedure systLBC is very similar to the one declared for the procedure multMat, that is, the matrix is a customization parameter. Furthermore, one can notice that if the procedure multMat is called to compute the redundant data, this context satisfies the BtmultMat scenario. Thus, the implementation of the procedure systLBC is

```
#include "multmat.h"
void
systLBC(int *v_in, int k, int n, int **matrix, int *v_out)
 {
  int i;
  for(i = 0; i < k; i++)
    v_out[i] = v_int[i];
  multMat(v_int, k, n - k, matrix, v_out, k);
 }
```

and the declaration module for LBC encoding with a systematic matrix is defined as follows.

```
Module lin_b_code_sys {
  Imports {
    From multmat.mdl {BtmultMat;}}
  Defines {
    From lin_b_code_sys.c {
      BtsystLBC :: intern systLBC(D(int[]) v_in, S(int) k, S(int) n,
                                  S(int[][]) matrix, D(int[]) v_out)
          {needs{BtmultMat;}};
    }
  }
  Exports {BtsystLBC;}
}
```

The keyword **needs** indicates that the invocation of multMat in systLBC satisfies the imported scenario BtmultMat declared in the module multmat.mdl. In fact, a scenario plays the role of a *customization contract* which refers to a precisely defined customization behavior. The customization context requirements specified by this contract are enforced by our analysis phase.

Once all the subcomponents of the encoder component and their associated declaration modules have been developed, they must be compiled to create a customizable component.

3   Making Customizable Components

Like any compiler, the module compiler processes the declarations to detect syntactic or semantic errors. It then verifies that the declarations are coherent with the C source code of the component. For example, it checks that customization scenarios match the type signatures of the associated C entities. The next step is the actual analysis of the component source code. Our analysis phase is automatically configured using information extracted during the module compilation, allowing the appropriate analyses to be carried out. The different analyses determine *how* to customize the component. Meanwhile, verifications are made to guarantee that this customization process will be coherent with the declared customization scenarios. A customization mismatch can either be intra-module or inter-module. In either case, it is caused by a program entity that is used in the wrong context. For example, a global variable that is declared static might incorrectly be assigned a dynamic value. In fact, solving a customization mismatch is similar to handling type problems. Our analysis phase provides the programmer with various aids to track these errors.

To assist the component programmer further, we have built a graphical environment, shown in Figure 2. It consists of a customizable component browser (bottom right corner), a component dependency visualizer (bottom left corner), and a customization scenario browser (top). The developer may use the component browser to access existing modules. When a module is selected, its cus-

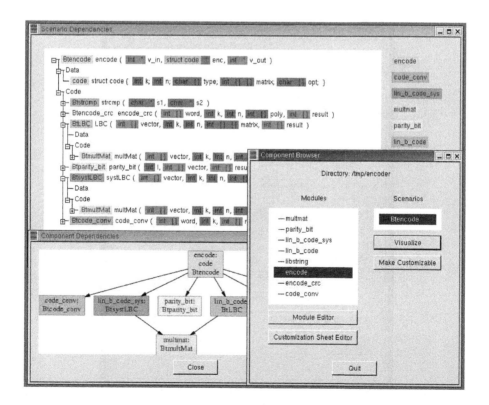

Fig. 2. Component developer interface

tomization scenarios are listed. For a given scenario, the corresponding hierarchy of components is displayed by the component dependency visualizer. This tool allows the developer to rapidly verify whether the component dependencies are as expected. Finer grain information are provided by the customization scenario browser: it shows the tree of sub-scenarios corresponding to a given scenario. The dependencies of a scenario consist of two parts: data and code. The data part groups the scenarios associated with data structures and global variables. The code part lists the required scenarios that are associated with procedures. Starting from the selected component scenario, the developer can recursively visit all the scenarios that are involved. Color-coded information help the developer to see how the customization parameters flow through all the scenarios. Once the developer is satisfied with the declarations, she can make the component customizable for the selected scenario. This action triggers the analysis phase.

Finally to package the customizable component, the programmer uses a customization sheet editor (see Figure 3) through which she gives a high-level description of the customization properties and defines how the user should enter the customization values: they might be typed in, or obtained through a procedure call when dealing with large values. Once the component has been made

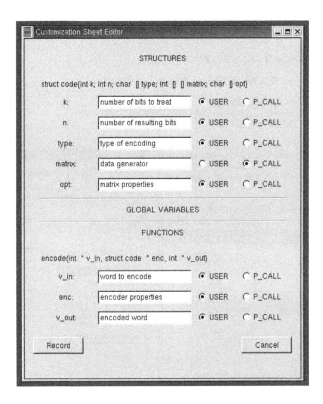

Fig. 3. Component editor

customizable, it can be distributed to component users to be custom-fitted for a particular application.

4 Generating Customized Components

Generating a customized component is performed by a transformation engine that takes two inputs: the customizable component and the customization values. As shown in Figure 4, the user may enter these values by filling in the customization sheet generated by the component developer. The customization process may be repeated as many times as there are customization values, creating each time a specific customized component. Once customized, the component is ready to be integrated in an application.

The transformation engine we use is a program specializer named Tempo [2,3]. Program specialization is an automatic technique that propagates information about a program's inputs throughout the program and performs the computations which rely on the available inputs. In our context, the propagated information is the component's customization parameters. Program specializers have been implemented for languages such as C [1,3] and Java [13], and have been successfully used for a large variety of realistic applications in domains such as operating systems [10,12], scientific algorithms [7], graphics programs [11] and software engineering [9,16,17].

However using a specializer is very complicated if one is not an expert in the domain. Furthermore, specialization was until now only applied to manually-isolated code fragments and offered no support for component specialization. Our approach enables component programmers to benefit from the power of a specializer engine without having to deal with its intricacies.

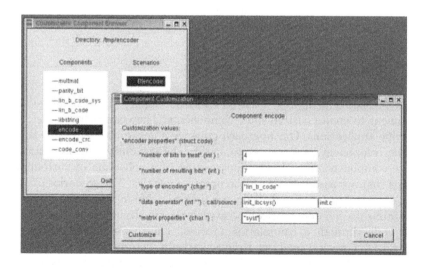

Fig. 4. Component user interface

5   Experimental Study

We have developed a customizable FEC component that covers several encoding algorithms: parity-bit (PB), cyclic redundancy check (CRC), convolutional coding (CONV), and linear block coding (LBC) for both systematic and non-systematic matrices. To assess the performance of the customized encoders, we have compared their execution time with both the execution time of manually written encoders (*e.g.,* hand-customized for a dedicated encoder configuration) and the execution time of the generic encoder.

In practice, FEC encoders are used on data of widely varying sizes, depending on the application. Thus, we have tested our encoders on very different sizes of data blocks, corresponding to real situations. For each encoder, we have measured the time spent to encode one thousand data segments. Our measurements, presented in Figure 5, were obtained using a Sun UltraSPARC 1 with 128 megabytes of main memory and 16 kilobytes of instruction and data cache, running SunOS version 5.7.

The numbers show that the encoders generated through customization are at least as efficient as the encoders manually written. The customized LBC encoder is even 4 times faster than the manually written LBC encoder (see graph 5-d). This speedup is mainly due to code optimization, like loop unrolling and constant folding, performed by our customization process but that are tedious to perform by hand. As expected, the hand-written encoders are more efficient than the generic one. However, the difference is negligible in the CRC case shown in the graph 5-f. This is due to the fact that the inefficiencies in the generic encoder are canceled by the cost of the other calculations that are performed.

We mentioned above that loop unrolling operations were performed. However, it may happen that such transformation is not desired when the number of loop iterations is high. To address such a situation, our declaration language provides a means to easily express constraints on the property value to propagate, and thus to avoid loop unrolling if needed.

6   Conclusion and Future Work

We have presented an approach that provides developers with a language and an environment to create customizable components. They can then be customized for specific applications. Our approach relies on a declaration language that enables the component programmer to specify the customization properties of a software component. The declarations consist of a collection of customization scenarios that are associated with the program entities. The scenarios of a component do not clutter the code; they are defined aside in a module.

Customizable components are created from the declarations and the component code through a compilation process. This phase mainly corresponds to carrying out several analyses to automatically determine how to customize the component accordingly to the declared customization values. Once generated, customizable components can be distributed to be tailored by application

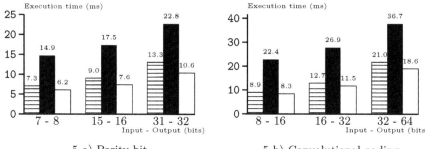

5-a) Parity-bit   5-b) Convolutional coding

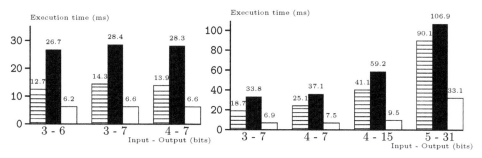

5-c) Linear block coding   5-d) Linear block coding
with systematic matrix

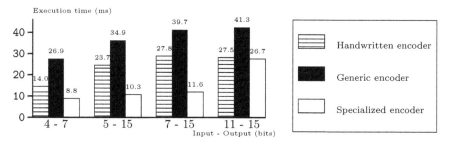

5-e) Cyclic redundancy check

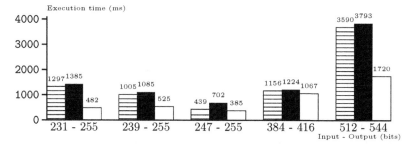

5-f) Cyclic redundancy check

Fig. 5. FEC encoder benchmarks

builders. The component customization values are set through a customization sheet. Besides the language compiler, we have developed a set of tools to assist the developer at each step of the process.

We have applied our approach to create a customizable forward error correction encoder. The customized components generated for various usage contexts have exhibited performance comparable to, or better than manually customized code.

We are now working on a larger scale experiment where our technology is applied to build audio applications from customizable components such as filters, buffers, *etc*. In the near future, we also plan to extend our approach to provide dynamic re-customization capabilities.

Acknowledgments

This work was partially supported by the ITEA project ESAPS.

References

1. L.O. Andersen. *Program Analysis and Specialization for the C Programming Language*. PhD thesis, Computer Science Department, University of Copenhagen, May 1994. DIKU Technical Report 94/19.
2. C. Consel, L. Hornof, J. Lawall, R. Marlet, G. Muller, J. Noyé, S. Thibault, and N. Volanschi. Tempo: Specializing systems applications and beyond. *ACM Computing Surveys, Symposium on Partial Evaluation*, 30(3), 1998.
3. C. Consel, L. Hornof, F. Noël, J. Noyé, and E.N. Volanschi. A uniform approach for compile-time and run-time specialization. In O. Danvy, R. Glück, and P. Thiemann, editors, *Partial Evaluation, International Seminar, Dagstuhl Castle*, number 1110 in Lecture Notes in Computer Science, pages 54–72, February 1996.
4. K. Czarnecki and U. W. Eisenecker. *Generative Programming - Methods, Tools, and Applications*. Addison-Wesley, 2000.
5. Red Hat. eCos : Embedded configurable operating system, 2000. http://sources.redhat.com/ecos.
6. B. W. Kernighan and D. M. Ritchie. *The C Programming Language*. Prentice-Hall, Englewood Cliffs, New Jersey, 1978.
7. J.L. Lawall. Faster Fourier transforms via automatic program specialization. In J. Hatcliff, T.Æ. Mogensen, and P. Thiemann, editors, *Partial Evaluation—Practice and Theory. Proceedings of the 1998 DIKU International Summerschool*, volume 1706 of *Lecture Notes in Computer Science*, pages 338–355, Copenhagen, Denmark, 1999. Springer-Verlag.
8. S. Lin and D. J. Costello. *Error Control Coding: Fundamentals and Applications*. Prentice Hall: Englewood Cliffs, NJ, 1983.
9. R. Marlet, S. Thibault, and C. Consel. Efficient implementations of software architectures via partial evaluation. *Journal of Automated Software Engineering*, 6(4):411–440, October 1999.
10. G. Muller, R. Marlet, E.N. Volanschi, C. Consel, C. Pu, and A. Goel. Fast, optimized Sun RPC using automatic program specialization. In *Proceedings of the 18th International Conference on Distributed Computing Systems*, Amsterdam, The Netherlands, May 1998. IEEE Computer Society Press.

11. F. Noël, L. Hornof, C. Consel, and J. Lawall. Automatic, template-based run-time specialization : Implementation and experimental study. In *International Conference on Computer Languages*, pages 132–142, Chicago, IL, May 1998. IEEE Computer Society Press. Also available as IRISA report PI-1065.
12. C. Pu, H. Massalin, and J. Ioannidis. The Synthesis kernel. *Computing Systems*, 1(1):11–32, Winter 1988.
13. U. Schultz, J. Lawall, C. Consel, and G. Muller. Towards automatic specialization of Java programs. In *Proceedings of the European Conference on Object-oriented Programming (ECOOP'99)*, volume 1628 of *Lecture Notes in Computer Science*, pages 367–390, Lisbon, Portugal, June 1999.
14. J. G. Siek and A. Lumsdaine. The matrix template library: A generic programming approach to high performance numerical linear algebra. In *International Symposium on Computing in Object-Oriented Parallel Environments*, 1998.
15. Java Sun. Javabeans component architecture. http://java.sun.com/products/javabeans/.
16. S. Thibault and C. Consel. A framework for application generator design. In *Proceedings of the Symposium on Software Reusability*, Boston, MA, USA, May 1997.
17. Scott Thibault, Renaud Marlet, and Charles Consel. A domain-specific language for video device driver: from design to implementation. In *Proceedings of the 1st USENIX Conference on Domain-Specific Languages*, Santa Barbara, California, October 1997.
18. T.L. Veldhuizen. Arrays in Blitz++. In *Proceedings of the International Symposium on Computing in Object-Oriented Parallel Environments*, number 1505 in Lecture Notes in Computer Science, Santa Fe, NM, USA, December 1998. Springer-Verlag.

Appendix

Let us consider the function **power** which raises **base** to the power of **expon**. The usual C code of this function looks like:

```
int power(int base, int expon)
{
  int accum = 1;
  while (expon > 0) {
    accum *= base;
    expon--;
  }
  return(accum);
}
```

Now let us suppose that the value of **expon** is known at compilation time. If the value of **expon** is not too large, it is thus interesting to optimize the code by unrolling the loop that depends on it.

Using our approach, the programmer writes the following customization scenario:

```
Btpower :: power(D(int) base, D(int) expon)
          { constraint{ expon : expon < 10; } };
```

which enables the loop to be unrolled if the value of **expon** is less than 10.

Thus, once customized, say for a value of **expon** equals to 3, the code of the power function is:

```
int power(int base)
{
  return base*base*base;
}
```

In C++, if the programmer decides that it is worth to unroll the loop in some cases, she must write, besides the generic code (which looks very much like the C version), yet another implementation of the **power** function. This other implementation explicitly tells the compiler to perform the desired transformations. In this situation, the "trick" is to use the compiler to recursively inline the function **power**. Here is how to do it:

```
template<int expon>
inline int power(const int& base)
{ return power<expon-1>(base) * base; }

template<>
inline int power<1>(((const int& base)
{ return base; }

template<>
inline int power<0>(const int& base)
{ return 1;}
```

This way, the call **power<3>(base)** is successively transformed by the compiler as follows: power<3>(base), power<2>(base) * base, power<1>(base) * base * base, and finally base * base * base.

There exist numerous examples of such situations where the programmer has to write the code to enable the compiler to perform the needed transformations [4].

In our approach, the programmer has just to declare *what* to optimize and does not have to worry about *how* to implement the optimization.

A Contract-Based Approach
of Resource-Constrained Software Deployment

Nicolas Le Sommer and Frédéric Guidec

VALORIA Laboratory, University of South Brittany, France,
{Nicolas.LeSommer|Frederic.Guidec}@univ-ubs.fr

Abstract. Software deployment can turn into a baffling problem when the components being deployed exhibit non-functional requirements. If the platform on which such components are deployed cannot satisfy their non-functional requirements, then they may in turn fail to perform satisfactorily. In this paper we propose a contract-based approach of resource-constrained software deployment. We thus focus on a specific category of non-functional requirements: those that pertain to the resources software components need to use at runtime. Ultimately, our objective is to provide software components with means to specify their requirements regarding hardware and/or software resources, and to design methods and models for utilising this kind of information at any stage of a component's life-cycle. The paper reports the design of JAMUS, an experimental platform we develop in order to support the deployment of mobile software components, while providing these components with guaranteed access to the resources they need. JAMUS implements a contract-based model so as to recognise and to allow for the requirements of components regarding resource access and consumption.

1 Introduction

When deploying software components on a target platform, one can wonder whether the requirements of these components can be satisfied by the runtime environment offered by the platform. Almost any software component exhibits specific non-functional requirements. Such requirements can in turn be categorised, depending on whether they refer to properties such as persistence, fault-tolerance, reliability, performance, security, etc. As observed in [17], "it is obvious that in most practical examples a violation of non-functional requirements can break [components] just as easily as a violation of functional requirements". Hence, if the platform on which a component is deployed fails to meet its non-functional requirements, then the component may in turn fail to fulfil its mission, which usually consists in providing a clearly defined set of services with a certain level of quality of service (QoS). The question of deciding whether the non-functional requirements of components can be satisfied is even more crucial on an open platform, for new components can be deployed on – or removed from – such a platform while other components are running. Dynamically loading or removing a single software component on such a platform may impact dramatically on all the components that share the same runtime environment.

J. Bishop (Ed.): CD 2002, LNCS 2370, pp. 15–30, 2002.

In this paper we focus on a specific category of non-functional requirements, that is, those that pertain to the resources a software component needs to use at runtime. All software components are not equivalent as far as resource access and consumption are concerned. Some components can do very well with sparse or even missing resources, while others require guaranteed access to the resources they need. In order to deal with non-functional requirements pertaining to resource utilisation we propose a contractual approach of resource management and access control. This idea is being investigated in the context of project RASC[1] *(Resource-Aware Software Components)*. This project aims at providing software components with means to specify their requirements regarding hardware and/or software resources, and to design methods and models for utilising this kind of information at any stage of a component's life-cycle.

This paper mostly reports the design of JAMUS, an experimental platform whose development is in progress within project RASC. The JAMUS platform supports the deployment of software components, provided that these components can specify their requirements regarding resource utilisation in both qualitative (eg access rights to parts of the file system) and quantitative terms (eg read and write quotas). JAMUS is actually most specifically dedicated to hosting simple mobile Java components, such as application programs and applets. These could be downloaded from remote Internet sites or received as Email attachments before being deployed on the platform. As a consequence, emphasis is put in JAMUS on providing a safe and guaranteed runtime environment for components of such dubious origin. (" JAMUS" is actually an acronym for *Java Accommodation of Mobile Untrusted Software*. Any mobile component deployed on this platform is considered as a potential threat throughout its execution.)

The remaining of this paper is organised as follows. Section 2 presents the general architecture of the JAMUS platform. It also gives an overview of RAJE, the runtime environment this platform relies on, and whose development is also carried out within project RASC. Section 3 introduces the notion of resource utilisation profile, and it shows how this notion is implemented and used in JAMUS. Resource utilisation profiles are important elements in the platform, as they make it possible to set restrictions on the resources it offers, while specifying the requirements of hosted components regarding these resources. The notion of resource usage profile is thus the key to resource contracting in JAMUS. This specific mission is under the responsibility of a resource broker, whose role and main features are detailed in Section 4. Since the mobile components deployed on the platform are perceived as inherently non-trustworthy, their execution is submitted to a constant monitoring, so that resource access violations can be readily detected and dealt with. Section 5 details the mechanisms that permit this monitoring in JAMUS. Related work is mentioned in Section 6. As a conclusion, Section 7 discusses some of the current limitations of the JAMUS platform, and gives an overview of the lines we plan to work along in the future.

---

[1] http://www.univ-ubs.fr/valoria/Orcade/RASC

2   Overview of the Jamus Platform

The general architecture of the platform is shown in Figure 1. The platform is implemented over RAJE, a *Resource-Aware Java Environment* whose development is also carried out in our laboratory.

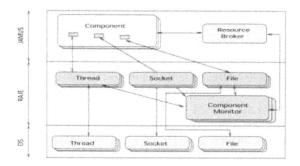

Fig. 1. Overview of the platform's architecture

2.1   Middleware Support for Resource Monitoring and Control

RAJE can be perceived as an extension of the traditional runtime environment of the Java 2 platform. This extension provides various facilities for monitoring the resources of a hardware platform, as well as for monitoring and controlling the resources used by Java application programs at runtime. It includes classes that reify system resources (CPU, network interfaces, etc.) as well as classes that model conceptual resources (sockets, files, etc.). Some of these classes are specific to RAJE, while others simply provide alternative implementations for classes of the standard Java API. For example, standard Java classes *Socket* and *File* are given specific implementations in RAJE, so that any access to the conceptual resources they model can be monitored and controlled at runtime.

Most of the code included in RAJE is pure Java and, as such, is readily portable. However, part of this code consists of C functions that permit the extraction of information from the underlying OS, and the interaction with inner parts of the JVM (Java Virtual Machine). To date RAJE is implemented under Linux, and the JVM it relies on is a variant of TransVirtual Technology's Kaffe 1.0.6. System resources are monitored by polling various files in the */proc* pseudo file-system of the Linux OS. The JVM is modified in such a way that Java threads are implemented as standard Linux native threads. This approach gives us better control over the CPU resource. For example, it makes it possible to monitor the amount of CPU consumed by each Java thread, since this information is readily available under */proc* for any Linux thread.

RAJE is dedicated to supporting high-level resource-aware applications, such as adaptive systems, security-oriented systems, or QoS-oriented systems. The JAMUS platform lies at the frontier between the two latter categories. It controls the resources used by Java application programs in order to ensure a secure runtime environment for these programs, as well as guaranteed QoS as far as resource availability is concerned.

2.2   Resource Contracting in Jamus

As mentioned in Section 1, resource control in JAMUS is based on a contractual approach. A four-level classification of the various kinds of contracts encountered in object-oriented programming has been proposed in [4]. According to this classification, the contracts we consider in JAMUS fall into the fourth level, which is that of contracts pertaining to non-functional properties and requirements.

Whenever a software component applies for being deployed on the platform, this component must specify explicitly what resources it will need at runtime, and in what conditions. Moreover access conditions can be specified in both a qualitative way (*eg* access permissions) and a quantitative way (*eg* access quotas). By specifying its requirements regarding resource access privileges and quotas, the candidate component requests a specific service from the JAMUS platform. At the same time it promises to use no other resource than those mentioned explicitly. Likewise, when the platform accepts a candidate component it promises to provide the component with all the resources it requires. At the same time it reserves the right to sanction any component that would try to access other resources than those it required.

The main originality of our approach with respect to related works (such as those mentioned in Section 6) lies in the fact that a specific contract must be subscribed between the JAMUS platform and each software component it accommodates. Based on these contracts, JAMUS provides some level of quality of service regarding resource availability. It also provides components with a relatively safe runtime environment, since no component can access or monopolise resources to the detriment of other components.

Contract subscription. Contract subscription in JAMUS relies on a two-step procedure. Any software component that applies for being deployed on the JAMUS platform must first pass an admission control examination. The requirements of a candidate component regarding resource utilisation must be expressed as a set of so-called resource utilisation profiles. Section 3 gives a detailed description of these profiles. The requirements of a candidate component are examined by a resource broker in order to decide if this component can be admitted on the platform. Admission control is based on a resource reservation scheme: a component is admissible only if the resources it requires are available on the platform in sufficient quality and quantity. When a component is declared admissible, the resource broker reserves the required resources for this component. The role and features of the resource broker are further detailed in Section 4.

When the admission control step and the resource reservation step are complete, a candidate component can start running on the platform. However the platform and the component are bound by a contract: the platform expects that the component will not attempt to access other resources than those it required, and the component expects that the platform will provide the resources it required.

Contract monitoring. Contract monitoring would not be necessary if the components deployed on the JAMUS platform could all be considered as trustworthy. If that was the case, any component could reasonably be expected to behave exactly as promised, and to use only those resources it required. Indeed, works are in progress that aim at providing so-called "trusted components" [15,12,14]. Hence, there is hope that, in the future, contract monitoring will not necessarily be required in all circumstances.

JAMUS is being developed in order to provide a safe and guaranteed runtime environment for components of dubious origin, such as application programs or applets downloaded from remote Internet sites. Consequently, any component deployed on the platform is considered as a potential threat throughout its execution.

Once a component has been accepted on the JAMUS platform, this does not necessarily mean that at runtime this component will respect the contract it subscribed with the platform. A component designed in a clumsy way – or in a malevolent perspective – may attempt to misbehave by accessing resources it did not explicitly ask for. In order to prevent such problems any component deployed on JAMUS is considered as non-trustworthy. Its execution is monitored so as to to check that it never attempts to access resources in a way that would violate the contract it subscribed with the platform during the admission control step. The mechanisms that permit the supervision of a component at runtime are presented in Section 5.

3   Describing Restrictions and Requirements: The Key to Contracts

At startup the JAMUS platform is given a description of the resources it can make available to hosted components, as well as instructions on how these resources should be used by components. RAJE and JAMUS together provide a series of interfaces and classes that enable modeling of resources and access conditions as so-called "resource utilisation profiles". Such profiles can thus be defined as Java code, and handled at runtime as standard Java objects.

Setting restrictions on the platform. The piece of code reproduced in Figure 2 shows how resource usage profiles can be defined in order to describe and to set restrictions on the resources available on the platform. In this example the platform is provided with three distinct profiles.

An instance of class *ResourceUtilisationProfile* basically aggregates three objects, which implement the *ResourcePattern*, *ResourcePermission*, and *ResourceQuota* interfaces respectively (see Figure 3).

```
int MB = 1024*1024;
ResourceUtilisationProfile C1, C2, C3;

// Global restrictions set on all socket-based
// communications: 200 MB sent, 500 MB received.
C1 = new ResourceUtilisationProfile(
            new SocketPattern(),
            new SocketPermission(SocketPermission.all),
            new SocketQuota(200*MB, 500*MB));

// Global restrictions set on any access
// to directory /tmp: 100 MB written, 100 MB read.
C2 = new ResourceUtilisationProfile(
            new FilePattern("/tmp"),
            new FilePermission(FilePermission.all),
            new FileQuota(100*MB, 100*MB));

// Selective restriction set on any access
// to directory /tmp/jamus: 15 MB written, 40 MB read.
C3 = new ResourceUtilisationProfile(
            new FilePattern("/tmp/jamus"),
            new FilePermission(FilePermission.all),
            new FileQuota(15*MB, 40*MB));
```

Fig. 2. Example of restrictions imposed on the JAMUS platform

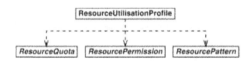

Fig. 3. Object-oriented modelling of resource utilisation profiles

JAMUS provides specific implementations of these interfaces for each resource type. For example, some of the classes that implement the ResourcePattern interface are shown in Figure 4. By including a given type of *ResourcePattern* in a *ResourceUtilisationProfile* one indicates that this profile is only relevant for those resources whose characteristics match the pattern, and that the *ResourcePermission* and *ResourceQuota* objects defined in this profile only pertain to this particular set of resources.

For example, the *SocketPattern* defined in profile *C1* (see Figure 2) specifies that this profile only concerns socket resources. The access permissions and transmission quotas defined in *C1* should thus be enforced only on sockets. The *FilePattern* defined in profile *C2* specifies that this profile concerns only file resources, and more precisely those files that are located under the */tmp* directory. The permissions and quotas defined in *C2* should thus be enforced only on runtime components attempting to accessing files in */tmp*. Profile *C3* sets

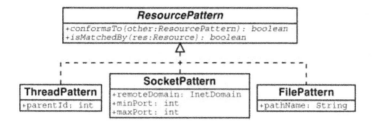

Fig. 4. Excerpt from the resource pattern hierarchy, as defined in JAMUS

further restrictions on directory */tmp/jamus*, imposing smaller quota values on this specific directory.

Specifying hosted components' requirements. Whenever a candidate component is submitted to the admission control step, it must specify its own requirements with respect to the resources offered by the platform. These requirements can also be modelled as instances of the class *ResourceUtilisationProfile*.

Figure 5 shows how a component can specify its requirements by defining the static method *getResourceRequirements()*, which returns a set of *ResourceUtilisationProfiles*. This method is systematically called by the platform's launcher in order to ask candidate programs for their requirements.

Checking requirements against restrictions. The interfaces *ResourcePattern*, *ResourcePermission* and *ResourceQuota* all define a boolean function *conformsTo()*, which can be used to check the conformity between two objects that implement the same interface (as shown in Figure 4 in the case of interface *ResourcePattern*). Conformity between patterns, permissions, and quotas is defined as follows:

- A pattern *Sa* is said to conform to another pattern *Sb* if any resource object whose characteristics satisfy the selection criterion defined in *Sa* also satisfy that of *Sb*.
- A permission *Pa* is said to conform to another permission *Pb* if any operation allowed in *Pa* is also allowed in *Pb*.
- A quota *Qa* is said to conform to another quota *Qb* if any amount (or rate) specified in *Qa* is smaller than (or equal to) that specified in *Qb*.

The function *conformsTo()* can thus be used at runtime to check a program's requirements against the restrictions imposed on the platform. With this function one can readily identify the requirements and restrictions that concern the same category of resources, and then verify that these requirements are compatible with those restrictions.

```
public class MyProgram {
  public static Set getResourceRequirements(String[] args) {
    int MB = 1024*1024;
    ResourceUtilisationProfile R1, R2, R3, R4;

    // Global requirement for all socket-based
    // communications: 20 MB sent, 80 MB received.
    R1 = new ResourceUtilisationProfile(
                new SocketPattern(),
                new SocketPermission(SocketPermission.all),
                new SocketQuota(20*MB, 80*MB));

    // Selective requirement for connections to the specified
    // Internet domain: 5 MB sent, 12 MB received.
    R2 = new ResourceUtilisationProfile(
                 new SocketPattern("univ-ubs.fr"),
                 new SocketPermission(SocketPermission.all),
                 new SocketQuota(5*MB, 12*MB));

    // Global requirement for the file system: access limited
    // to directory '/tmp': 30 MB written, 40 MB read.
    R3 = new ResourceUtilisationProfile(
                 new FilePattern("/tmp"),
                 new FilePermission(FilePermission.all),
                 new FileQuota(30*MB, 40*MB));

    // Selective requirement concerning access to directory
    // /tmp/jamus/data: 5 MB read, write access not required.
    R4 = new ResourceUtilisationProfile(
                 new FilePattern("/tmp/jamus/data"),
                 new FilePermission(FilePermission.readOnly),
                 new FileQuota(0, 5*MB));

    Set req = new HashSet();
    req.add(R1); req.add(R2); req.add(R3); req.add(R4);
    return req;
  }

  public static void main(String[] args) { ... }
}
```

Fig. 5. Example of an simple application program that specifies its own requirements regarding the resources it plans to use at runtime

4   Admission Control and Resource Reservation: Contract Subscription

The resource broker implemented in JAMUS is inspired by that described in [13]. It implements a reservation mechanism in order to guarantee the availability of resources for hosted components.

Initialisation of the resource broker. At startup, the broker receives the set of resource utilisation profiles that describe the restrictions imposed on the platform's resources. This information is used by the broker to build its own "perception" of the resources initially available on the platform, and of the conditions set on any access to these resources.

Admission of a candidate component. Whenever a candidate component is submitted to the admission control test, the resource broker examines the requirements of this component. For each basic requirement, the broker must decide if this requirement is admissible. A requirement is declared admissible if it violates none of the restrictions imposed on the platform. The candidate component itself is declared admissible if all its requirements are admissible. A component can be hosted on the JAMUS platform only after it has been declared admissible by the resource broker.

Consider the requirements $R2$ and $R3$ expressed by the candidate component reproduced in Figure 5, and assume that the broker is checking these requirements against the platform's restrictions defined in Figure 2. Since the pattern defined in $R2$ only conforms to that of $C1$, the permission and quota conditions required in $R2$ should only be checked against those imposed in $C1$. The broker must thus check that the access permissions (resp. quotas) required in $R2$ do not violate the restrictions imposed in $C1$. In the present case, $R2$ can be declared admissible by the broker.

The pattern defined in $R3$ conforms to those defined in both $C2$ and $C3$. Access to the part of the file-system considered in $R3$ should thus be performed according to the restrictions imposed in both $C2$ and $C3$.

Analysis of the access permissions required in $R3$ shows that they contradict neither the restrictions imposed in $C2$, nor those imposed in $C3$. On the other hand, although the access quotas required in $R3$ are compatible with those imposed in $C2$, they do not conform to those imposed in $C3$. Requirement $R3$ should thus be declared as non-admissible by the resource broker: the requirement expressed in $R3$ could not be satisfied by JAMUS without violating at least one of the restrictions imposed on the platform. As a consequence, the candidate component shown in Figure 5 should be declared as non-admissible by the platform, assuming that this platform is bound by the restrictions shown in Figure 2.

The former example shows that admission control in JAMUS is currently based on a quite pessimistic approach. More "optimistic" admission control policies may however be considered and implemented in JAMUS in the future, as discussed in Section 7.

Resource reservation and release. When a candidate component has successfully passed the admission control test, it can start running on the platform. However, JAMUS commits itself to providing hosted components with the resources they require. The resource broker is responsible for this commitment on behalf of the entire platform. Resource reservation is achieved by dynamically updating the broker's "perception" of the resources available on the platform.

Once a component has been declared admissible by the broker, and before this component actually starts running, the broker updates the quota values in the platform's restrictions, based on the component's requirements. Hence, whenever the requirements of a new candidate component are examined by the broker, these requirements are actually checked against a set of profiles that model the currently available resources, rather than the resources that were available when the broker was first initialised.

Likewise, when a component reaches completion the broker updates the quota values in the platform's restrictions accordingly, so as to account for the release of the resources that were reserved for this component.

5   Resource Access Supervision: Contract Monitoring

5.1   Monitoring Entities

Every component hosted by the JAMUS platform runs under the control of a component monitor. This monitor uses the resource utilisation profiles provided by the component to instantiate as many resource monitors.

A resource monitor admits a *ResourceUtilisationProfile* as a construction parameter. Its mission is to monitor the resources whose characteristics match the pattern defined in this profile, and to enforce the profile's access permissions and quotas on these resources.

JAMUS includes different kinds of resource monitors. For example, the class *SocketMonitor* implements a resource monitor dedicated to socket resources. When monitoring the resources used by a hosted component, the role of a *SocketMonitor* is to check that the socket resources that satisfy the selection criterion defined in its *SocketPattern* are used according to the conditions specified in its *SocketPermission* and *SocketQuota*.

As an example, consider the component shown in Figure 5, and assume that this component has been admitted by the JAMUS platform. When loading this component, the platform creates a component monitor. This monitor examines the requirements of the component, and since these requirements are expressed as four resource utilisation profiles, it creates four resource monitors. Two of these resource monitors are *SocketMonitors*, and the other two are *FileMonitors*. The first *SocketMonitor* receives profile *R1* as a construction parameter. From this time on it is thus dedicated to monitoring the use of all the *Socket* resources the hosted component may create at runtime, while enforcing the global quotas specified in *R1* (no more than 20 MBytes sent, no more than 80 MBytes received) on these sockets. The second *SocketMonitor* receives *R2* as a construction parameter: it will thus have to monitor only sockets connected to hosts of the remote Internet domain *"univ-ubs.fr"*, enforcing the quotas specified in *R2* (no more than 5 MBytes sent, no more than 12 MBytes received) on these sockets.

Notice that at runtime any socket monitored by the second *SocketMonitor* shall be also monitored by the first one, as its characteristics will match the patterns defined in both *R1* and *R2*. A resource may thus be supervised by several monitors, just like a single monitor may have to supervise several resources simultaneously.

The remainder of this section gives an overview of the mechanisms component monitors and resource monitors rely on.

5.2 Resource Tracking

In JAMUS all resources are modelled as Java objects (instances of classes *Socket*, *File*, *CPU*, etc.), which can be created and destroyed (or, more precisely, de-referenced) dynamically by a hosted component. As a consequence, the component monitor that is responsible for monitoring a given hosted component must be informed about any creation or destruction of a resource object by this component. The JAMUS platform implements a resource register, whose role is to identify and to keep track of all resource objects used by a hosted component.

In the current implementation of the platform a distinct resource register is associated with each hosted component. Moreover, each component is loaded using a distinct *ClassLoader*. This approach ensures that resource objects used by different components are registered separately. It also guarantees that two hosted components do not share the same name-space, hence preventing resource capture and corruption between concurrent components.

5.3 Monitoring Models

Resource monitoring is said to be achieved synchronously when any attempt to access a given resource can be intercepted and checked immediately by the monitors associated with this kind of resource. Synchronous monitoring can be obtained quite easily when a resource is modelled by an accessor object, that is, when accessing a resource comes down to calling a method on a Java object that represents this resource in the Java environment. Classes *Socket*, *Datagram-Socket*, *File*, etc. are accessor classes: they model conceptual resources, and as such they define accessor objects that can be submitted to synchronous monitoring.

All resources cannot be monitored using the synchronous approach, though. For example, although all Java components (or, more precisely, all Java threads) consume shares of the CPU resource, they do not do so explicitly by calling methods on an object that would model the underlying hardware CPU. Instead, access to the CPU is controlled exclusively by the scheduler of the Java Virtual Machine, or by that of the underlying operating system. In order to deal with resources that cannot be monitored synchronously, such as the CPU, we propose to do with asynchronous monitoring. Monitoring a resource asynchronously consists in consulting the state of this resource every now and then, in such a way that the time of the observation does not necessarily coincide with the time of an attempt to use the resource.

RAJE provides abstractions and implementation alternatives for performing both kinds of monitoring. Some of these facilities are used in JAMUS to put resources under the control of resource monitors.

Implementation of the synchronous model. Synchronous monitoring is obtained in RAJE by implementing a call-back mechanism in resource classes. Any resource object admits a set of listeners. Whenever a method is called on a resource object by an application component, the resource object informs all its registered listeners that an attempt is being made to access the resource it models. A listener can refuse that a certain operation be performed on a resource by returning a *ResourceAccessException* signal to the corresponding resource object. In such a case the resource object must abort the operation considered, and return the appropriate exception signal to the application component.

With this approach a resource monitor that implements the synchronous model can keep informed about any operation attempted on the resource objects it monitors.

Implementation of the asynchronous model. In order to be observable asynchronously, an object that models a resource must be able to produce an observation report on demand. In RAJE, an observation report is an object that implements the *ObservationReport* interface. RAJE provides a specific implementation of this interface for each type of resource considered to date. Moreover, each resource class defines a method *observe()* that returns the appropriate kind of *ObservationReport*.

For example, a *Thread* object (threads are considered as resources in JAMUS) can produce a *ThreadReport*, which reports the current priority level of this thread, as well as the amount of CPU it consumed during the last observation period. Likewise, the method *observe()* implemented in class *Socket* returns a *SocketReport*, which reports the current characteristics of the corresponding socket (remote address and port, number of bytes sent and received since this socket was opened, etc.).

RAJE also provides mechanisms for controlling resources. For example many resource classes defined in RAJE implement interface *Lockable*. When a resource object is locked, utilisation of this object by an application component is denied, and any attempt to access the associated resource raises an exception signal.

Notice that observation and locking facilities have been kept separate in RAJE. The reason for this separation is that although all resources can be observed quite easily, there are resources (such as the system CPU) that can hardly be locked.

5.4 Dealing with Faulty Components

Resource monitors in JAMUS rely on either the asynchronous or the synchronous facilities implemented in RAJE in order to monitor the resources whose characteristics match their pattern. Each monitor enforces the access permissions and quotas defined in its profile on the resource objects it monitors. Whenever a transgression is observed, the monitor notifies the resource broker. The broker then terminates the faulty component. Release of the resources this component used is accounted by the broker, so that these resources can later be reassigned to new candidate components.

6 Related Work

The Java Runtime Environment (JRE) implements the so-called *sandbox* security model. In the first versions of the JRE, this security model gave local code –considered as safe code– full access to system resources, while code downloaded from the Internet (for example under the form of an applet) was considered as untrusted, and was therefore only granted access to a limited subset of resources [9]. With the Java 2 platform this restrictive security model was abandoned for a new model that relies on the concept of protection domain [9,10]. A protection domain is a runtime environment whose security policy can be specified as a set of permissions. An access controller is associated with each protection domain. It checks any resource access performed from this domain, and it implements the security policy as defined by the permissions associated with the domain.

J-Kernel extends this approach by permitting communication and data sharing between protection domains [11]. Communication between domains is however limited to method calls on so-called capability objects.

The security models implemented in J-Kernel and in the JRE rely on stateless mechanisms. Access to a specific resource cannot be conditioned by whether the very same resource was accessed previously, or by how much of this resource was consumed previously. Hence, quantitative constraints (amount of CPU, I/O quotas, etc.) cannot be set on the resources accessed from protection domains. As a consequence, the security mechanisms implemented in J-Kernel and in the JRE cannot prevent abnormal operations resulting from an abusive consumption of resources (denial of service attacks, etc.).

Environments such as JRes [3,5], GVM [2], and KaffeOS [1] partially solve the above-mentioned problem. They include mechanisms that permit the counting and the limiting of the amounts of resources used by an active entity (a thread for JRes, a process for GVM and KaffeOS). However, resource accounting is only achieved at coarse grain. For example it is possible to count the number of bytes sent and received by a thread (or by a process) through the network, but it is not possible to count the number of bytes exchanged with a given remote host, or with a specific remote port number. Similarly, it is possible to count how many bytes have been written to (or read from) the file system, but it is not possible to set particular constraints on the use of specific directories or files.

Projects Naccio [7,6] and Ariel [16] are dedicated to security. Both provide a language for defining a security policy, as well as mechanisms for enforcing this policy while an application program is running. Security policy enforcement is carried out statically, by rewriting the application program byte-code as well as that of the Java API. An advantage of this approach is that the cost of the supervision of a program is kept at a minimum, for code segments that check the access to a particular kind of resource are inserted in Java API classes only if the selected security policy requires it. However, the generation of an API dedicated to a specific security policy is a quite expensive procedure. The approach proposed in Naccio and Ariel is thus mostly dedicated to the generation of predefined Java APIs that each enforce a generic security policy. Unlike the JAMUS platform, though, Naccio and Ariel can hardly ensure the supervision of an application program, when the security policy must be derived from the resource requirements specified by the application program itself.

[8] presents a resource-constrained sandboxing approach that shows much similitude with ours. The sandbox described in this paper relies on standard shared system libraries available in Windows NT and in Linux, in order to provide sandboxing for executable programs. The resulting sandbox can enforce qualitative and quantitative restrictions on the system resources used by application programs, while providing these programs with soft guarantees of and fairness of resources. It monitors the application's interactions with the underlying operating system, pro-actively controlling these interactions in order to enforce the desired behaviour. The paper distinguishes between implicit and explicit requests to the OS, and it shows that resource utilisation can be constrained either by intercepting explicit requests to the OS, or by monitoring the frequency of implicit requests. This distinction obviously compares with our observation that resource monitoring should be performed either synchronously or asynchronously, depending on the kind of resource considered, and on the desired level of control. Unlike the JAMUS platform, though, the sandbox described in [8] is not dedicated to the accommodation of Java mobile components. As a consequence it cannot take benefit of one of the most interesting possibilities offered by Java-based software environments, namely, cross-platform mobility. Moreover an advantage of JAMUS is that the resource patterns it relies on make it easy to obtain almost any grain of monitoring: single resource, group of resources, resource type, etc.

7   Discussion and Perspectives

The development of the JAMUS platform (and of the underlying environment RAJE) is still in progress. As a consequence, JAMUS is obviously still limited and quite perfectible. In the following we list some of the problems we should address shortly, as well as some of the lines we plan to work along in the future.

In the current implementation, resource usage profiles must be expressed as Java source code (as shown in Section 3). This is a rather crude, and sometimes not-so-convenient creation procedure. We should soon raise this limitation, though, as it would be most interesting if profile objects could be stored in files, and retrieved from these files at startup. An approach to achieve this goal would be that all *ResourceUtilisationProfile* objects implement the standard Java interface *Externalizable*. Another interesting approach would be to define a dedicated

XML-based language, so that profiles can be defined and edited using some of the tools developed around the XML technology.

The current syntax, grammar, and semantics associated with resource utilisation profiles have not been formerly defined. Besides, they could certainly be improved so as to gain expressiveness and flexibility. For example it would be interesting if resources could be reserved for groups of components, rather than for individual components. Another possibility would be to complement the mechanism of resource reservation with alternative access schemes (such as best effort, priority-based access, etc.).

Resource contracting in JAMUS relies on a quite simplistic model: the requirements of a component must all be known and fully expressed *before* this component can be admitted on the platform. In many cases, though, the requirements of a component can hardly be defined statically, because they depend on parameters the component should only discover at runtime, or because they are likely to change dynamically while the component is running. The architecture of JAMUS gives provision for more flexible contract-management mechanisms. New facilities should be included in the platform in the near future so as to permit that contracts be subscripted, cancelled, or modified dynamically throughout a component's lifetime.

Since the development of the platform is not complete, no extensive performance evaluation has been performed so far. However, preliminary experiments have shown that the overhead of resource monitoring in JAMUS remains quite low. For example, in order to evaluate the specific overhead of network activity monitoring performance, measurements have been realized with a Java-based FTP server[2]. During this experiment the network transmissions achieved by the server were monitored and constrained by JAMUS. File uploads and downloads realized by the server in these conditions showed no detectable degradation of performance.

JAMUS constitutes a demonstrator platform, with which we experiment with the idea of resource-constrained software deployment. It is our conviction that many other application domains and systems (such as agent-based systems, or adaptive systems) could benefit of – or take inspiration from – the models and mechanisms we develop in this particular context.

References

1. Godmar Back, Wilson C. Hsieh, and Jay Lepreau. Processes in KaffeOS: Isolation, Resource Management, and Sharing in Java. In *The 4th Symposium on Operating Systems Design and Implementation*, October 2000.
2. Godmar Back, Patrick Tullmann, Legh Stoller, Wilson C. Hsieh, and Jay Lepreau. Techniques for the Design of Java Operating Systems. In *USENIX Annual Technical Conference*, June 2000.

---

[2] JFTPd server developed by the MIT *(http://jftpd.prominic.org/index.html)*. Experiment achieved using two workstations (with PII processors) directly connected by a point-to-point 100 Mbps Fast Ethernet link.

3. Nataraj Bagaratnan and Steven B. Byrne. Resource Access Control for an Internet UserAgent. In *The 3th USENIX Conference on Object-Oriented Technologie and Systems*, 1997.
4. Antoine Beugnard, Jean-Marc Jézéquel, Noël Plouzeau, and Damien Watkins. Making components contract-aware. In IEEE, editor, *Computer*, page 38 44. IEEE, June 1999.
5. Grzegorz Czajkowski and Thorsten von Eicken. JRes: a Resource Accounting Interface for Java. In *ACM OOPSLA Conference*, 1998.
6. David Evans. *Policy-Directed Code Safety*. PhD thesis, Massachussets Institute of Technology, February 2000.
7. David Evans and Andrew Twyman. Flexible Policy-Directed Code Safety. In *IEEE Security and Privacy*, May 1999.
8. Fangzhe Chang and Ayal Itzkovitz and Vijay Karamcheti. User-level Resource-constrained Sandboxing. In -. The 4 th USENIX Windows Systems Symposium, August 2000.
9. Li Gong. Java Security: Present and Near Future. *IEEE Micro*, -:14–19, May 1997.
10. Li Gong and Roland Schemers. Implementing Protection Domains in the Java Development Kit 1.2. In *Internet Society Symposium on Network and Distributed System Scurity*, March 1998.
11. Chris Hawblitzel, Chi-Chao Chang, Grzegorz Czajkowski, Deyu Hu, and Thorsten von Eicken. Implementing Multiple Protection Domains in Java. In *USENIX Annual Technical Conference*, June 1998.
12. J.-M. Jézéquel, D. Deveaux, and Y. Le Traon. Reliable Objects: a Lightweight Approach applied to Java. *IEEE Software*, 18(4):76–83, July/August 2001.
13. Kihun Kim and Klara Nahrstedt. A Resource Broker Model with Integrated Reservation Scheme. In *IEEE International Conference on Multimedia and Expo (II)*, pages 859–862, 2000.
14. U. Lindqvist, T. Olovsson, , and E. Jonsson. An Analysis of a Secure System Based on Trusted Components. In *Proc. 11th Ann. Conf. Computer Assurance*, pages 213–223. IEEE Press, 1996.
15. B. Meyer, C. Mingins, and H. Schmidt. Providing Trusted Components to the Industry. *IEEE Computer*, pages 104–15, May 1998.
16. Raju Pandey and Brant Hashii. Providing Fine-Grained Access Control for Java Programs. In *The 13th Conference on Object-Oriented Programming, ECOOP'99*. Springer-Verlag, June 1999.
17. Clemens Szyperski. *Component Software: Beyond Object-Oriented Programming*. ACM Press, Addison-Wesley, 1998.

Architecture-Level Support for Software Component Deployment in Resource Constrained Environments

Marija Mikic-Rakic and Nenad Medvidovic

Computer Science Department,
University of Southern California,
Los Angeles, CA 90089-0781,
{marija,neno}@usc.edu

Abstract. Software deployment comprises activities for installing or updating an already implemented software system. These activities include (1) deployment of a system onto a new host, (2) component upgrade in an existing system, (3) static analysis of the proposed system configuration, and (4) dynamic analysis of the configuration after the deployment. In this paper, we describe an approach that supports all four of these activities. The approach is specifically intended to support software deployment onto networks of distributed, mobile, highly resource constrained devices. Our approach is based on the principles of software architectures. In particular, we leverage our lightweight architectural implementation infrastructure to natively support deployment in resource constrained environments.

Keywords. Software deployment, software architecture, architectural style, software connector, multi-versioning, Prism

1 Introduction

Software deployment involves the activities needed for installing or updating a software system, after the software has been developed and made available for release. Software systems of today often have complex architectures that are characterized by large numbers of potentially pre-fabricated ("off-the-shelf") components. Over a long lifespan, these systems are likely to have many installed versions and experience numerous and frequent updates. The components that comprise these systems are more commonly being developed and released independently by third-party organizations (i.e., vendors). The vendors of components are themselves usually distributed, heterogeneous, and their locations may change over time. Due to the time-to-market pressures, component vendors frequently release new versions that need to be deployed to large numbers of sites. However, the vendors usually have no control over a majority of the systems in which their deployed components reside. Moreover, multiple versions of such systems (referred to as *target* systems below) are likely to exist in various locations simultaneously. For these reasons, human-operated deployment becomes impossible, and support for automated software deployment becomes critical. This picture has become even more complex with the recent emergence of inexpensive, small, heterogeneous, resource-constrained, highly

J. Bishop (Ed.): CD 2002, LNCS 2370, pp. 31–50.

distributed, and mobile computing platforms that demand highly efficient software deployment solutions.

If considered from the perspective of the effects of deployment on the target system, software deployment deals with at least four problems. These problems are independent of the application domain, or nature and configuration of hardware platforms on which the software is to be deployed. The four problems are:

1. initial deployment of a system onto a new host (or set of hosts);
2. deployment of a new version of a component to an existing target system;
3. static analysis, prior to the deployment, of the likely effects of the desired modifications on the target system; and
4. dynamic analysis, after the deployment, of the effects of the performed modifications on the running target system.

Several existing approaches have been aimed at providing support for one or more of these four activities. Typically, software deployment has been accomplished via large-scale "patches" that replace an entire application or set of applications (e.g., new version of MS Word or MS Office). These patches do not provide control over the deployment process beyond the selection of optional features available for a given application (e.g., optional installation of MS Equation Editor in MS Office). Some existing approaches (e.g., [5]), have addressed this problem by providing support for deployment at a finer-grain component level. However, these approaches have typically taken a configuration management perspective on the deployment problem, tracking dependencies among versions of *implemented* modules. With one notable exception [6], these approaches have rarely taken into account system architectures, their evolution over time due to the frequent component upgrades, or the relationship of the deployed multiple versions of a given system to that system's architecture. Furthermore, these approaches have often required sophisticated deployment support (e.g., deployment agents [5]) that uses its own set of facilities, provided separately from the application's implementation infrastructure, thereby introducing additional overhead to the target host. For these reasons, these approaches are usually not applicable in an emerging class of light-weight, resource constrained, highly distributed, and mobile computational environments.

In this paper, we propose an approach that attempts to overcome the shortcomings of previous work and address all four deployment problems discussed above. Our approach directly leverages a software system's architecture in enabling deployment. Specifically, we have been able to adapt our existing architectural implementation infrastructure to natively and inexpensively support deployment, both at system construction-time and run-time. Our solution is light weight and is applicable in a highly distributed, mobile, resource constrained, possibly embedded environment. A key aspect of the approach is its support for intelligent, dynamic upgrades of component versions. We have provided a graphical software deployment environment, and have evaluated our approach on a series of applications distributed across a variety of desktop, lap-top, and hand-held devices.

The rest of the paper is organized as follows. Section 2 briefly describes an example application used to illustrate the concepts throughout the paper. Section 3 summarizes the architectural style used as the basis of this work and its accompanying infrastructure for implementing, deploying, migrating, and dynamically reconfiguring applications. Section 4 discusses our approach to supporting component deployment, while Section 5 describes in more detail a technique for supporting upgrades of component versions. The paper concludes with overviews of related and future work.

2 Example Application

To illustrate our approach, we use an application for distributed, "on the fly" deployment of personnel, intended to deal with situations such as natural disasters, military crises, and search-and-rescue efforts. The specific instance of this application depicted in Figure 1 addresses military Troops Deployment and battle Simulations (TDS). A computer at *Headquarters* gathers all information from the field and displays the complete current battlefield status: the locations of friendly and enemy troops, as well as obstacles such as mine fields. The *Headquarters* computer is networked via a secure link to a set of hand-held devices used by officers in the field. The configuration in Figure 1 shows three *Commanders* and a *General*; two

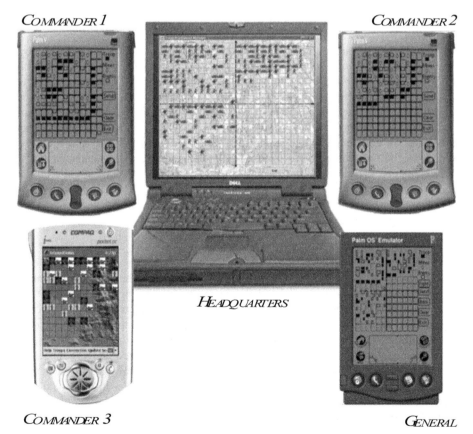

Fig. 1. TDS application distributed accross multiple devices.

Commanders use Palm Pilot Vx devices, while the third uses a Compaq iPAQ; the *General* uses a Palm Pilot VIIx. The *Commanders* are capable of viewing their own quadrant of the battlefield and deploying friendly troops within that quadrant to counter enemy deployments. The *General* sees a summarized view of the entire battlefield (shown); additionally, the *General* is capable of seeing detailed views of each quadrant. Based on the global battlefield situation, the *General* can issue direct troop deployment orders to individual *Commanders* or request transfers of troops among the *Commanders*. The *General* can also request for deployment strategy suggestions from *Headquarters*, based on current positions of enemy troops, mines, and the number of friendly troops at disposal. Finally, the *General* can issue a "fight" command, resulting in a battle simulation that incrementally determines the likely winner given a configuration of troops and obstacles.

The TDS application provides an effective platform for illustrating our ideas. It has been designed, implemented, and deployed using the approach described in this paper. In the instance of TDS shown in Figures 1 and 2, sixteen software components deployed across the five devices interact via fifteen software connectors.

3 Architectural Basis for Software Deployment

We are using a software architectural approach as the basis of our support for deployment. *Software architectures* provide high-level abstractions for representing structure, behavior, and key properties of a software system [18]. They are described in terms of components, connectors, and configurations. Architectural *components* describe the computations and state of a system; *connectors* describe the rules and mechanisms of interaction among the components; finally, *configurations* define topologies of components and connectors. Software *architectural styles* involve identifying the types of elements from which systems are built, the characteristics of these elements, the allowed interactions among the elements, and the patterns that guide their composition [15]. The specific architectural style upon which we are relying in this work is Prism [10].

3.1 Architectural Style

The Prism style is targeted at heterogeneous, highly distributed, highly mobile, resource constrained, possibly embedded systems. In formulating the Prism style, we have leveraged our extensive experience with the C2 architectural style, which is intended to support highly distributed applications in the graphical user interface (GUI) domain [19]. Prism-style *components* maintain state and perform application-specific computation. The components may not assume a shared address space, but instead interact with other components solely by exchanging messages via their three communication *ports* (named *top*, *bottom*, and *side*). *Connectors* in the Prism style mediate the interaction among components by controlling the distribution of all messages. A *message* consists of a name and a set of typed parameters.

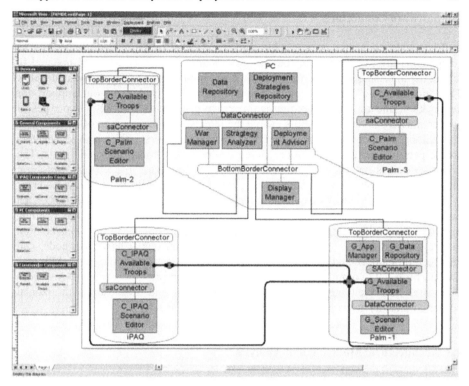

Fig. 2. Architecture of the TDS application, displayed in the Prism deployment environment (Prism-DE). The unlabeled circles connecting components across the hand-held devices represent peer connectors.

A message in the Prism style is either a *request* for a component to perform an operation, a *notification* that a given component has performed an operation and/or changed its state, or a *peer* message used in direct (peer-to-peer) communication between components. Request messages are sent through the top port, notifications through the bottom port, and peer messages through the side port of a component. The distinction between requests and notifications ensures Prism's principle of *substrate independence*, which mandates that a component in an architecture may have no knowledge of or dependencies on components below it. In order to preserve this property, two Prism components may not engage in interaction via peer messages if there exists a vertical topological relationship between them. For example, *DataRepository* on the *PC* and *G_ScenarioEditor* on the *Palm-1* in Figure 2 may not exchange peer messages since one component is above the other; on the other hand, no vertical topological relationship exists between *C_iPAQ_AvailableTroops* on the *iPAQ* and *G_AvailableTroops* on the *Palm-1*, meaning that they may communicate via peer messages.

3.2 Software Connectors

A Prism-style connector does not have an interface at declaration-time; instead, as components are attached to it, the connector's interface is dynamically updated to reflect the interfaces of the components that will communicate through the connector. This "polymorphic" property of connectors is the key enabler of our support for deployment, and run-time reconfiguration. Prism distinguishes between two types of connectors. *Horizontal* connectors enable the request-notification type of communication among components through their top and bottom ports, while *peer* connectors enable peer-to-peer communication among components through their side ports. The Prism style does not allow a peer and a horizontal connector to exchange messages; this would, in effect, convert peer messages into requests/notifications, and vice versa.

The Prism style directly supports connectors that span device boundaries. Such connectors, called *border connectors*, enable the interactions of components residing on one device with components on other devices (e.g., *BottomBorderConnector* on the *PC* in Figure 2). A border connector marshals and unmarshals data, code, and architectural models, and dispatches and receives messages across the network. It may also perform data compression for efficiency and encryption for security. A *Border Connector* may facilitate communication via requests and notifications (horizontal border connector) or via peer messages (peer border connector).

3.3 Architectural Modeling and Analysis

Prism supports architectures at two levels: application-level and meta-level. The role of components at the Prism meta-level is to observe and/or facilitate different aspects of the deployment, execution, dynamic evolution, and mobility of application-level components. Both application-level and meta-level components obey the rules of the style. They execute side-by-side: meta-level components are aware of application-level components and may initiate interactions with them, but not vice versa.

In support of this two-level architecture, Prism currently distinguishes among three types of messages. *ApplicationData* messages are used by application-level components to communicate during execution. The other two message types are used by Prism meta-level components: *ComponentContent* messages contain mobile code and accompanying information (e.g., the location of a migrant component in the destination configuration), while *ArchitecturalModel* messages carry information needed to perform architecture-level analyses of prospective Prism configurations (e.g., during deployment).

We have extensively used special-purpose components, called *Admin Components*, whose task is to exchange *ComponentContent* messages and facilitate the deployment and mobility of application-level components across devices. Another meta-level component is the *Continuous Analysis* component, which leverages *ArchitecturalModel* messages for analyzing the (partial) architectural models during the application's execution, assessing the validity of proposed run-time architectural changes, and possibly disallowing the changes.

In support of this task, we have recently added architecture description language (ADL) support to Prism. We have extended our existing ADL (C2SADEL [11]) and

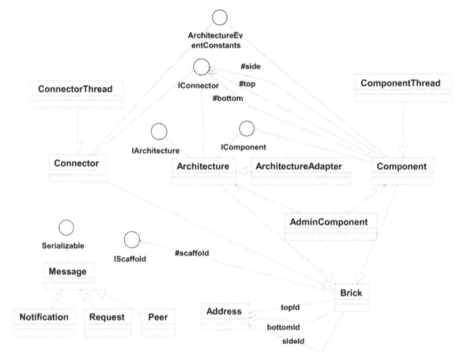

Fig. 3. Class design view of the Prism implementation framework.

tool support (DRADEL [11]) with a set of new capabilities for modeling and analyzing Prism-style architectures. Specifically, the *Continuous Analysis* component is built using a subset of DRADEL to assess the proposed architectural (re)configurations. That assessment is carried out by matching the interfaces and behaviors (expressed via component invariants and operation pre- and post-conditions) of the interacting components [11].

3.4 Architectural Implementation

Prism provides stylistic guidelines for composing large, distributed, mobile systems. For these guidelines to be useful in a development setting, they must be accompanied by support for their implementation. To this end, we have developed a light-weight architecture implementation infrastructure. The infrastructure comprises an extensible framework of implementation-level modules representing the key elements of the style (e.g., architectures, components, connectors, messages) and their characteristics (e.g., a message has a name and a set of parameters). An application architecture is then constructed by extending the appropriate classes in the framework with application-specific detail. The framework has been implemented in several programming languages: Java JVM and KVM [20], C++ and Embedded Visual C++ (EVC++), and Python.

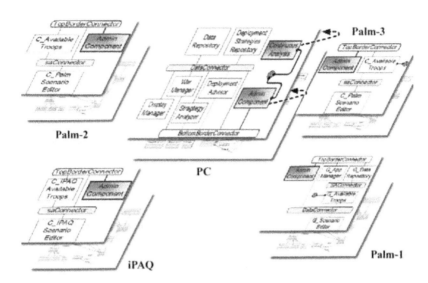

Fig. 4. Layered construction of an application using the Prism implementation framework. The application is distributed across five devices, each of which is running the framework. Meta-level components (highlighted in the figure) may control the execution of application-level components via Prism messages or via pointers to the local *Architecture* object (shown in the subarchitecture on the *PC*).

A subset of the Prism framework's UML class diagram is shown in Figure 3. The classes shown are those of interest to the user of the framework (i.e., the application developer). Multiple components and connectors in an architecture may run in a single thread of control (*Component* and *Connector* classes), or they may have their own threads (*ComponentThread* and *ConnectorThread*). The *Architecture* class records the configuration of its constituent components and connectors, and provides meta-level facilities for their addition, removal, replacement, and reconnection, possibly at system run-time. A distributed application, such as TDS, is implemented as a set of interacting *Architecture* objects as shown in Figure 4.

The first step a developer (or tool generating an implementation from an architectural description [11]) takes is to subclass from the *Component* or ComponentThread framework classes for all components in the architecture and to implement the application-specific functionality for them. The next step is to instantiate the *Architecture* classes for each device and define the needed instances of thus created components, as well as the connectors selected from the connector library. Finally, attaching components and connectors into a configuration is achieved by using the *weld* and *peerWeld* methods of the *Architecture* class. At any point, the developer may add meta-level components, which may be welded to specific application-level connectors and thus exercise control over a particular portion of the *Architecture* (e.g., *Admin Component* in Figure 4). Alternatively, meta-level components may remain unwelded and may instead exercise control over the entire *Architecture* object directly (e.g., *Continuous Analysis* component in Figure 4).

4 System Deployment

Our support for deployment addresses problems 1 and 3 stated in the Introduction (initial system deployment and static analysis prior to deployment) by directly leveraging the Prism implementation infrastructure. We have developed a custom solution for deploying applications instead of trying to reuse existing capabilities (e.g., [5]) because of the facilities provided by the Prism style (*ComponentContent* messages, *Admin Components*, meta-level architecture) and the light weight of the Prism implementation framework, which is critical for small, resource constrained devices (e.g., Palm Pilot, which has 256KB of dynamic heap memory). We use the same infrastructure for the initial deployment of a system onto a new host (or set of hosts) and for deploying a new version of a component to an existing target system.

4.1 Basic Requirements

In order to deploy the desired architecture on a set of target hosts, we assume that a skeleton (meta-level) configuration is preloaded on each host. The configuration consists of the Prism implementation framework, with an instantiated *Architecture* object that contains a *Border Connector* and an *Admin Component* attached to the connector. The skeleton configuration is extremely lightweight. For example, in our Java implementation, the skeleton uses as little as 8KB of dynamic memory. Since the Prism framework, *Architecture* object, and *Border Connector* are also used at the application level, the actual memory overhead of our basic deployment support (i.e., the *Admin Component*) is only around 3KB.

The *Admin Component* on each device contains a pointer to its *Architecture* object and is thus able to effect run-time changes to its local subsystem's architecture: instantiation, addition, removal, connection, and disconnection of components and connectors. *Admin Components* are able to send and receive from any device to which they are connected the meta-level *ComponentContent* messages through *Border Connectors*. Each *Admin Component* can request the components that are to be deployed in its subsystem's architecture. Finally, each *Admin Component* has the knowledge of the set of components that are available in the local configuration via a pointer to the *Architecture* object.

4.2 Deployment Process

The *current* configuration of a system describes its current topology. The *desired* configuration represents a configuration that needs to be deployed. If there is a difference between the current and desired configurations, the deployment process will be initiated. The information about the current and desired configurations can either be stored on a single host (*centralized* ownership) or each subsystem may have the knowledge of
its current and desired configurations (*distributed* ownership). In the first scenario, the *Admin Component* on the host storing the descriptions of configurations will

initiate the deployment on all hosts. In the second scenario, each *Admin Component* will initiate the deployment on its local host.

```
architecture TDS is {
    component_types {
    component PC_StrategyAnalyzer is extern {
        C:\spec\PC_StrategyAnalyzer.Prism;}
        ...
    component C_AvailableTroops is extern {
        C:\spec\C_AvailableTroops.Prism;}
        ...}}
    architectural_topology {
    component_instances {
        pcStratAnalyzer : PC_StrategyAnalyzer;
        pcDataRepository : PC_DataRepository;
        cAvailableTroops: C_AvailableTroops;
        cAvailableTroops1: C_AvailableTroops;}
    connector_instances {
        BottomBorderConn : RegularConn;}
    peer_connector_instances {
    PeerCon : PeerComm;}
    connections {
        connector BottomBorderConn {
            top  pcStratAnalyzer;
            bottom pcDataRepository;}}
    peer_connections{
    peer_connector PeerCon {
    side cAvailableTroops, cAvailableTroops1;}}
}}
```

Fig. 5. Partial architectural specification of the TDS application in the Prism ADL. Individual components are specified in separate files denoted by the extern keyword.

In order to support centralized ownership of the application's architecture, the skeleton configuration on the central host should also contain a *Continuous Analysis* component. The centralized *Continuous Analysis* component has the knowledge of the current and desired configurations for all subsystems. Figure 5 shows the partial description of the TDS application configuration used by the central *Continuous Analysis* component.

Distributed ownership of the application's architecture requires that the skeleton configuration on each host contain a *Continuous Analysis* component (attached to the local *Border Connector*), which is aware of its subsystem configuration. Each *Continuous Analysis* component is capable of analyzing the validity of architectural configurations either by performing the analysis locally or by requesting the analysis of a given configuration remotely (e.g., on a more capacious host that can perform such analysis). Additionally, the *Continuous Analysis* component is capable of storing the desired (but not yet deployed) local configuration.

```
add(DataRepository: source PC): PC
add(DeploymentStrategiesRepository: source PC): PC
add(DataConnector: source none): PC
add(C_IPAQAvailableTroops: source local): iPAQ
add(C_IPAQScenarioEditor: source PC): iPAQ
add(SaConnector: source none): iPAQ
weld(DataRepository,DataConnector): PC
weld(DeploymentStrategiesRepository,DataConnector): PC
weld(C_IPAQAvailableTroops,SaConnector): iPAQ
weld(TopBorderConnector,C_IPAQAvailableTroops): iPAQ
weld(SaConnector,C_IPAQScenarioEditor): iPAQ
peerWeld(G_AvailableTroops,SideBorderConnector):Palm-1
```

Fig. 6. Partial description of the configuration created by Prism-DE for the TDS application. Component source and destination devices are shown. Sources are denoted as "none" in the case of connectors that use the base implementation (asynchronous message broadcast) provided by the Prism framework.

Table 1.

Centralized Ownership	Distributed Ownership
1. The central *Continuous Analysis* component receives the desired configuration as part of an *ArchitecturalModel* message, analyzes it, and after ensuring that the configuration is valid, invokes the *Admin Component* on the local host.	1. Each *Continuous Analysis* component receives the desired configuration of the local subsystem, analyzes it, and, after ensuring that the configuration is valid, invokes the *Admin Component* on the local host.
2. The *Admin Component* packages the components (e.g., .class files in Java) to be deployed into a byte stream and sends them as a series of *ComponentContent* messages via its local *Border Connector* to the target hosts.	2. *(a)* Each *Admin Component* issues a series of requests to other *Admin Components* (using either request or peer messages) for a set of components that are to be deployed locally. *(b) AdminComponents* that can service the requests package the required component(s) into byte streams and send them as a series of *ComponentContent* messages via their local *Border Connectors* to the requesting device.
3. Once received by the *Border Connector* on each destination device, the *ComponentContent* messages are forwarded to the *Admin Component* running locally. The *Admin Component* reconstitutes the migrant components from the byte stream contained in each message.	
4. Each *Admin Component* invokes the *add*, *weld*, and *peerWeld* methods on its *Architecture* object to attach the received components to the appropriate connectors (as specified in the *ComponentContent* message) in its local subsystem.	
5. Each *Admin Component* sends a message to inform the centralized *Continuous Analysis* component that the deployment has been performed successfully. The central *Continuous Analysis* component updates the model of the configuration accordingly. Update to the model is made only after successful deployments.	5. Each *Admin Component* sends a peer message to inform its local *Continuous Analysis* component (see Figure 4) that the deployment has been performed successfully. The local *Continuous Analysis* component updates the model of the local configuration accordingly.
6. Finally, each *Admin Component* invokes the *start* methods of all newly deployed components to initiate their execution.	

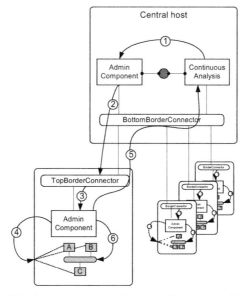

Fig. 7. Deployment process using centralized ownership.

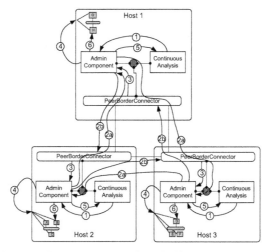

Fig. 8. Deployment process using distributed ownership.

Table 1 and Figures 7 and 8 describe the deployment process in the Java version of our implementation and deployment framework for both the cases of centralized and distributed ownership of the application's architecture.

4.3 Deployment Environment

We have integrated and extended the MS Visio tool to develop *Prism-DE*, the Prism architectural modeling and deployment environment (see Figure 2). Prism-DE contains several toolboxes (shown on the left side of Figure 2). The top toolbox enables an architect to specify a configuration of hardware devices by dragging their icons onto the canvas and connecting them. Prism-DE currently assumes that the available devices and their locations are known; we are extending Prism-DE with support for automated discovery of network nodes. The remaining toolboxes in Figure 2 supply the software components and connectors that may be placed atop the hardware device icons. Once a desired software configuration is created and validated in Prism-DE, it can be deployed onto the depicted hardware configuration with a simple button click.

Prism-DE supports deployment using centralized ownership of the application's architecture. Recall that this is *not* the case with our implementation framework, which also supports decentralized ownership as discussed in Section 4.2. Our current implementation assumes that the locations of the compiled code for all the needed components and connectors are known, and specified inside Prism-DE. Each software component in the toolboxes is associated with its compiled code location and its architectural description. Once the desired configuration is created, its validity can be assured automatically: Prism-DE generates the appropriate architectural description in the Prism ADL (e.g., recall Figure 5) and invokes its internal *Continuous Analysis* component to ensure that the description is valid. Once the user requests that the architecture be deployed, Prism-DE generates a series of deployment commands as shown in Figure 6. These commands are used as invocations to the skeleton configuration on the device on which Prism-DE resides. The local *Admin Component* initiates the deployment process on all hosts as specified in the left column of Table 1.

5 Component Upgrade

Prism and its integrated analysis capabilities provide assurance that the specified con-figuration of components and connectors is valid according to the architectural specification. However, implemented components may not preserve all the properties and relationships established at the architectural level (e.g., due to accidental coding errors) [12]. This section describes a run-time approach to supporting reliable upgrades of existing component versions [2,16] and reliable deployment of new com-ponents, addressing problems 2 and 4 stated in the Introduction.

When upgrading a component, vendors try to maintain the old component version's key properties (e.g., granularity, implementation language, and interaction paradigm), while enhancing its functionality (by adding new features) and/or reliability (by fixing known bugs). However, component upgrades raise a set of questions, including whether the new version correctly preserves the functionality carried over from the old version, whether the new version introduces new errors, and whether there is any performance discrepancy between the old and new versions. Depending on the kinds of problems a new component version introduces and the remedies it provides for the old version's problems, this scenario can force a user to make some interesting choices:

- deploy the new version of the component to replace the old version;
- retain the old version; or
- deploy both the old and new versions of the component in the system.

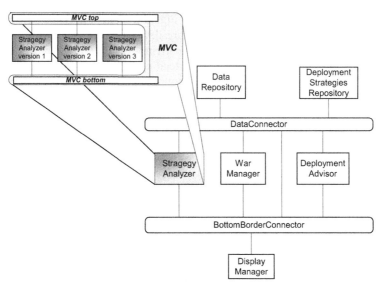

Fig. 9. Partial architecture of the TDS application. The internal structure of MVC is highlighted.

Prior to making one of these choices, the user must somehow assess the new component in the context of the environment within which the old component is running, and, once the choice is made, the running system needs to be updated.

```
Component: StrategyAnalyzer
Operations:
analyzeStrategy(int[][]):boolean;
calculateProbabilities(int[][]):int[][];
determineWinner(int[][]):String;
fight(int[][]):int[][];
```

Fig. 10. Operations of the Strategy Analyzer component.

5.1 Multi-Versioning Connectors

We illustrate our approach in the context of the example application described in Section 2. Figure 9 shows the partial architectural configuration of the TDS application. In this configuration, a *Strategy Analyzer* component provides several operations as illustrated in Figure 10. Let us assume that, after this application is deployed, we obtain two new versions of *Strategy Analyzer* that are claimed to be improvements over the old version. We would like to assess both new versions before deciding which one to deploy in our system.

Figure 9 depicts the essence of our approach: a component (*Strategy Analyzer*) is replaced by a set of its versions encapsulated in a wrapper. The wrapper serves as a connector between the encapsulated component versions and the rest of the system [13]. We say that *Strategy Analyzer* is multi-versioned and call the wrapper *multi-versioning connector (MVC)*. The MVC is responsible for "hiding" from the rest of the system the fact that a given component exists in multiple versions. The role of the MVC is to relay to all component versions each invocation that it receives from the rest of the system, and to propagate the generated result(s) to the rest of the system. Each component version may produce some result in response to an invocation. The MVC allows a system's architect to specify the component authority [2] for different operations. A component designated as authoritative for a given operation will be considered nominally correct with respect to that operation. The MVC will propagate *only* the results from an authoritative version to the rest of the system. At the same time, the MVC will log the results of all the multi-versioned components' invocations and compare them to the results produced by the authoritative version.

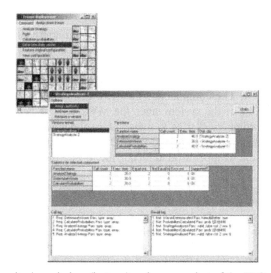

Fig. 11. MVC monitoring window (bottom) and a screenshot of the TDS application (top).

We are allowing authority specification to be at the level of the entire invocation domain (e.g., for each invocation, the entire component version *v1* will be considered nominally correct). We are also supporting authority specification at the level of individual operations (e.g., component version *v1* is authoritative for *analyzeStrategy*, while *v2* is authoritative for *calculateProbabilities*). For each possible invocation, we are assuming that there is going to be exactly one component designated as authoritative.

In addition to this "basic" functionality of insulating multi-versioned components from the rest of a system, the MVC provides several additional capabilities. It allows component authority for a given operation to be changed at any point. It also allows insertion of a new component version into the system during run-time without removing the old version. The MVC can monitor the execution of the multiple component versions and perform comparisons of their performance (i.e., execution speed), correctness (whether they are producing the same results as the authoritative version) and reliability (number of thrown exceptions and failures). Furthermore, the MVC logs the execution history as a sequence of invocations of the multi-versioned component. In case a failure has occurred, this information can be used to determine which sequence of invocations has led to the failure. The MVC also periodically records the state of each component version. The execution history and state "snapshots" can be used to roll back the execution of a multi-versioned component to any point in its past [16].

MVC's monitoring mechanism (logging of component invocations, comparisons of their results, and component state "snapshots") can help a user decide among replacing the old component version with the new, retaining the old version, and simultaneously deploying multiple versions of a single component in the system. In the first two cases, the MVC can be removed from the system to reduce the overhead introduced by its insertion. In the last case, the MVC will be retained and used to "simulate" the functionality of a single conceptual component. In that case, the monitoring can be disabled to minimize the overhead.

To date, we have primarily focused on the use of our approach in the case of component upgrades. However, the same infrastructure can be used when an entirely new component needs to be reliably deployed into a system. The wrapped component can be deployed at the desired location in the system's architecture in the manner discussed in Section 4. The component's behavior can then be assessed with minimal disturbance to the rest of the system since the MVC will be configured to "trap" all the invocations the component tries to make. Once the new component is assessed in the context of the deployed system and it is established that the component produces satisfactory results, the wrapper around it (i.e., the MVC) may be removed.

5.2 Implementation of MVC

We have directly leveraged Prism's implementation infrastructure in constructing the MVC. In particular, we have implemented three special-purpose, reusable software connectors, called *MVC-Top*, *MVC-Bottom*, and *MVC-Side*. Each connector serves as an intermediary between the multi-versioned component and the corresponding port through which the component is attached to the rest of the system. Depending on which ports are used by the multi-versioned component, one, two, or all three MVC connectors would be required to create the wrapper. Figure 9 shows one possible wrapping scenario, in which the multiversioned component is communicating using the top and bottom, but not side ports. *MVC-Top* and *MVC-Bottom* connectors encapsulate multiple versions of a component, allowing their parallel execution and monitoring. The intrinsic support of the Prism framework for dynamic addition and removal of components [10,14] is leveraged in the context of the MVC to add and remove component versions during run-time.

When a message is sent to a multi-versioned component (e.g., *Strategy Analyzer* in Figure 9) from any component below the *MVC-Bottom* or above the *MVC-Top* connectors, the corresponding connector invokes within each component version the operation that is responsible for processing that message. Even though the operation is invoked on all the installed versions, only the messages generated by the authoritative version are propagated by the two MVC connectors to the rest of the system. In our example, whenever a *determineWinner* request message is sent from the *Display Manager* component, MVC-Bottom will return to *Display Manager* only the result produced by (the authoritative) version *v2*; the results produced by versions *v1* and *v3* are compared with those of *v2* and logged, but are not propagated to the rest of the system.

The GUI of our implementation of the MVC is shown in the bottom window of Figure 11. This window is separate from an application's UI, such as that of TDS, partially depicted in the top window. The MVC window shows the list of component versions in the upper left frame. The table in the upper right frame shows the current authority specification and the total (cumulative) execution time, in milliseconds, for each invoked operation of a selected component version (in this case, version *v1* of *Strategy Analyzer*).

The table in the middle frame displays the execution statistics for the selected component version. For each operation, the table shows the number of times the operation has been invoked, the average execution time for that operation (-1 if the operation is not implemented by the component version), and the number of times the operation produced identical and different results in comparison to the authoritative version. The table also displays the number of times an error (an exception or a failure) occurred during the execution of the operation, and whether the invoked operation is implemented by the component version.

The bottom two frames in the MVC window display the call and result logs as sequences of generated messages. Using these logs, the *Undo* button can revert the states of a given set of multi-versioned components to any point in the past. This capability is achieved by taking "snapshots" of and storing the versions' states at regular intervals and by logging each message sent to the multi-versioned component. A detailed description of the undo process is given in [16].

The overhead of MVC is linearly proportional to the number of operations of the multiversioned component, and can be calculated using the following formula:

$Mem(MVC)=1208+44*num\_op$ (in bytes)

where *Mem(MVC)* is the memory usage of a single MVC and *num_op* is the total number of operations provided by the multi-versioned component. For example, the overhead of a single MVC for a component with 10 operations is around 1.6KB. The overhead of MVC's GUI is 680KB since it uses an off-the-shelf GUI framework (Java Swing). While this overhead is acceptable on desk-top and even some hand-held platforms (e.g., the iPAQ), it is too expensive for devices with significant resource constraints (e.g., the Palm Pilot). We are currently developing a simplified version of the UI that is targeted for such, less capacious platforms.

6 Related Work

In addition to software architectures, discussed in Section 3, this section outlines other relevant research. Carzaniga et. al. [1] proposed a comparison framework for software deployment techniques. They identified the activities in the software deployment process and provided an extensive comparison of existing approaches based on their coverage of the deployment activities. Our approach has similar coverage of the deployment process to application management systems [1]. Below, we briefly describe two approaches most closely related to ours.

Software Dock [5] is a system of loosely coupled, cooperating, distributed components. It supports software producers by providing a Release Dock and a Field Dock. The Release Dock acts as a repository of software system releases. The Field Dock supports a software consumer by providing an interface to the consumer's resources, configuration, and deployed software systems. The Software Dock employs agents that travel from a Release Dock to a Field Dock in order to perform specific software deployment tasks. A wide area event system connects Release Docks to Field Docks. The entire infrastructure of Software Dock introduces substantial overhead, and is therefore not directly applicable for the classes of applications that need to be deployed onto resource constrained devices.

Cook and Dage [2] have developed an approach to reliable software component upgrades that is most closely related to ours. Their component upgrade framework, HERCULES, treats only individual procedures as components, allows multiple such procedures to be executed simultaneously, and provides a means for comparing their execution results. Unlike our MVC, HERCULES does not provide any support for inserting and removing component versions at system run-time, or reverting a multi-versioned component to its past execution state.

7 Conclusions and Future Work

Software deployment is a central activity in the software development lifecycle. The deployment process changes the architecture of the target systems, as well as the systems' behavior. In order to ensure the desired effects of deployment, these changes need to be analyzed and controlled. The recent emergence of inexpensive, lightweight, resource constrained, highly distributed and mobile platforms additionally demands highly efficient software deployment solutions.

This paper has presented an approach that addresses these issues. Our approach directly leverages a system's architecture in enabling deployment. We have adapted our existing architectural implementation infrastructure to natively support the four deployment activities outlined in the Introduction. Our solution is extremely lightweight and has been successfully ported to a number of desk-top and hand-held platforms. While our experience thus far has been very positive, a number of issues remain areas of future work.

The issue of trust is central to the deployment of Prism applications due to their increased distribution, heterogeneity, and (possibly wireless) communication. We believe that explicit, first-class software connectors may be used to effectively support secure deployment in the Prism setting. The connectors may be used to implement various security protocols, including authentication, authorization, encryption, certificates, and sessions [13]. To date, we have implemented an encryption module inside *Border Connectors*. We plan to extend and directly apply this capability in our deployment support in the near future.

Another critical issue associated with highly distributed, mobile, possibly embedded systems is performance [7]. Our longer term goal is to develop techniques for actively assessing Prism applications and suggesting deployment strategies that minimize network traffic and maximize performance and availability. This includes estimation of optimal component locations in a distributed configuration, estimation of which components should be deployed, and, finally, when the deployment should occur. We intend to integrate Prism's support for architectural self-awareness and run-time monitoring with existing tools for system resource analysis [4] in order to enable these estimations.

References

1. A. Carzaniga et. al. A Characterization Framework for Software Deployment Technologies. Technical Report, Dept. of Computer Science, University of Colorado, 1998.
2. J. E. Cook and J. A. Dage. Highly Reliable Upgrading of Components. *21st International Conference on Software Engineering (ICSE'99)*, Los Angeles, CA, May 1999.
3. F. DeRemer and H. Kron. Programming-in-the-Large Versus Programming-in-the-Small. *IEEE Transactions on Software Engineering*, June 1976.
4. P. H. Feiler and J. J. Walker. Adaptive Feedback Scheduling of Incremental and Design-To-Time Tasks. 23rd *International Conference on Software Engineering (ICSE 2001)*, Toronto, Canada, May 2001.
5. R. S. Hall, D. M. Heimbigner, and A. L. Wolf. A Cooperative Approach to Support Software Deployment Using the Software Dock. *21st International Conference on Software Engineering (ICSE'99)*, Los Angeles, CA, May 1999.
6. J. Kramer and J. Magee. Constructing Distributed Systems In Conic. *IEEE TSE*, Vol. 15, No. 6, 6 1989.
7. E. A. Lee. Embedded Software. Technical Memorandum UCB/ERL M001/26, UC Berkeley, CA, July 2001
8. T. Lindholm and F. Yellin. The Java Virtual Machine Specification. *Addison Wesley* 1999.
9. N. Medvidovic, et al. Reuse of Off-the-Shelf Components in C2-Style Architectures. *19th International Conference on Software Engineering (ICSE'97)*, Boston, MA, May 1997.
10. N. Medvidovic and M. Mikic-Rakic. Architectural Support for Programming-in-the-Many. Technical Report, USC-CSE-2001-506, University of Southern California, October 2001.
11. N. Medvidovic, et al. A Language and Environment for Architecture-Based Software Development and Evolution. *21st International Conference on Software Engineering (ICSE'99)*, Los Angeles, CA, May 1999.
12. N. Medvidovic and R. N. Taylor. A Classification and Comparison Framework for Software Architecture Description Languages. *IEEE Transactions on Software Engineering*, January 2000.
13. N. Mehta, N. Medvidovic, and S. Phadke. Towards a Taxonomy of Software Connectors. *22nd International Conference on Software Engineering (ICSE 2000)*, Limerick, June 2000.
14. P. Oreizy, N. Medvidovic, and R. N. Taylor. Architecture-Based Runtime Software Evolution. *20th International Conference on Software Engineering (ICSE'98)*, Kyoto, Japan, April 1998.
15. D.E. Perry, and A.L. Wolf. Foundations for the Study of Software Architectures. *ACM SIGSOFT Software Engineering Notes*, October 1992.
16. M. Rakic and N. Medvidovic. Increasing the Confidence in Off-the-Shelf Components: A Software Connector-Based Approach. *Symposium on Software Reusability*, Toronto, Canada, May 2001.
17. B. Shannon, et al. Java 2 Platform, Enterprise Edition: Platform and Component Specifications. *Addison Wesley* 2000.

18. M. Shaw, and D. Garlan. Software Architecture: Perspectives on an Emerging Discipline. *Prentice Hall*, 1996.
19. R.N. Taylor, N. Medvidovic, et al. A Component- and Message-Based Architectural Style for GUI Software. *IEEE Transactions on Software Engineering*, June 1996.
20. Sun Microsystems. K Virtual Machine (KVM). http://java.sun.com/products/kvm.

Evolution of Distributed Java Programs

Susan Eisenbach, Chris Sadler, and Shakil Shaikh

[1] Department of Computing, Imperial College, London, UK SW7 2BZ,
[sue, sas97]@doc.ic.ac.uk
[2] School of Computing Science, Middlesex University, London, UK N14 4YZ,
c.sadler@mdx.ac.uk

Abstract. A major challenge of maintaining object-oriented programs is to find a means of evolving software that already has a distributed client base. This should be easier for Java developers than for most, because dynamic linking has been designed into the runtime system.
It turns out however that things are not so straightforward as they seem, since a given modification can leave a remote client in one of a number of states, not all of which are tolerable, let alone desirable. In this paper we attempt to delineate these states, and to consider ways of avoiding the worst of them. We describe our utility, which offers library developers a transparent version control system, to protect their remote clients.

1 Introduction

In this paper we consider the choices faced by a programmer who wishes to develop code for use by a community of heterogeneous and dispersed application developers. We refer to the code as a *library* and to its developer as the *library developer*. The users of the library we call the *client developers*.

The main issue of concern in this paper is the maintenance, or evolution of the library over time. We envisage that from time-to-time, the library developer will modify the code in the library and that different groups of client developers will initially join the user community at different points in its lifetime (different *generations*). We make a number of assumptions which it will be useful to clarify here:

1. The library developer is concerned to support all clients, no matter what generation of the library they are currently using.
2. The library developer has no idea which parts of the library are being used. The consequences of this is that, whenever a modification is made, no matter how obscure, the library developer must consider the *potential* impact, whether or not there are any clients who will *actually* be affected.
3. When the library developer makes a modification, he or she knows what is to be achieved, knows how to achieve it, and modifies the code in such a way as to achieve the desired result. We say such modifications are *intentional* and *effective*. Many library developers can and do make modifications which produce unintentional effects or which are not effective. We are not trying to solve this problem – if we could solve it, we would eliminate much of software maintenance altogether.

J. Bishop (Ed.): CD 2002, LNCS 2370, pp. 51–66, 2002.

4. When a library developer has modified the library, they will want to make it available to client developers and they will take any steps necessary to do so.

5. When a client developer needs to modify the client code as a result of a modification made to the library, the re-coding will be done with full knowledge about the nature of the library modification and the developer will continue re-coding until the modification has been successfully accommodated.

An early choice facing the library developer is how to distribute the code. On the one hand there is a very mature software engineering technology, which involves delivering a *static* version of the library on a physical medium or, with improved communications technology, by downloading from a network. The library developer can take care of his (or her) clients by imposing a good version control system [26] and offering frequent upgrades. Once downloaded, the software resides on the client system. For most of the history of software development this has been the standard method of distribution. It is still in use today (for example, by Sun Microsystems for delivering updated versions of the Java Development Kit [21]).

On the other hand, improved communication technology has given rise to a number of developments in software technology, which offer the library developer some alternatives. These include the concept of *object request brokering* [4,5,2]. Here the library developer never loses control of the library since the code to be executed resides at the library developer's site. Clients wishing to make use of the library must connect with the system and the library functions will be executed there. Provided that the integrity of the software interface is not compromised, this arrangement offers the library developer considerably more control over the immediate functionality of the library. Instead of waiting for the next 'release' to implement bug-fixes or enhancements, the library developer can implement these *in situ* to the immediate benefit of all concerned.

However, there are some disadvantages. Firstly, the library developer must have a system sufficiently powerful to deliver reasonable performance for an unknowably large community of client developers *and* their application users, and must be willing to pay for this. This is the *processor problem*. Secondly, if the system goes down or there are network problems, applications will not run at all, so all clients developers and users will be vulnerable – the *downtime problem*. Lastly, object request brokering doesn't allow for the software re-use that comes about through mechanisms that permit sub-classing (and sub-interfacing).

In this paper we consider *dynamic loading* which lies between the extremes of static library distribution and object request brokering. Dynamic libraries have a long history of providing support to executables at the operating system level [20]. However, these were usually distributed statically. Today's most prominent manifestation, the Windows dynamic link library (DLL) allows for a more incremental approach to updating, but imposes some restrictions and acknowledges some problems [1] compared with a more static approach to linking. Modern object oriented programming languages (specifically Java) incorporate similar dynamic loading capabilities into the runtime system and it is this technology we investigate here.

In section two we describe how Java's dynamic loading mechanism can give the library developer more control over the immediate functionality of his (or her) library and also some of the pitfalls which relying on this may entail. The main contribution of this paper is made in section three where we develop a scheme to help the library developer keep track of the different modification effects that can arise as the library evolves, and in section four which describes the design and development of a utility conceived to assist library developers in their task in such a way that even solves the downtime problem. In section five we report on other recent work, which has addressed this problem and in section six give some indications of where we want to take this work in the future.

2   Using Remote Libraries

2.1   Dynamic Loading

In most programming language environments linking occurs at compile-time and at runtime the system loads the complete binary. In Java environments, the compiler embeds only symbolic references into the binary and the Java Virtual Machine (JVM) uses this information to locate and load individual classes and interfaces 'on demand' – that is, *dynamically* [12,9]. This makes for a much more complex loading process but there are advantages:

- There is a faster start-up because less code needs to be loaded (at least initially). In particular, there is 'lazier' error detection since exceptions only need to be thrown when there is an actual attempt to link with unsafe code.
- At runtime, the program can link to the latest version of the binary, even if that version was not available at the time of compilation.

It is this last feature that we are interested in and it makes Java sound like the perfect solution for library developers with remote clients. Java is pretty good, but it is not perfect. In the first place, the designers of the JVM could not (quite rightly) just leave the loading mechanism at that – between loading the code and executing it, the Verifier must be run to ensure that any changes that may have been made to the code do not break the type checks that were originally performed by the compiler. If they do a *link error* occurs.

Secondly, even if the Verifier can be persuaded to accept a modified library class, it is possible to introduce modifications which will

- not be 'felt' at all by the client application;
- compromise the safe execution of the client application;
- put the code in such a state that further recompilation on the part of the client developer will result in failure – that is, an executable application cannot be re-created from the existing sources.

2.2 Binary Compatibility

If the Verifier detects no link errors at run time we say that the (new) library is *binary compatible* with the client [12]. Every individual modification that led to the existence of the new version must have been such as to maintain binary compatibility and so is a *binary compatible modification*.

Binary compatible modifications have been the subject of some study [10,11,7,8]. The way binary compatibility works is that at compile-time the compiler embeds symbolic references (not binary code!) into the client binaries. These references record the location of the library binaries together with type information (field types and method signatures). When the library source is modified and re-compiled, if the symbolic references are unchanged the new binary can still link to previously compiled clients.

Figure 1 lists some important types of modifications, which do not interfere with the symbolic references. There are also (see Figure 2) significant and common modifications that *do* interfere with symbolic information and which must be assumed to be binary *incompatible* with old clients.

Binary compatibility is a powerful concept, which, through the mechanism of dynamic loading, can offer the library developer a great deal of support in propagating the benefits of library evolution directly to clients. However, library developers should not be too comforted by binary compatibility because there are a number of traps waiting for unwary old clients.

Any modification made to anything private.
Any modifications which improve performance or correct errors without modifying field types, method signatures or the positions of classes, interfaces or members within the class hierarchy.
Any new classes, interfaces or members. Any modification which relaxes control over the class hierarchy. Thus `abstract` − > non-abstract permitting instantiation, `final` − > non-final permitting subclassing and any increases in the accessibility of classes, interfaces and members (`private` − > `protected` − > `public`).
Any modification, which moves a field up the class hierarchy. At runtime, the system attempts to resolve unresolved field references by searching up the class hierarchy.

Fig. 1. Some Binary Compatible Modifications

2.3 Old Clients

New clients of course experience a 'virgin' library and are not our concern here. It is the existing clients that we want to try to help to keep up-to-date. Those old clients that are likely to experience link (and other) errors are considered in a subsequent section. In earlier work [11], we considered those old client developers who may be beguiled by error-free linking into believing that their users

Any modification, which removes (deletes) an accessible class or interface. If no old clients actually subclass or instantiate that class, they will in fact link without error. However, since the library developer cannot know which features and facilities his (or her) clients are using he (or she) must assume that all features and facilities are being used.

Any modification, which changes field types or method signatures in situ.

Any modification, which strengthens control over the class hierarchy. Thus non-abstract $->$ `abstract` preventing instantiation, non-final $->$ `final` preventing subclassing and decreases in the accessibility of classes, interfaces and members (`public` $->$ `protected` $->$ `private`).

Any modification, which repositions a field further down the class hierarchy.

Fig. 2. Some Binary Incompatible Modifications

1. will benefit immediately from recent modifications;
2. will run trouble-free; or
3. will be able to continue evolving their applications without difficulty.

In some cases a client binary will link to a modified library binary without error, but the client user will not experience the effect of the modification until re-compilation. We called these *blind* clients. Situations in which blind clients can occur include the introduction into the library of a shadowing field and the modification of a compile-time constant. In other cases a client binary will link to a modified library binary but will no longer compile without error. Examples of such *fragile* clients include the use of shadowing fields when the field type is changed, the introduction of a more limited access modifier and the introduction of a new method into an interface [11].

3   Modification Effect Analysis

In order that modifications should not lead to such surprises, it is important to understand the possible effects of all types of modifications. In this analysis of modification effect *outcomes* we distinguish between effects that will occur without any action on the part of the client developer, save simply executing the client code (*link-time effects*); and effects which occur after client developer action (i.e. re-coding and/or recompilation) – *compile-time effects*.

3.1   Link-Time Effects

Once the modification has been made, the library will be rebuilt and the next time the client runs it will be dynamically linked with the new library. There are three possible effects:

LE0: The client links without error and runs without any discernible modification effect;

LE1: The client links without error and the modification effect is immediately discernible;

LE2: The modification is not binary compatible and consequently a link error occurs.

In relation to 'smooth' evolution, clearly the states LE0 and LE1 are desirable in the sense that the immediate client execution is not compromised by the modification, whilst LE2 is undesirable.

3.2   Compile-Time Effects

At some point (probably immediately in the case of a link-time or run-time error) the client is likely to recompile. The compilation may be trouble-free or it may be troublesome (i.e. there are compilation errors). In the case of troublesome compilation, it is assumed in the model that the client developer will re-code until compilation succeeds, and that re-coding will be done in the light of full knowledge about the library modification and with a view to benefiting from the modification. This gives rise to three possible effects:

CE0: The client rebuilds without error and runs without any discernible modification effect;

CE1: The client rebuilds without error and the modification effect appears (or persists if it was previously discernible);

CE2: The client encounters a compilation error, and, after re-coding achieves the desired modification.

CE0 is a desirable outcome if the modification made was not intended for these clients at all, but for a new species of client. CE1 is also desirable. CE2 places the burden of achieving a desirable modification effect on the client developer. We delineate all possible states by combining all LE and CE states as in Figure 3.

3.3   Classifying Reaction Types

On the assumption therefore that the client is bound to use the current version of the library (as dynamic linking presupposes), any individual modification to a library class can result in one of nine distinct outcomes for the client. However, from the library developer's point of view they can be classified into four *reaction types*.

Type I. The client can link to the new library and continue operations without hindrance. This category covers four distinct outcomes. In some cases (00 and 11) there are no further implications for the library developer provided that the actual outcome is the desired one.

In the case of 00 for instance, if the library developer had introduced a new class, which was not intended for old clients, then the fact that the old clients would never see the class is a desirable outcome.

LE	CE	Description	Reaction Type
0	0	The client experiences nothing (ever).	I
0	1	The client experiences nothing until a trouble-free re-compilation makes the modification discernible.	I
0	2	The client must re-code in order to experience the modification.	II
1	0	The client experiences the modification but it disappears after a trouble-free compilation.	I
1	1	The client experiences the modification immediately.	I
1	2	The client experiences the modification but the client developer will need to re-code as soon as recompilation occurs.	II
2	0	The client experiences an immediate linking problem. On recompilation, the problem disappears, but the modification never appears.	III
2	1	The client experiences an immediate linking problem which a trouble-free compilation resolves.	III
2	2	The client experiences an immediate problem, which the client developer will need to re-code to fix.	IV

Fig. 3. Modification Effects

In the case of 11, the modification would be discernible for old clients. If the effect is intended (for example, if it achieved improved performance of an algorithm, or corrected a spelling mistake in an error message) then the outcome is desirable.

However, the library developer could introduce a modification, which caused old clients to compute incorrect results (for example, changing a method so that it returned financial data in Euros rather than Pounds). Although the modification is discernible, its effect is an undesirable one and further intervention is indicated.

For outcome 01, the modification will only become discernible after rebuilding. It may be that no action is required on the part of the library developer, but if the modification *corrects* an error, which threatens future runs of the client, it would be desirable for the client developer to deal with it urgently. Another case may arise when the developer introduces an unintentional name-clash. On re-compilation the client binary may link to the wrong entity. Since it was unintentional, the library developer is unlikely to be aware of this and the client developer will have to detect the error and recover.

Type II. The modification does not threaten the running of the existing client, but when the client code is re-built, the modification will compromise the resulting binaries unless further client coding is done. Since it is not possible for the library developer to dictate precisely when the client recompiles, it would be safer if the client were to continue to link to the previous version.

Type III. Even though the re-build will be trouble-free, any execution before it is done will compromise the client. Once again, because the library developer cannot force the client to rebuild, a conservative policy dictates that the client should continue to link to the previous version of the library.

Type IV. The modification has compromised the client binaries – the client cannot link with the new library and cannot recompile without further coding. This is the least desirable scenario of all.

3.4   An Evolutionary Development Strategy

How can Java library developers evolve their classes without forcing their distributed clients into undesirable reaction states? One possibility is to restrict modifications so that they are only Type I. To help library developers to achieve this, we want to be able to determine, for any particular modification, whether

1. the client code will link and run (i.e. the modification is binary compatible, LE=0 or LE=1);
2. the client code will compile without error (CE=0 or CE=1);
3. the client code will execute correctly (LE=1, CE=1 and the discernible effect is desirable).

In any utility designed to assist Java library developers with distributed evolution, it should be possible to implement (1) and (2), although (3) will always be the developer's responsibility.

The restriction to Type I modifications is severely limiting for developers and we need to find a way to overcome this limitation. One idea is to devise a method of compromising the dynamic loading mechanism so that, under controlled conditions, potentially incompatible clients can link to earlier versions of the library (with which they are compatible). This can be incorporated relatively easily into any utility for the evolution of distributed Java programs. Another idea would be to develop techniques for embedding the code of undesirable modifications into structures that can mitigate their effects.

Finally, the discussion above identified several situations when it would be highly desirable for the library developer to be able to communicate with the client developer – for example to advise of an essential bug-fix which can be made discernible by means of a simple rebuild (01 or 21) or to warn not to rebuild (12). To achieve this it is not necessary to maintain a large contact list of clients or to require clients to go through a registration process, since every time a client runs, it 'touches base' with the library. We would like a Java evolution utility to help the library developer achieve this communication.

In the next section we discuss the design of a Distributed Evolution for Java Utility DEJAVU which has been developed to implement and experiment with some of the ideas discussed above.

4   DEJAVU – The Distributed Evolution for Java Utility

We set out to design a utility to help library developers and their client application developers to overcome the problems discussed above. To limit the scope and also to exploit the potential embedded in its design, we decided to restrict ourselves to distributed program development using Java. We assume furthermore that any modification made by the library developer is intentional (in the sense that it does what the library developer wanted it to do) and effective (in the same sense). A number of other stipulations were made to determine the scope of the utility:

1. All modifications are to be made to source code. No bit-twiddling of the binaries or other hacking can be permitted.
2. Evolution and access are to be mutually asynchronous. Any concept of 'releases' should be utterly transparent to clients.
3. Clients should be able to access and use the library without having to identify themselves or 'register' in any other way.
4. No changes to the Java language definition or to Java technical standards should be imposed.
5. Both library developers and client developers should be able to develop their code in standard Java development environments.
6. Library developers and client developers should not have to modify their programming style in order to use the tool.
7. Library developers and client developers should have access to version information.
8. The existence and operation of the tool should be transparent to all client application users.

From these indications we deduce the operation of the utility as follows:

1. The utility should accept versions of libraries from the library developer.
2. Having accepted a new version, it must compare it with the existing version. In making this comparison, it must detect significant modifications and must assess their impact at some level. (Initially Response Type I.)
3. The utility must report its findings to the library developer.
4. On the basis of the report (or otherwise), it must permit the library developer to publish the new version – that is to make it available to clients.
5. When a client developer wishes to compile, the utility must provide access to the appropriate library code.
6. When a client application attempts to link at runtime, the utility must determine whether or not the compile-time library version corresponds to the current runtime version. If not, it must ensure that the client application links to (and hence runs with) the appropriate (updated if necessary) version of the library.

7. The utility must be able to report to the client developer where and how the client application's most recently compiled version of the library diverges from the latest published version.

4.1   Architecture

Providing the client developer with a custom classloader, which is sensitive to the various versions of the library, could solve this problem. When this classloader detects a class that had been updated since the last build or run, it could analyze subsequent versions of the library to determine the most recent compatible one from which to load the class.

However, this is not a feasible solution for distributing libraries because of the way the current JVM works (see [24]). Either the client developer or the library developer would have to alter their programming style quite radically for such a system to work. (The client developer would need to use reflection to invoke methods. The library developer would need to establish fixed static interfaces). Instead we adopted the idea of updating at the level of the library as a whole. On the library developer side, we proposed a Controller component, which allows developers to maintain multiple versions of the library. One version is labelled 'latest' and this is the default version with which all new clients will link. Older clients will originally have compiled using an earlier version. The Controller needs to know, for any given client, whether the linked version is compatible with the latest version, and if not, which is the most recent version that it is compatible with.

The crucial question here is to determine what constitutes 'compatible' in these circumstances. In our system we define compatibility via a set of 'rules' governing one or more differences between versions of a class. If all the rules are satisfied the two versions will be considered compatible. By enunciating new rules and expanding the ruleset, we plan to extend the support, which the utility can provide to developers. The component of the system that applies Rules to two versions of a any library class is the RuleEngine. The overall architecture can be represented schematically as in Figure 4.

4.2   The Rule Engine

In order to drive the RuleEngine, an abstract Rule class was developed. This contains a number of fields and methods whose explanation will serve to describe the structure of the class.

1. `Vector newClasses, oldClasses`. When the RuleEngine attempts to apply a rule, it needs to compare two versions of a class library. The Vectors store all the classnames of each version, so each rule can be applied in turn to all the classes in the library.
2. `Vector ruleBreakingClasses`. Once it has been determined that a rule has been broken, the RuleEngine needs to be able to identify those classes where this has been detected.

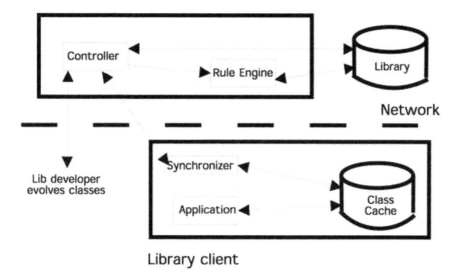

Fig. 4. Tool architecture

3. `String rule, ruleName, ruleExp`. These are designed to store specific reporting data for each specific rule, respectively the rule's operation, name and a description of the nature of the breakage.
4. `void setClasses (Vector nc, Vector oc)`. This method establishes the classnames of classes in the two versions of the library to be compared.
5. `static Class extract (Class c, Vector v)`. This method is used to extract corresponding classes from the two libraries.
6. `abstract Boolean checkRule()`. This method applies the (concrete) rule to the current set of library versions.
7. `abstract String diagnose()`. Rreturns a diagnostic message when a rule is broken.
8. `abstract Vector getDetails()`. Returns ruleBreakingClasses to report where the rule was broken.

Some rules cover classes as a whole – for example, there are rules to detect deleted public classes; classes that have become abstract, final and other than public; and a rule to determine whether the inheritance chain has been changed. Others are concerned with members of classes - deleted public fields and methods; deleted constructors; reduction of access to fields and methods.

Using this scheme, a set of such Rules can be implemented and passed to the RuleEngine, which iterates through, reporting its findings. The RuleEngine works with java.lang.reflect to examine and compare class versions. To do this the relevant classes must be loaded in the normal way. However the routine classloader provided with the JVM [18] is not capable of loading two classes with the same name from different locations. To bypass this a server-based custom classloader was developed capable of loading named classes from arbitrary locations.

4.3   The Controller and Synchroniser

On the client side, the system provides a Synchronizer component, which must be invoked as a part of the client application initialization. The client developer must start with an initial version of the library, downloaded into a local Class-Cache, and containing the `Synchroniser` class `ClassSynchr` with the method `syncClasses()`. It is this method that must be invoked early in the execution of the client application. At compile time the client code will link to the local version of the library and build the binaries accordingly. At runtime, the call to `syncClasses()` will create a connection to the remote `RuleServer` to test to see if the library needs updating. If it does then the entire library is replaced by the latest compatible version before loading continues once again from the local ClassCache.

In order to implement this, it is essential that the `syncClasses()` enquiry (about version compatibility) can be quickly dealt with. To enable this a number of persistent 'settings' files are maintained by the utility. These are

1. RuleSettings. This file is maintained by the `RuleServer` and covers all versions of the library as a whole – thus it records a list of all 'currently published' versions.
2. ServerVersionSettings. This file resides in the directory of each version. It stores the version number together with a record of the latest compatible version and also the latest version with which it has been compared.
3. LocalVersionSettings. This records the most recently copied local version of the library.

The Controller provides the interface for all the users of the system. It must be able to

1. accept updated versions of the library and, when requested, publish these.
2. interact with the `ClassSyncr` object of each client to determine whether a new library version is required and, if so, which one to download.

To manage multiple simultaneous clients, the `Controller` is implemented by a Controller/Slave pattern. Library developer requests cause a `RuleRemoteObj` to be created. This manages the upload of the new library files and invokes the `RuleEngine` to generate the version compatibility data.

This is not an ideal arrangement since the library developer cannot deduce the precise compatibility circumstances governing the current modifications in any interactive way, but must instead wait until the new library has been uploaded. For this reason the upload occurs in two stages. First the library is uploaded. Then it can be checked by the RuleEngine and a report for the library developer generated. Only then may the library developer 'publish' the new version, making it available to external clients. Correspondingly, on receiving a request from a remote ClassSyncr object, the controller creates a slave RuleRemoteCL to retrieve and examine the LocalVersionSettings file of the requester and choose an appropriate library version to download to the remote ClassCache. This can be represented schematically as in Figure 5.

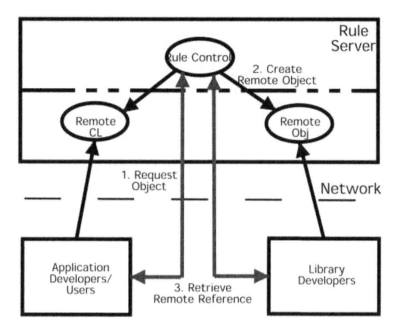

Fig. 5. Rule controller and slave objects

5 Related Work

The work described here arose directly out of theoretical work on binary compatibility done in collaboration with Drossopoulou and Wragg [7,8]. As binary compatibility was conceived to assist with the development of distributed libraries [10,11], we examined its effect on evolving libraries. Drossopoulou then went on to model dynamic linking in [6] and we looked at the nature of dynamic linking in Java [9]. We have looked at the problems that arise with binary compatible code in [10] and built a less powerful tool, described in [11]. Other formal work on distributed versioning has been done by Sewell in [23], but this work does not consider the issue of binary compatibility.

Other groups have studied the problem of protecting clients from unfortunate library modifications. [25] identified four problems with 'parent class exchange'. One of these concerned the introduction of a new (abstract) method into an interface. As discussed in [11], this is a 02 modification effect since the client will not compile correctly until the method has been implemented. The other issues all concern library methods which are overridden by client methods in circumstances where, under evolution, the application behaviour is adversely affected. To solve these problems, *reuse contracts* are proposed in order to document the library developer's design commitments. As the library evolves, the terms of the library's contract change and the same is true of the corresponding client's contract. Comparison of these contracts can serve to identify potential problems.

Mezini [19] investigated the same problem (here termed horizontal evolution) and considered that conventional composition mechanisms were not sophisticated enough to propagate design properties to the client. She proposed a *smart* composition model wherein, amongst other things, information about the library calling structure is made available at the client's site. Successive versions of this information can be compared using reflection to determine how the client can be protected. These ideas have been implemented as an extension to Smalltalk.

[17,3,27] have done work on altering previously compiled code. Such systems enable library code to be mutated to behave in a manner to suit the client. Although work on altering binaries preceded Java [27] it came into its own with Java since Java bytecode is high level, containing type information. In both the Binary Component Adaptation System [17] and the Java Object Instrumentation Environment [3] class files are altered and the new ones are loaded and run. One of the main purposes of this kind of work is extension of classes for instrumentation purposes but these systems could be used for other changes. We have not taken the approach of altering library developers' code because it makes the application developer responsible for the used library code. Responsibility without source or documentation is not a desirable situation. There is also the problem of integrating new library releases, which the client may not benefit from.

Often configuration management is about configuration per se – technical issues about storage and distribution; or management per se – policy issues about what should be managed and how. Network-Unified Configuration Management (NUCM) [13,14] embraces both in an architecture, incorporating a generic model of a distributed repository. The interface to this repository is sufficiently flexible to allow different policies to be manifested.

World Wide Configuration Management (WWCM) [15,22] provide an API for a web based client-server system. It is built around the Configuration Management Engine (CME) to implement what is effectively a distributed project. CME allows elements of a project to be arranged in a hierarchy and working sets to be checked in and out, and the project as a whole can be versioned so several different versions may exist concurrently.

In this paper we have mostly discussed changes that should propagate without requiring such explicit management. Where there are more major modifications, which will need substantial rebuilding, Configuration Management systems such as those described will be necessary.

6   Conclusions and Future Work

We have attempted to address the problems faced by a library developer who wishes to support remote clients by means of Java's dynamic loading mechanism. Although we started by considering binary compatibility as a key criterion for safe evolution, our analysis indicates that the situation is more complicated and that there is a greater variety of modification effects. We have developed a utility that helps to manage some of the issues raised and which we believe has the potential to be extended to cover a wider range of the issues.

In contemplating the further development of our project we see a number of ideas, which could serve to enhance the utility. These include:

1. Support for library development at the package level [16]. We have considered a library to be simply a hierarchy of classes. The Java language designers envisage libraries more in terms of Packages and we need to consider what issues this raises.

2. Library clients. It is possible that the client developer is developing a library for use by downstream clients. This leads to a multi-layered development model and we need to consider how our utility might work when a downstream client tries to link to several libraries each linked to a different version of the original.

3. Touching Base. Every time a client application runs, dynamic loading causes it to 'touch base' with the library's home system. There are many ways in which this communication could be exploited, such as

   (a) transmitting warnings and other updating information;
   (b) collecting information about the numbers of users and frequency of use of different versions of the library;
   (c) managing licenses and intellectual property data;
   (d) charging users on a 'per use' basis. Sun is developing support for this via its JMX (Java Management Extensions) specification [16]. We need to see whether this technology can serve our purposes.

Acknowledgements

We acknowledge the financial support of the EPSRC grant Ref GR/L 76709. Some of this work is based on more formal work done with Sophia Drossopolou. We thank the JVCS implementation team Y. Lam, K. Lin, Y. Gojali, C. Xu and D. Woo for their contributions to the predecessor tool of DEJaVU.

References

[1] R. Anderson, *The End of DLL Hell*, Microsoft Corporation, http:msdn.microsoft.comlibrarytechartdlldanger1.htm, January 2000.

[2] D. Box, D. Ehnebuske, G. Kakivaya, A. Layman, N. Mendelsohn, H. F. Nielsen, S. Thatte, D. Winer, *SOAP: Simple Object Access Protocol*, http://msdn.microsoft.com.

[3] G. Cohen, J. Chase, and D. Kaminsky, *Automatic Program Transformation with JOIE*, USENIX Annual Technical Symposium, New Orleans, 1998.

[4] *CORBA*, http://www.corba.org/.

[5] DCOM, http://www.microsoft.com/com/tech/DCOM.asp.

[6] S. Drossopoulou, *An Abstract Model of Java Dynamic Linking*, Loading and Verification, Types in Compilation Montreal, September 2001.

[7] S. Drossopoulou, S. Eisenbach and D. Wragg, *A Fragment Calculus – towards a model of Separate Compilation, Linking and Binary Compatibility*, IEEE Symposium on Logic in Computer Science, Jul. 1999, http://www-dse.doc.ic.ac.uk/projects/slurp/.

[8] S. Drossopoulou, D. Wragg and S. Eisenbach, *What is Java Binary Compatibility?*, OOPSLA'98 Proceedings, October 1998, http://www-dse.doc.ic.ac.uk/projects/slurp/.

[9] S. Eisenbach and S. Drossopoulou, *Manifestations of the Dynamic Linking Process in Java*, June 2001, http://www-dse.doc.ic.ac.uk/projects/slurp/dynamic-link/linking.htm.

[10] S. Eisenbach and C. Sadler, *Ephemeral Java Source Code*, IEEE Workshop on Future Trends in Distributed Systems, Cape Town, Dec. 1999.

[11] S. Eisenbach and C. Sadler, *Changing Java Programs*, IEEE Conference in Software Maintenance, Florence, Nov. 2001.

[12] J. Gosling, B. Joy, G. Steele and G. Bracha, *The Java Language Specification Second Edition*, Addison-Wesley, 2000.

[13] D. Hoek, M. Heimbigner, and A.L. Wolf, *A Generic, Peer-to-Peer Repository for Distributed Configuration Management*, ACM 18th International Conference on Software Engineering, March 1996.

[14] D. Hoek, M. Heimbigner, and A.L. Wolf, *Versioned Software Architecture*, 3rd International Software Architecture Workshop, Orlando, Florida, November 1998.

[15] J. J. Hunt, F. Lamers, J. Reuter and W. F. Tichy. *Distributed Configuration Management Via Java and the World Wide Web*, In Proc 7th Intl. Workshop on Software Configuration Management", Boston, 1997.

[16] *Java Management Extensions (JMX)*, java.sun.com/products/JavaManagement/, Jul. 2000.

[17] R. Keller and U. Holzle. *Binary Component Adaptation*, Proc. of the European Conf. on Object-Oriented Programming, Springer-Verlag, July 1998.

[18] T. Lindholm and F. Yellin, *The Java(tm) Virtual Machine Specification*, http:java.sun.comdocsbooksvmspec2nd-editionhtmlChangesAppendix.doc.html.

[19] M. Mezini, *Maintaining the Consistency of Class Libraries During Their Evolution*, Proc. of OOPSLA, 1997.

[20] J. Peterson and A. Silberschatz, *Operating System Concepts*, Addison Wesley, 1985.

[21] *Products and APIs*, http://java.sun.com/products/.

[22] J. Reuter, S. U. Hanssgen, J. J. Hunt, and W. F. Tichy. *Distributed Revision Control Via the World Wide Web*, In Proc. 6th Intl. Workshop on Software Configuration Management", Berlin, Germany, March, 1996.

[23] P. Sewell, Modules, *Abstract Types, and Distributed Versioning*, Proc. of Principles of Programming Languages, ACM Press, London, Jan. 2001.

[24] S. Shaikh, *Distributed Version Control for Java*, June, 2001, http://www-dse.doc.ic.ac.uk/projects/slurp/.

[25] P. Steyaert, C. Lucas, K. Mens and T. D'Hondt, *Reuse Contracts: Managing the Evolution of Reusable Assets*, Proc. of OOPSLA,1996.

[26] W. Tichy. *RCS: A System for Version Control*, Software – Practice and Experience, 15(7):637–654, July 1985.

[27] R. Wahbe, S. Lucco, and S. Graham. *Adaptable binary programs*, Technical Report CMU-CS-94-137, Carnegie Mellon University, School of Computer Science, Pittsburgh, PA 15213, Apr. 1994.

Reconfiguration in the Enterprise JavaBean Component Model

Matthew J. Rutherford, Kenneth Anderson, Antonio Carzaniga,
Dennis Heimbigner, and Alexander L. Wolf

Department of Computer Science, University of Colorado,
Boulder, Colorado 80309-0430 USA,
{matthew.rutherford,kena,carzanig,dennis,alw}@cs.colorado.edu

Abstract. Reconfiguration is the process of applying planned changes to the communication, interconnection, componentization, or functionality of a deployed system. It is a powerful tool for achieving a variety of desirable properties of large-scale, distributed systems, including evolvability, adaptability, survivability, and continuous availability. Current approaches to reconfiguration are inadequate: some allow one to describe a system's range of configurations for a relatively broad class of system architectures, but do not provide a mechanism for actually carrying out a reconfiguration; others provide a mechanism for carrying out certain kinds of limited reconfigurations, but assume a specialized system architecture in order to do so. This paper describes our attempt at devising a reconfiguration mechanism for use with the popular and widely available Enterprise JavaBean (EJB) component container model. We describe extensions to the basic services provided by EJB to support the mechanism, a prototype implementation, and a case study of its application to a representative component-based distributed system.

1   Introduction

Subsequent to their development, software systems undergo a rich and complex set of management activities referred to as the *deployment life cycle* [3,6]. These activities include the following.

- *Release:* packaging all artifacts and configuration descriptions needed to install a system on a variety of platforms.
- *Install:* configuring and assembling all artifacts necessary to use a released system. Typically this involves selecting from the release the configuration that is compatible with the specifics of the intended operating environment.
- *Activate:* putting installed software into a state that allows it to be used. Typically this involves allocating resources.
- *Deactivate:* putting installed software into a state that makes it unable to be used. Typically this involves deallocating resources.
- *Reconfigure:* modifying an installed and possibly activated system by selecting a different configuration from an existing release. Typically this activity is intended to satisfy an anticipated variation in operational requirements and, thus, is driven by external pressures.

J. Bishop (Ed.): CD 2002, LNCS 2370, pp. 67–81, 2002.

- *Adapt:* modifying an installed and possibly activated system by selecting a different configuration from an existing release. This activity differs from *reconfigure* in that it is intended to maintain the integrity of the system in the face of changes to the operating environment and, thus, is driven by internal pressures.
- *Update:* modifying an installed and possibly activated system by installing and possibly activating a newly released configuration.
- *Remove:* removing from the operating environment the installed artifacts of a system.
- *Retire:* making a release unavailable for deployment.

Many commercial tools exist to address the "easy" part of the problem, namely the activities of release, install, remove, and retire (e.g., Castanet, InstallSheild [7], netDeploy [12], and RPM [1]), but none that covers all the activities. Research prototypes have made strides at addressing dynamic reconfiguration, but are generally conceived within restricted or specially structured architectures [2,8,9,11].

In this paper we present our attempt at improving support for the activities of reconfigure, adapt, and update. Although the context and drivers for these three activities differ substantially, they clearly share many of the same technical challenges with respect to the correct and timely modification of a system. Therefore, in this paper we simply refer to the three activities collectively as "reconfiguration", using the individual activity names only when necessary.

In earlier work, we developed a tool called the Software Dock to automate the configuration and reconfiguration of distributed systems [3,4,5]. However, the Software Dock is currently restricted to the reconfiguration of installed systems that are not active. Activated systems complicate support for reconfiguration in at least three ways: (1) maintaining consistent application state between modifications; (2) coordinating modifications to concurrently active components; and (3) ensuring minimum disruption or "down time".

To help us better understand the challenges of reconfiguring activated systems, we embarked on an effort to study the problem in a particular context. The context we chose is the widely used Enterprise JavaBean (EJB) component framework [10]. EJBs are distributed components and, thus, further raise the level of complexity of software deployment activities, since the activities may have to be coordinated across multiple network nodes.

Further framing the problem, we delineated a space of reconfigurations that we wished to address in the study (Table 1). We consider three media of modifications leading to reconfiguration: parameters, implementations, and interfaces. We also consider whether or not modifications to multiple EJBs are dependent or independent; a dependency implies the need for transactional modification. In fact, the modifications should be both synchronized and transactional, since the system could be unstable if the reconfiguration is not successful on all nodes. On the other hand, there may be modifications that do not change the contract between components, and while it may be desirable for these changes to be made on all nodes, the changes do not need to be coordinated.

Table 1. Kinds of Reconfigurations

	Independent	**Dependent**
Parametric	Preprogrammed modification applied to a single component.	Preprogrammed modification applied to multiple components.
Implementation	Modification to the implementation of a component that does not require a modification to the implementation of its clients.	Modification to the implementation of a component that requires a modification to the implementation of its clients.
Interface	Modification to the interface of a component that does not require a modification to its clients.	Modification to the interface of a component that requires a modification to its clients.

A parametric reconfiguration is one that a component is itself designed to handle. It reflects a common way of planning for change in software systems, namely by having certain options specified as parameters through some external means such as a property file or database entry. By changing the parameter values, modifications can be made to the behavior of a software system without having to modify any of its executable software components. This type of reconfiguration might have to be coordinated across multiple nodes. For example, a parameter might be used to control whether or not a communication channel is encrypted, requiring distributed, communicating components to coordinate their response to a modification in this parameter.

An implementation reconfiguration is one in which only the implementation of a component is modified, but not its interface. Of course, the goal of separating implementation from interface is, in part, to isolate implementation modifications. Nevertheless, in some cases the effect of the modification does indeed propagate to the clients of the component. For example, a component may expose a method that takes a single string as its argument. The format of this string is important, and an implementation modification in the component may alter the expected format of this argument. This would require all client components to also modify their implementation to conform to the new format, even though the exposed interface did not change.

Finally, an interface reconfiguration results from the most pervasive modification to a component, affecting both the interface and implementation. Typically, an interface modification must be coordinated with client components. But this need not always be the case. For example, the modification may simply be an extension to the interface.

While this space may not be a complete expression of reconfiguration scenarios, it is sufficiently rich to exercise our ideas. In the next section we provide some background on the EJB framework, pointing out some of its shortcomings with respect to reconfiguration. Following that we introduce BARK, a prototype infrastructure for carrying out sophisticated EJB reconfigurations. We then demonstrate BARK by applying it to the reconfiguration of a distributed application that we built. The demonstration covers the six kinds of reconfigurations described above.

2   Background: Enterprise JavaBeans

The Sun Microsystems Enterprise Java initiative is a suite of technologies designed to provide a standard structure for developing component-based enterprise applications. The technologies address issues such as database connectivity, transaction support, naming and directory services, messaging services, and distribution. EJBs are the cornerstone of the Enterprise Java initiative. EJBs are distributed components, intended to execute within so-called *containers* that handle much of the complexity inherent in multi-threaded, database-driven, transactional applications; theoretically, the use of the EJB framework should allow developers to concentrate on the business logic of applications. The EJB specification provides strict guidelines about how EJB components must be packaged, and how they can reference other components. These guidelines provide a structure in which an automated deployment system can handle various management tasks.

EJBs come in three flavors: stateless session beans, stateful session beans and entity beans. The EJB 2.0 specification also defines a fourth flavor, message-driven beans, which are invoked by the arrival of a message to a specific topic or queue; here we only deal with the first three types of EJB. Stateless session beans are components that do not maintain any state between invocations. Essentially, stateless session beans provide utility functions to clients. Stateful session beans are components that need to maintain a conversational state on a per-client, per-session basis. That is, a different instance of a stateful session bean implementation class is used for each client, and its state is maintained between method invocations until the session is terminated. Entity beans are used to handle persistent business objects. This means that they are used to represent objects whose state can be shared across all the clients of the system. Typically, entity beans are used as a software representation of a single row of a query into a relational database.

Part of the EJB framework relates to the so-called "life cycle" stages that an EJB implementation instance goes through as it is servicing requests. Stateless session beans have a very simple life cycle, since the same instance can repeatedly service requests from different clients without the special handling that is required for stateful beans. For stateful beans, the life cycle is a bit more complicated, since the instance must be associated either with a particular client across multiple method calls or with a particular persistent entity. EJB containers maintain the state of component implementation instances using the following four EJB life-cycle methods.

- *Activate:* the first method called after a stateful EJB is deserialized from secondary storage. Any resources that it needs should be allocated.

- *Passivate:* the last method called before a stateful EJB is serialized to secondary storage. Any resources that it holds should be released.
- *Load:* valid for entity beans only, this method instructs the instance to retrieve current values of its state from persistent storage.
- *Store:* valid for entity beans only, this method instructs the instance to save current values of its state to persistent storage.

Note that in EJB terminology, "deployment" is the process by which an EJB server loads an EJB package and passes it to the container to make it available to clients. In this paper we avoid this restricted definition of deployment, since it can be confused with the broader meaning described in Section 1.

Once the classes that comprise an EJB have been developed, they then must be packaged in a standard fashion so that EJB servers can install them properly. Typically, all the classes that are needed for the EJB to run (excluding system classes that are available to all components) are assembled into a JAR (Java Archive) file that includes deployment descriptors identifying the standard set of classes that permit the EJB to be managed and used (the so-called home, remote, and implementation classes). The descriptors also typically include the JNDI (Java Naming and Directory Interface) name to which the interfaces to these classes are bound. Another important part of the standard deployment description includes information about any other EJBs upon which the given component depends.

The packaging specification for EJBs allows multiple EJBs to be packaged together in a single EJB JAR file. An EJB container handles all of the EJBs packaged together as a single application unit; once EJBs are packaged together, they cannot be maintained separately from the other EJBs with which they were packaged. In our work we therefore assume that a single EJB JAR file is described as containing a single component, with each EJB in the package representing a different view onto that component. Thus, the decision made by the software producer about the packaging of EJBs essentially drives the granularity of how the deployment life cycle of those EJBs can be managed.

Deployment in EJB-based systems involves various combinations of a small set of common actions.

- *Retrieve* a new component package from a software producer (*install* and *update*).
- *Load* a component package into an EJB server (*activate, reconfigure, update,* and *adapt*).
- *Unload* a component package from an EJB server (*update, deactivate,* and *reconfigure*).
- *Reload* a component package into an EJB server to freshen its bindings to other components (*reconfigure, update,* and *adapt*).
- *Modify* a database schema, database data, or content file (*activate, update, reconfigure,* and *adapt*).

One of the major problems with these actions is that they can be heavy handed. This is especially true of the actions that must be taken to reconfigure, update, or adapt an activated system, where component packages must be reloaded just to make sure the bindings are up to date. This invasive process implies that some or even all of the components in a system must be shut down for some period of time, which is simply unacceptable in high-volume, high-availability applications such as the electronic-commerce infrastructure systems that EJBs were largely meant to support.

To a certain extent, this problem of heavy handedness is dictated by the way that component package descriptors are used to specify the dependencies among EJBs. Included in the package descriptor for a component is the well-known naming service name of all other referenced components. When a referenced component is loaded by its EJB application server, the well-known name is bound into the naming service and the component is available. This presents a problem when updating a component that has dependent clients: If the same well-known name is chosen for the new version of the component, then the existing version must first be unloaded before the new version can be loaded, meaning that the system will effectively be unable to satisfy requests for a time. If instead a different well-known name is chosen for the new version of the component, then the package descriptors for all of its clients must be updated to be told of this new name, which means that they must be reloaded by their EJB application servers, again resulting in down time.

3   Approach: The BARK Reconfiguration Tool

Our approach to the problem is embodied in a prototype tool we call BARK (the Bean Automatic Reconfiguration frameworK). It is designed to facilitate the management and automation of all the activities in the deployment life cycle for EJBs. BARK provides some basic functions, such as the ability to download component packages over the Internet and load them into the EJB container. Other, more sophisticated aspects of the framework manipulate the component package descriptors to provide fine-grained control over a system formed from EJBs, even down to the level of individual bindings between components. In a sense, the functionality that BARK presents to its users defines an "assembly language" for EJB deployment management.

It is important to note that BARK is only a management tool; it does not provide any analysis of the running system, nor does it make recommendations or determine automatically what steps need to be taken to reconfigure a system in a particular way. As a management tool, it provides a certain level of checking to make sure that the user does not put the system into an unstable state unwittingly. However, BARK generally allows the user to force any action, thereby allowing the user to fully control the reconfiguration of the system as they see fit.

3.1   Architecture

The high-level architecture of BARK is depicted in Figure 1 and consists of the following major components.

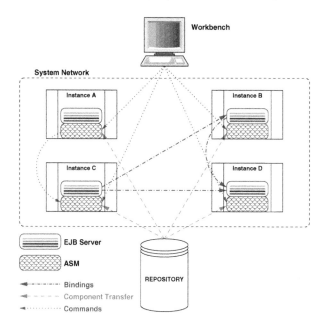

Fig. 1. The BARK Architecture

– *Application Server Module (ASM):* works in cooperation with an EJB application server instance to provide management of the components that it serves. The ASM is installed with every application server instance that is involved in the system being managed. The division of labor between an ASM and its application server is clear. The ASM is responsible for all the processing involved with managing the deployment life cycle of the components, including downloading packages, tracking deployment state and component versions, and managing reconfiguration transactions. In turn, the application server is responsible for handling the normal running of the software. An ASM only interacts with the application server directly when it activates or deactivates components. To achieve the necessary granularity for bindings, the ASM also adjusts the values stored in the JNDI naming service that is typically running as part of the application server.

– *Repository:* a central location for storing component software packages. ASMs download software packages from the repository when required. The repository is a conceptual part of the BARK system; there is no specialized repository software provided as part of BARK. In practice the repository can be any file server that is available to the ASMs. This represents the location to which a software producer would release software components.

– *Workbench:* provides a system administrator with a tool for directly controlling ASMs, serving as a bridge between the repository, which is controlled by software producers, and the ASMs, which represent the software consumers.

The bindings depicted in Figure 1 represent client/server relationships between components. Knowledge about such bindings are important for deployment activities, since it is changes in these bindings that are often involved in reconfiguration. The commands represent requests for deployment actions. Most of the commands depicted in Figure 1 are shown as originating from the workbench. However, inter-ASM commands are also necessary to ensure that any changes to bindings are approved by both the client and the server before they are completed.

BARK provides the ability to execute individual deployment actions or to execute scripts that combine multiple actions. Aside from conveniently grouping related sequences of actions, scripts are used to indicate transactional actions directed at one or more ASMs. In fact, a script is treated just as any other component and, therefore, its actions are managed by the ASM and the EJB application server. Scripts can also contain code for making changes to database structures or file contents.

3.2 Commands

Each command executed by an ASM is atomic and affects a single component or binding. Following are the primary ASM commands.

- *Add:* directs an ASM to download to the local node a particular EJB component package from a repository. After the package is downloaded, the ASM processes its contents and makes changes to the package descriptor that will allow the component to be properly controlled by subsequent commands.
- *Delete:* directs an ASM to remove a package from the local node.
- *Load:* directs an ASM to trigger its local application server to enable a component to make bindings to other components and accept client requests. The implementation of this command is EJB-vendor specific, since each vendor has their own notion of how to "deploy" component packages.
- *Unload:* directs an ASM to disable a component from making bindings to other components and accept client requests. A component cannot be unloaded if it still has active bindings and/or bound clients.
- *Bind:* directs an ASM to make a client relationship to a server component. If the two components are managed by different ASMs, then the ASM first contacts the server ASM directly to make sure that both the client and server were correctly specified and can create the binding. After a component is fully bound, it is available to accept clients. In situations where there are circular dependencies among components, the *Bind* command can force a server to accept clients before it is fully bound.
- *Rebind:* directs an ASM to update the binding of a component. Unlike the *Bind* command, the client component must already be bound to a server component.
- *Unbind:* directs an ASM to remove a relationship between two components. This command normally cannot be used until all clients of a component are removed, but can force the removal of a relationship in cases of circular dependencies.

- *Execute:* directs an ASM to begin execution of a loaded and fully bound component.
- *Stop:* directs an ASM to suspend execution of an executing component.
- *Reload parameters:* directs an ASM to cause a component to reload its parameters.
- *Refresh bindings:* directs an ASM to cause a component to refresh its bindings.

The last two commands are specifically intended to reduce the down time suffered by a running application when undergoing reconfiguration. However, unlike the other commands, they are predicated on cooperation from component designers, who must expose interfaces explicitly supporting these two non-standard life-cycle activities. With conventional EJB application servers, the only way to cause a freshening of bindings or reloading of parameter values is to force the server to reload the entire component package. Either that or the component could be programmed to always refresh or reload before each use, just in case there was a change. Both these approaches exhibit performance problems. The alternative that we advocate through BARK is a compromise that allows a refresh or reload directive to come from outside the component when necessary to support reconfiguration.

3.3   Transactions

The programmatic interface of BARK is modeled through a class called Connection. Instances of Connection provide strongly typed methods for executing commands on the ASM with which it is associated. In order to get proper transactional processing, some care must be taken when using Connection. To illustrate this, the steps taken by the scripting engine within an ASM are described below.

1. *Retrieve Connection object from primary ASM instance.* If multiple ASMs are involved in the execution of a script, one of them needs to be chosen as the primary instance. This can be done arbitrarily, since there is no special processing that must be performed.
2. *Retrieve Connection objects for other ASMs.* The primary Connection object is used to open connections onto the other ASMs. These new, secondary Connection objects are all considered to be in the same transaction context as the primary Connection object.
3. *Issue commands.* With the proper connections established, commands can be issued to any of the ASMs.
4. *Commit or rollback.* Using the primary Connection object, the entire transaction can be committed or rolled back.

Thus, a key feature of BARK is its support for transactional reconfigurations, since it is easy to see how a partial reconfiguration could render a software system unusable. The requirements on BARK's transactions are as follows: all of the configuration changes must be committed or rolled back as a unit; none of the configuration changes can be visible to other transactions until they are committed; and configuration changes made to one component during the transaction must be visible to the other components that are involved in the transaction.

BARK uses an optimistic concurrency control scheme, which effectively means that the first transaction to modify an object will succeed, while subsequent modifications will fail on a concurrency violation error. When a transaction is committed through a primary `Connection` object, all the secondary `Connection` objects are committed using a standard two-phase commit protocol. Although application servers that support EJBs must provide a transaction manager that implements Sun's Java Transaction Service, BARK manages its own transactions. This was an implementation decision driven by the desire to keep ASMs cleanly separated from application servers.

3.4   Scripts

Scripts are XML descriptions defining sequences of BARK commands that should be carried out in a single transaction. The script first defines all of the ASMs that are involved in the script, and then provides the sequence of actions that must be performed on each of them.

Figure 2 contains a sample BARK script. In this script, only one node is being managed. The script first retrieves two component packages from the repository, giving them script-local names `compA` and `compB`. In steps 3 and 4, both components are loaded into the EJB application server. Step 5 binds `compB` to `compA`.

```
<?xml version="1.0" standalone="no"?>
<!DOCTYPE bark-script SYSTEM ''bark-script.dtd" >
<bark-script name="SampleScript">
    <!-- host declarations -->
    <instance id="moleman" url="moleman:1099" />
    <!-- actions -->
    <get sequence="1" instance-id="moleman" id="compA"
        remote-url="http://repository/bark/ComponentA.jar" />
    <get sequence="2" instance-id="moleman" id="compB"
        remote-url="http://repository/bark/ComponentB.jar" />
    <load sequence="3" instance-id="moleman" component-id="compA" />
    <load sequence="4" instance-id="moleman" component-id="compB" />
    <bind sequence="5" instance-id="moleman" force="false"
        client-component-id="compB" client-view-name="ComponentB"
        server-component-id="compA" server-view-name="ComponentA" />
</bark-script>
```

Fig. 2. A BARK Script

3.5   Name Binding

Most EJB application servers use JNDI as a mechanism to make the developer-defined name of the server's (home) interface available to clients. Clients of the component "know" this name, and use it to do their lookups. This arbitrary name poses some problems when maintaining components in a server. For one thing, the clients have this name hard coded somewhere in their software or in their deployment descriptors. This effectively means that the component must always be installed with this name, or clients will not know how to look up references to it. For another, JNDI only allows one object to be bound to a particular name, so new versions of a component force prior versions to be unloaded.

The primary mechanism that BARK uses to achieve finer control over component bindings, and thereby greater flexibility in changing those bindings, is to transform the JNDI bindings after a component has been loaded by a server. In essence, the idea is to create an internally unique name that is known to BARK. For example, BARK might generate the internal name `bark/7730183/12876309` for a component whose original JNDI name was `componentb/ComponentB`. This JNDI name rewriting is handled automatically.

One drawback of this approach is that a client of a component managed by BARK, but that is not itself managed by BARK, does not have any way of binding to that component directly. To alleviate this problem, BARK provides an alias mechanism through which a name can remain unchanged while its association with internally generated names can change. The commands *Bind-name* and *Unbind-name* are provided to manipulate such aliases. For example, if there was a non-BARK application that needed to use the BARK-managed EJB `componentB`, and it was expecting its interface to be bound to the JNDI name `componentb/ComponentB`, then the *Bind-name* command could be used to automatically create an alias from `componentb/ComponentB` to the BARK-generated name `bark/7730183/12876309`.

3.6   Implementation

As mentioned above, the ASM software was designed to run in conjunction with an EJB application server. We use the open-source JBoss EJB application server in our prototype implementation of BARK. This server, as are other major servers such as BEA's WebLogic, is built using the Sun Microsystems JMX framework. JMX organizes services as so-called Manageable Beans (MBeans) that can be plugged together easily in a single application and so provide services to each other. The ASM software was integrated into the JBoss server as an MBean. This allows the ASM to have direct access to some of the important services that it needs, particularly the JNDI naming service and the EJB loading service. By being incorporated directly into the server application, the ASM is started and stopped when the server is, allowing for explicit control of the components it manages during those events.

4   Example Application: Dirsync

We developed an application called Dirsync as an exercise in the use of BARK. Dirsync provides a service for synchronizing the contents of shared directories on remote computers. It is a component-based distributed system built from a number of interdependent EJB components. Figure 3 shows the use relationships among the components; unfortunately, space does not permit an explanation of their individual functionality. A separate instance of Dirsync resides on each node in a network and is responsible for the directories on that node. The relationship between any two such instances, which is mediated by bound instances of `DataChannel` on either end, can be master/slave or peer-to-peer. Several versions of Dirsync were developed to drive a representative case study of how such a distributed component-based system can be evolved over time.

Most of the components that comprise the system are session beans, both stateless and stateful. A few entity beans are used to handle persistence of directory state, component parameters, and logging information. None of the entity beans are accessed directly by clients of a component. Instead, clients bind to a session bean that hides some of the details of the entity bean from the clients.

Although there are not a large number of components in Dirsync, complexity arises out of the relationships among them (both within a local machine and across the network), the changeable nature of the network topology, and the state that must be maintained on each local machine. These combine to make Dirsync a reasonable reconfiguration challenge. Some of the specific features of Dirsync that are representative of many real-world applications are as follows.

– *Both client/server and peer-to-peer relationships.* Client/server architectures are common, so any solution must be able to deal with them. But they are also easier to reconfigure, since they embody a clear hierarchy and, therefore, it is usually straightforward to determine an ordering for changes. With peer-to-peer architectures, certain reconfigurations need to occur on multiple nodes at once, making the coordination of reconfiguration more difficult.

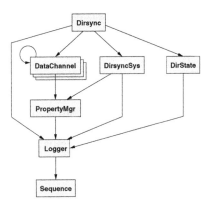

Fig. 3. The Dirsync Component Uses Hierarchy

- *A non-stop service.* This is a very common characteristic of multi-user distributed systems: there must always be something running that is ready to accept requests. This presents a reconfiguration challenge because changes must be made with minimal disruption to the service.
- *Network topology is dictated by application settings.* A dynamic network topology is fairly common, and presents a reconfiguration challenge because inter-node dependencies can only be determined based on the current configuration. This also means that some changes to the application parameters will require new bindings to be made between remote components.
- *There is persistent state.* The use of a database, or some other persistence resource, is very common in distributed systems, particularly for business applications. This presents a reconfiguration challenge because changes must be coordinated between an external software application and the software components of the system.

Table 2 summarizes a sequence of reconfigurations that we applied to a simple scenario of Dirsync running on two nodes, N-1 and N-2. Those particular reconfigurations were chosen because they represent a range of modifications commonly applied to component-based distributed systems and because they cover the space of reconfigurations outlined in Table 1 of Section 1.

We collected some initial performance statistics that indicate reasonable overhead in carrying out the reconfigurations. For example, the *Bind*, *Rebind*, and *Unbind* commands generally took on the order of 30 to 50 milliseconds. The *Add* and *Load* commands took much longer, consuming on the order of 1000 to 2500 milliseconds in our experiments. Our analysis shows that the *Add* command is dominated, not surprisingly, by network latency and repository implementation issues, while the *Load* command is dominated by time spent inside the JBoss server implementation of component activation. Clearly, more experiments are needed to validate these preliminary results.

5 Conclusion

The contribution of the work described in this paper lies primarily in the experience gained engineering advanced reconfiguration capabilities into an established component management framework. The challenge was to work within the confines of the services that the framework already provided. In fact, we saw the need to extend that framework in only two ways (reloading parameters and refreshing bindings), yet those extensions are really only for the purposes of reducing system down time and are not required functionality.

The next step for this work is to feed our experience back into the design of a next-generation Software Dock deployment system. Our intention is to create a version that is in some sense parametric with respect to the underlying component model, whether it be EJB, .NET, OSGi, or some other "standard" infrastructure. This requires the development of architectural principles that can be instantiated for the particular situation at hand.

Table 2. Dirsync Reconfigurations and Associated BARK Commands

---

Release 1: Initial Deployment

Establishes the sharing of `dir1` in a client/server relationship between `N-1` and `N-2`

a. *Add* all components from the repository
b. *Add, Load, Bind,* and *Execute* a script to create the database schemas
c. *Load* all components
d. *Bind* all local and remote components
e. *Execute* all local and remote components

Release 2: Independent Parametric Reconfiguration

The name `dir1` is changed on `N-2`

a. *Add, Load, Bind,* and *Execute* a script on `N-2` that can *Stop* `Dirsync`, rename directory `dir1`, and change `DirsyncSys` parameters
b. *Reload parameters* of `DirsyncSys` on `N-2`
c. *Execute* component `Dirsync` on `N-2`

Release 3: Dependent Parametric Reconfiguration

`dir2` is added as a new directory to be synchronized in a peer-to-peer fashion

a. *Add, Load, Bind,* and *Execute* a script on `N-1` and `N-2` that can *Stop* `Dirsync` and create properties for directory `dir2`
b. *Reload parameters* of `DirsyncSys` on `N-1` and `N-2`
c. *Execute* `Dirsync` on `N-1` and `N-2`

Release 4: Independent Implementation Reconfiguration

The file-change algorithm is enhanced to include a checksum of file contents

a. *Add, Load, Bind,* and *Execute* a script on `N-2` that alters the database schema to include a new field `Checksum`
b. *Add, Load,* and *Bind* a new version of `DirState` on `N-2` having the checksum algorithm
c. *Rebind* `Dirsync` on `N-2` to the new version of `DirState`

Release 5: Dependent Implementation Reconfiguration

The format of the command file is changed to include the time of last modification

a. *Add, Load, Bind,* and *Execute* a script that can *Stop* `Dirsync` on `N-1` and `N-2`
b. *Unbind, Unload,* and *Delete* `Dirsync` on `N-1` and `N-2`
c. *Add, Load, Bind,* and *Execute* a new version of `Dirsync` on `N-1` and `N-2`

Release 6: Independent Interface Reconfiguration

A method is added to `PropertyMgr` for easier access to integer properties

a. *Add, Load,* and *Bind* a new version of `PropertyMgr` on `N-1`
b. *Add* and *Load* a new version of `DirsyncSys` on `N-1` and *Bind* it to new version of `PropertyMgr`
c. *Rebind* `Dirsync` on `N-1` to the new version of `DirsyncSys`

Release 7: Dependent Interface Reconfiguration

A subcomponent of `DataChannel` is enhanced for more efficient data transmission

a. *Add, Load,* and (locally) *Bind* a new version of `DataChannel` on `N-1` and `N-2`
b. *Bind* instances of new versions of `DataChannel` to each other on `N-1` and `N-2`
c. *Refresh bindings* of `Dirsync` on `N-1` and `N-2`

Acknowledgments

The work described in this paper was supported in part by the Defense Advanced Research Projects Agency, Air Force Research Laboratory, and Space and Naval Warfare System Center under agreement numbers F30602-01-1-0503, F30602-00-2-0608, and N66001-00-1-8945. The U.S. Government is authorized to reproduce and distribute reprints for Governmental purposes notwithstanding any copyright annotation thereon. The views and conclusions contained herein are those of the authors and should not be interpreted as necessarily representing the official policies or endorsements, either expressed or implied, of the Defense Advanced Research Projects Agency, Air Force Research Laboratory, Space and Naval Warfare System Center, or the U.S. Government.

References

1. E.C. Bailey. *Maximum RPM*. Red Hat Software, Inc., February 1997.
2. L.J. Botha and J.M. Bishop. Configuring Distributed Systems in a Java-Based Environment. *IEE Proceedings – Software Engineering*, 148(2), April 2001.
3. R.S. Hall, D.M. Heimbigner, A. van der Hoek, and A.L. Wolf. An Architecture for Post-Development Configuration Management in a Wide-Area Network. In *Proceedings of the 1997 International Conference on Distributed Computing Systems*, pages 269–278. IEEE Computer Society, May 1997.
4. R.S. Hall, D.M. Heimbigner, and A.L. Wolf. Evaluating Software Deployment Languages and Schema. In *Proceedings of the 1998 International Conference on Software Maintenance*, pages 177–185. IEEE Computer Society, November 1998.
5. R.S. Hall, D.M. Heimbigner, and A.L. Wolf. A Cooperative Approach to Support Software Deployment Using the Software Dock. In *Proceedings of the 1999 International Conference on Software Engineering*, pages 174–183. Association for Computer Machinery, May 1999.
6. D.M. Heimbigner and A.L. Wolf. Post-Deployment Configuration Management. In *Proceedings of the Sixth International Workshop on Software Configuration Management*, number 1167 in Lecture Notes in Computer Science, pages 272–276. Springer-Verlag, 1996.
7. InstallShield Corporation. *InstallShield*, 1998.
8. J. Kramer and J. Magee. Dynamic Configuration for Distributed Systems. *IEEE Transactions on Software Engineering*, SE-11(4):424–436, April 1985.
9. J. Kramer and J. Magee. The Evolving Philosophers Problem: Dynamic Change Management. *IEEE Transactions on Software Engineering*, 16(11):1293–1306, November 1990.
10. R. Monson-Haefel. *Enterprise JavaBeans*. O'Reilly and Associates, 2000.
11. K. Ng, J. Kramer, J. Magee, and N. Dulay. The Software Architect's Assistant – A Visual Environment for Distributed Programming. In *Proceedings of the Twenty-Eighth Annual Hawaii International Conference on System Sciences*, 1995.
12. Open Software Associates. *OpenWEB netDeploy*, 1998.

A Component Framework for Dynamic Reconfiguration of Distributed Systems

Xuejun Chen[1,2] and Martin Simons[2]

[1] University of Stuttgart, Faculty of Computer Science, IPVR,
D-70049 Stuttgart, Germany,
xnchen@rupert.informatik.uni-stuttgart.de
[2] DaimlerChrysler AG, Telematics and E-Business Research, HPC T728,
D-70546 Stuttgart, Germany,
{xuejun.chen, martin.simons}@daimlerchrysler.com

Abstract. The growing popularity of wired and wireless Internet requires distributed systems to be more flexible, adaptive and easily extendable. Dynamic reconfiguration of distributed component-based systems is one possible solution to meet these demands. However, current component frameworks that support dynamic reconfiguration either place the burden of preparing a component for reconfiguration completely on the component's developer or impose strong restrictions on the component model and the communication mechanisms. We investigate a middle ground between these two extremes and propose a component framework that supports a framework guided reconfiguration and places minimal burden on the component's developer. This component framework offers mechanisms to analyze and treat the interactions between the target component and other components during a dynamic reconfiguration.

1 Introduction

Today, not only conventional computers, but also many electronic appliances, such as PDAs, mobile phones, TV boxes, and telematics systems in vehicles are becoming "internet-enabled". With the growing popularity of wired and wireless Internet, the use of dynamically reconfigurable distributed component-based systems is increasing. The ability to dynamically reconfigure the applications enhances the flexibility and adaptability of distributed systems.

In long running distributed systems, it is undesirable to fix the exact location of a component, since its operating conditions may change. It is also difficult for such systems to decide which application components should be available throughout the whole lifecycle of the systems. In these cases, dynamic reconfiguration provides the necessary flexibility: a component can be dynamically loaded into the system, migrated from one location to another, and unloaded from the system at runtime. An additional advantage is that a component can be updated dynamically. Therefore, a dynamically reconfigurable distributed system can quickly adapt to changing environmental conditions.

J. Bishop (Ed.): CD 2002, LNCS 2370, pp. 82–96.
© Springer-Verlag Berlin Heidelberg 2002

When we want to optimize the performance of a distributed system, we have to consider the following factors: machine load, memory capability and network bandwidth. In a dynamically reconfigurable distributed system, we have the possibilities to optimize the performance, for example, we can migrate components from an overloaded computer to an underloaded computer. In addition, if two components communicate closely with each other, we can locate them in the same computer, so that the communication costs in a network can be reduced. This point makes sense particularly for wireless communication.

However, in building a dynamically reconfigurable component-based distributed system, how to deal with interactions among components during a reconfiguration is a challenge. The current component frameworks (e.g. CORBA Component Model [15], Enterprise JavaBeans [20] and Distributed Component Object Model (DCOM) [9]) or service frameworks such as OSGi [16] provide little support for dynamic reconfiguration of distributed systems. If a dynamically reconfigurable distributed system is built on these component frameworks, the burden of preparing a component for reconfiguration is completely placed on the component's developer.

When reconfiguring a component, for example, migrating a component from one location to another, the consistency of the system has to be maintained. As a result, before a component is migrated, ongoing interaction between the target component and other components must be completed. After a successful migration of a component, the references to the migrated component must be updated. Therefore, a component framework should provide mechanisms that monitor the interactions among the components and automatically update invalid references.

Most of the component frameworks that offer location transparency use remote invocation mechanisms for the interactions among components, although the components are in the same location. Such location transparency degrades the system performance, because of the incurred serialization and deserialization overhead. Our component framework realizes not only distribution transparency, but can also dynamically switch invocations from remote to local and vice versa. Remote method invocation is used only if two components are really in different locations. In this way, the system performance can be improved. In the paper, we will present our measurement results of method invocations in our component framework.

This article describes a novel component framework that efficiently supports dynamic reconfiguration of distributed systems. The rest of the paper is organized as follows: Section 2 surveys related work. Section 3 describes the challenges of dynamic reconfiguration on component framework. Section 4 presents a component model for dynamic reconfiguration. Section 5 describes a component framework that meets the challenges of dynamic reconfiguration. The last section gives a summary of the main points and discusses issues for future work.

2   Related Work

In this section we describe the related work in the areas of component models and dynamic reconfiguration of distributed systems.

2.1   Current Component Models

Currently, three major component models are well-known in distributed systems: the Component Object Model (COM) [9], Enterprise JavaBeans (EJB), and the CORBA Component Model (CCM). COM is a component model provided by Microsoft for designing components dynamically bound to each other with multiple interfaces. Distributed Component Object Model (DCOM) is an application-level protocol that enables location transparent communication among COM applications in distributed systems.

EJB is a server-side component model for building distributed Java application systems. Similar to EJB, the CCM is a component model for building and deploying CORBA applications. It is developed to provide a distributed component model using programming languages other than Java and at the same time achieve interoperability with EJB components. In both EJB and CCM, components are executed in a container. Containers themselves run on application servers, offering services such as transactions, security, persistence and events. Each component provides a home interface and a remote interface. The home interface is used by the container for managing its life-cycle such as creation, migration and destruction, while the remote interface is used for providing functionality of a component. Both EJB and CCM allow system services to be implemented by the container provider rather than the application developer.

However, all of the above mentioned component models do not support dynamic reconfiguration of components, because these component models only provide the infrastructure that forms the basic building blocks for component systems. The internal design of components, particularly the aspect related to component reconfiguration is not addressed by conventional component models.

Currently, a new component model called OSGi service platform is attracting the attention of industries. The Open Services Gateway Initiative (OSGi) created open specifications for the network delivery of managed services to local networks and devices[16]. OSGi specification contains a specification for a service framework that provides an execution environment for downloadable components, called bundles. OSGi service platform claims that it allows a bundle to be dynamically updated. However, this framework does not guarantee the consistency of a dynamic update, because the ongoing interactions between the bundle to be updated and other bundles are not treated during a reconfiguration.

2.2   Dynamic Reconfiguration of Distributed Systems

Dynamic reconfiguration has been discussed in the research area of distributed systems. In Conic [8], Kramer and Magee defined that a node reaches a reconfigurable state, if this node is quiescent. However, in Conic, during the reconfiguration of a node, other nodes that require a service from the target node are completely blocked, where some activities are blocked unnecessarily. In Conic and in [23], the co-operation among components is realized by atomic transaction that simplifies the treatment of interactions among components during a dynamic reconfiguration. However, communication based on transaction has restrictions: since not every system is transactional, a lot of applications need to take concurrency and partial failure into consideration [10]. Other research projects in this field, for example [2, 17], tried to minimize the system interruption during a reconfiguration of a component, where a configuration manager deals with the interactions among components. In such approaches, the centralized configuration manager is the bottleneck for communication among components. The work [5, 6] introduced a component configurator that carried out a dynamic reconfiguration at the application level, consequence of which is that the programmers must implement the configurator of each component.

3   Challenges of Dynamic Reconfiguration

As mentioned in the introduction, a component in a dynamically reconfigurable component-based distributed system can be loaded into the system, migrated from one location to another, and unloaded from the system at runtime. Moreover, a component can be replaced during its execution. In this section, we discuss what challenges must be met by a component framework for supporting a dynamic reconfiguration.

The consistent state of a component has to be guaranteed during a dynamic reconfiguration of the component. We define in this paper that a component is consistent, if the integrity of interactions between the component and other components is guaranteed. In other words, there are no pending interactions between the target component and other components. Similar to the work [8], we define that a component can be consistently reconfigured, only when the following conditions are fulfilled:

- Its clients carry out no new invocation on it.
- The invocations of its clients on it have been completed.
- It carries out no new invocation on any other components.
- Its invocations on its server component have been answered.

When a component fulfills the above conditions, we say, the component reaches a reconfigurable state. However, how to recognize when the target component reaches a reconfigurable state is a challenge. To meet this challenge, the component framework must offer mechanisms to analyze and treat the interactions among components during a dynamic reconfiguration. Before a dynamic reconfiguration is carried out, at first, we have to determine what interactions between the target component and other components will be affected by the reconfiguration. Then, we must decide how we deal with these interactions, so that the target component reaches the reconfigurable state. Thus, we can carry out the reconfiguration safely.

If a consistent reconfiguration is guaranteed, there are still some optimization challenges in dynamic reconfiguration that we must take into account. First, we must try to minimize the interruption that accrues during the reconfiguration. Second, we must try to minimize the system overhead of the dynamic reconfiguration capability. Finally, the burden that component developers take for the dynamic reconfiguration must also be minimal, because the developers should only concentrate on the application logic.

In conclusion, a component framework must meet the following demands to support a dynamic reconfiguration of component-based distributed systems:

(1) The framework must provide supports for analyzing and treating interactions among components during a dynamic reconfiguration. The framework must know between which two components an interaction takes place. If a component is being reconfigured, the framework must at first block new invocations between the target component and other components, but let the ongoing invocations between the target component and other components complete, so that the target component can reach its reconfigurable state. If the framework blocks only necessary interactions, the system interruption is minimized. After the target component has been reconfigured, the framework must be able to automatically update the reference to the reconfigured component, and rebuild the blocked interaction to the reconfigured component. In addition, it is desirable that the framework can measure the invocation rate among components. The invocation rate is an important factor to decide on a dynamic migration.

(2) The communication between components should be location transparent, and the components that are in the same location should communicate locally with each other. However, if a component is migrated, for example, from location A to location B, the geometry structure of the distributed system is changed. The components in location A must now communicate with the target component remotely, while the components in location B can locally communicate with it. In this case, the framework should automatically switch invocations from remote to local and vice versa, in order to support the location transparency, and at the same time, to improve the system performance.

In the next sections, we will describe our component model and framework that efficiently support dynamic reconfiguration of distributed systems.

4   Component Model for Dynamic Reconfiguration

A component model specifies design rules and conventions that are imposed on component developers. There is some terminological confusion in the literature concerning component models and frameworks. We follow the CMU/SEI terminologies [1] which state that component-based systems rely upon well-defined standards and conventions (what is called a component model) and a support infrastructure (what is called a component framework).

4.1   Component Structure

A software component is a unit of composition with specified interfaces [22]. In our component model, a component consists of the following (see Figure 1):
• service interfaces
• service implementation
• control interfaces
• control implementation

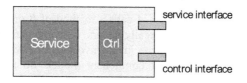

Fig. 1. Component structure

A component offers other components services through the service interfaces, so that the components can cooperate with each other. Conventional interface specification expresses functional properties that include services provided by a component and the signatures of these services - the types of arguments to the services and the manner in which results are returned from the services [1]. We call this kind of interface *service interface*. The *service interfaces* can be divided into *provided interface* and *required interface*. The *provided interface* is an interface that enables the component to provide other components the implemented functionality. The *required interface* describes the functionality that must be provided by other components or by the system to the component.

The *service implementation* ("*Service*") implements the services provided by the component. The *control implementation* ("*Ctrl*") of a component allows the component framework to control and reconfigure the components at runtime through the *control interface*, which defines the following methods: start(), stop(), update(), extractState(), restoreState(),and destroy(). These methods must be implemented by the programmers.

4.2   Intercomponent Dependencies

The current component models do not require explicit specification of dependencies among components and also do not manage the dependencies. However, if dependencies among components are not explicitly specified, it is difficult to build a robust component-based system, especially for a dynamically reconfigurable system. For example, without a dependence management, a new component probably cannot work after its installation, or the other components perhaps can not function after the installation of the component, because their requirements may not be fulfilled any more.

At design-time of a component, it must be determined on which components, which resources and which hardware this component depends. Such dependency is defined as *static dependency*. At compose-time of a component, for example, loading the component into a system, the component framework has to fulfill these static dependencies.

At dynamic reconfiguration-time of a component, we must answer the following questions: when a component is reconfigured, which other components are actually affected? How must we deal with these components? The static dependencies of components can not offer sufficient answers to the above questions, because a component does not actually depend on the components described in its static dependencies at an arbitrary point of time. For example, component *A* needs a service offered by component *B*. Only when the component *A* calls a method of component *B*, *A* is in fact dependent on *B*. Before *A* calls a method of *B* or after the method call is terminated, component *A* does not really depend on component *B*. We define the kind of runtime dependency that happens in an invocation between two components as *dynamic dependency*. The current component models do not distinguish between static and dynamic dependencies. In our component model, by the use of management of the dynamic dependencies among components we can determine which components are actually affected by a reconfiguration. This is a necessary condition for achieving such a dynamic reconfiguration that leads only to a minimal disruption of the system.

4.3   Intercomponent Interaction

Today's component frameworks often use RPC or its object oriented variant RMI (Remote Method Invocation) as communication mechanism. A client component holds references to its server components. If a server component is migrated or replaced, its reference that is held in its client components is not any longer valid. If the client component uses the reference, an exception will be thrown. The client components have to treat the exception, for example, updating the reference to the server component and repeating the call. Such a task is arduous and error-prone for the component developers. Preferably, the component framework can update an invalid reference just in time and automatically. In addition, as mentioned in Section 3, during a dynamic reconfiguration the interactions between the target component and other components must be monitored. For these purposes, we suggest a novel approach in which a component does not communicate with a normal stub of its server component, but with a virtual stub of the server component. A virtual stub is a local object and always valid for the client component. It holds the real reference to the server component, and updates this real reference immediately if the server component is reconfigured.

The advantages of a virtual stub are listed as follows: (1) A virtual stub can be manipulated by the component framework, for example, it can be dynamically loaded into the framework, and the real stub held in a virtual stub can be easily updated. (2) A virtual stub can automatically monitor the invocations between components. (3) A virtual stub can be automatically generated by a compiler (similar to the Java RMIC) from the provided interface of a server component.

A programmer can use a virtual stub like a normal Java RMI stub. The interface implemented by the RMI stub is also implemented by the virtual stub. The following example describes how a virtual stub *v_stub* is used in a program.

5   Component Framework for Dynamic Reconfiguration

In this section, we describe a novel component framework that supports dynamic reconfiguration. The component framework is an implementation of system services that supports and enforces the component model described in the last section.

```
public void testCall(){
  String info;
  TestInterface v_Stub = (TestInterface)
          componentContext.lookup("TestServer");
  try {
      info = v_Stub.testMethod("a test call");
      System.out.println(info);
      } catch (Exception e) {
            e.printStackTrace();
      }
}
```

Fig. 2. An example for using a virtual stub

5.1   Interaction Treatment During a Dynamic Reconfiguration

In this subsection we show how the proposed component framework analyzes and treats the interactions among components during a dynamic reconfiguration. The component framework provides a component runtime environment that is based on the Java Virtual Machine and implements the following system services: configuration management (CM), CM agents, and dependence management.

5.1.1   Configuration Management

A dynamically reconfigurable distributed system needs a CM that is responsible for initiating and performing a dynamic reconfiguration and guaranteeing the system integrity during the dynamic reconfiguration. Reasons for dynamic reconfiguration are the following: addition of a component; removal of a component; migration of a component; update of a component.

The CM is a core service in the distributed component-based system. The primary task of a CM is to check whether a configuration is consistent. The auxiliary tasks include version management and change management. These tasks are similar to software configuration management of conventional software systems and we no longer treat them in this paper. Instead, we emphasize the treatment of interactions among components during a dynamic reconfiguration.

When the CM decides to reconfigure the system, it must cooperate with its agents, in order to carry out the reconfiguration consistently. It informs the CM agents about the reconfiguration, so that the CM agents can control the interactions between the target component and other components, and let the target component reach its reconfigurable state. How exactly CM agents do their jobs will be described in the next subsection.

5.1.2   CM Agent

Residing in each component runtime environment, a CM agent is responsible for managing the components located in the same runtime environment, for example, loading a component into the runtime environment, starting, stopping, updating, and removing it from the system. In addition, a CM agent provides services for the managed components and guarantees the consistency of a dynamic reconfiguration in cooperation with the CM. The CM agent implements a component loader that is an extension of the Java class loader. After the CM agent has loaded a component into the runtime environment, the CM agent registers the component and stores the reference to the component, in order to manage the life-cycle of the component through its *control interface*.

When a component looks up a server component, the virtual stub of the server component is dynamically loaded by the CM agent into the runtime environment. The CM agent stores the reference to the loaded virtual stubs. Thus, the CM agent can control virtual stubs through the reference. Once a server component is able to be reconfigured, the CM agent asks the server component's virtual stubs to block any new invocations initiated by its client components. After the reconfiguration, the CM agent signals the virtual stubs to update the real reference to the server component and to resume the blocked communication. These operations are transparent to the clients.

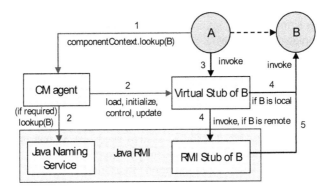

Fig. 3. Cooperation between CM agent and virtual stub

If a component is invoking a method on another component, we say, it is dynamically depending on the callee. The dynamic dependencies are registered by the virtual stubs. In order to provide support information for analyzing the dynamic dependencies among components, the virtual stubs must be aware which component uses it. A virtual stub is initialized by a CM agent as follows. First, a client component looks up a server component by calling *componentContext.lookup(serverName)*, where *serverName* represents the server component (see Figure 3). The *componentContext* is the interface to the framework's services. Next, the CM agent checks whether the server component is local. If the server component is local, the reference to the server component is already stored by the CM agent. If not, the CM agent asks for the address of the server component from the CM and invokes the method *java.rmi.Naming.lookup* in order to get the remote reference to the server component. The CM agent initializes the loaded virtual stub with three arguments: *clientName*, *serverName* and the local or remote reference to the server component, where *clientName* is given by the *componentContext*. Thus, the virtual stub is aware between which two components an interaction takes place and obtains a real reference to the server component. Finally, the virtual stub is returned to the client component. Thus, the client component can invoke a method on the server component through the virtual stub.

We have designed a super class called *VirtualStub*, from which all special virtual stubs are derived. The super class *VirtualStub* provides an interface, through which the CM agent can control the virtual stubs. This interface is presented as following:

- *initialization(clientName, serverName, target_ref)*: This method initializes a virtual stub. *clientName* and *serverName* have already been explained. *target_ref* is the reference to the callee (if the callee is located in the same runtime environment) or to the Java RMI stub of the callee. A method on the server component is actually invoked only by *target_ref*. *clientName* and *serverName* are used for analyzing the dynamic dependencies and controlling the interactions between the client component and the server component during a dynamic reconfiguration.

- *updateTargetRef(newTargetRef)*: This method is used after the reconfiguration of a server component, so that the real reference to the target component can be updated.

- *setLock(boolean)*: If the method *setLock(true)* is called, newly initiated invocations by the client component on the server component are blocked. If the method *setLock(false)* is called, the blocked invocations are resumed.

5.1.3   Managing *Dynamic Dependencies* among Components

As mentioned in Section 3, a component can be consistently reconfigured only if it is in a reconfigurable state. Dependence management monitors interactions among components, so that it determines when a target component reaches a reconfigurable state. Interactions that are affected by a reconfiguration are separated into two classes: newly initiated interactions and ongoing interactions. Before a dynamic reconfiguration, newly initiated invocations between the target component and other components are blocked by calling the method *setLock(true)* of the virtual stubs. After a dynamic reconfiguration, blocked invocations are rebuilt. On the other hand, ongoing interactions between the target component and other components must be completed. In order to monitor, when these interactions are completed, we have designed two methods in the super class *VirtualStub*. They are *addDependency* and *removeDependency*:

- *addDependency(clientName, serverName, serverMethod)*: When a virtual stub invokes a method on the server component, the *dynamic dependency* between the client component and the server method of the server component is registered in a dependence list. The argument *serverMethod* is used to analyze the call paths by a nested invocation. How this argument is used will be explained later.

- *removeDependency(clientName, serverName, serverMethod)*: After a virtual stub has finished the method invocation on the server component, the registration of the *dynamic dependency* between the client and the server method is removed from the dependency list.

The following simple method illustrates how a virtual stub supports dependence management.

```
public String testMethod(String info){
  if (lock == true) componentContext.block();
  try{
      TestInterface ref = (TestInterface)targetRef;
      addDependency(clientName, serverName, "testMethod");
      String str;
      if (remote == true)
          str = (String)ref.testMethod(info);
      else
          str = (String)ref.testMethod(copy(info));
      removeDependency(clientName,serverName, "testMethod");
      invocationCounter++;
      if (remote == true) return str;
          else return copy(str);
  } catch (Exception e){
      e.printStackTrace();
      return null;
  }
}
```

Fig. 4. Managing active dependency in a method of a virtual stub

Before a reconfiguration, all CM agents periodically check the dependency list in the related virtual stubs by calling the method *getDependencyInfo()*. If there is no ongoing interaction, the dependency list is empty, otherwise the CM agents allow the ongoing interactions to be completed. Thus, the four conditions in the definition of *reconfigurable state* mentioned in Section 3 are fulfilled, that is to say, the target component reaches its reconfigurable state.

However, it is not easy to decide which newly initiated invocations on the target component must be blocked. If we block a newly initiated invocation that participates in a nested invocation during a reconfiguration, this may lead to a deadlock (if there is cycles in the nested invocation), since the target component maybe can not reach a reconfigurable state forever. To solve this problem, *internal call paths* of a component are used by analyzing call paths in the dependence management. An internal call path describes a call path from an in-port to an out-port of a component. In order to determine the entire call paths for an invocation on a server component, the dependence management needs to know which method on the server component is being invoked by the client component and which internal call paths of the server component participate in this call path. That is the reason why the argument *serverMethod* is used in the method *addDependency*. By analyzing the entire call paths between the target component and other components, the CM can exactly determine during a dynamic reconfiguration, which invocations can be blocked and which must not. Due to space limitations, we do not describe this in detail.

By controlling invocations among components, the component framework can measure proximity among the components. For this purpose, an invocation counter is defined in the super class *VirtualStub* (see Figure 4). The counter registers the number of the invocations between the client and the server component. This information is useful for a decision of migration. If two components communicate frequently with each other and they are located in different runtime environments, we can move one of them to another. As a result, the communication costs can be reduced. However, after a migration of a component, the interactions between the target component and other components should be switched from remote to local or vice versa. The next subsection discusses this demand.

5.2   Switching Invocations from Remote to Local and Vice Versa

The current middleware, for example, DCE [18], CORBA [14], and Java RMI [21], use RPC or Remote Method Invocation to support location transparent communication between components. Even though two components are located in the same runtime environment, they communicate with each other by using remote method invocation. For example, Java RMI does not distinguish whether two components are located in the same Java Virtual Machine (JVM) or not. Therefore, serialization is always carried out, although both components are in the same JVM. In this subsection we show how our component framework meets the second demand of dynamic reconfiguration with respect to switching invocations from remote to local and vice versa. In the component framework, the remote method invocation is used only if two components are located in different runtime environments.

Notice that the parameters and results of inter-component invocations are always passed by value, in order to guarantee the semantic of regular Java RMI. If two components that communicate with each other are located in the same location, the parameters and results of invocations between both components are copied in the virtual stubs before being used (see Figure 4).

Automatically Switching Local/Remote Invocations

In our component framework, each component is dynamically loaded into the runtime environment by the CM agent. The CM agent retains the references of the loaded components. When a client component looks up a server component, the CM agent loads an appropriate virtual stub of the server component and returns it to the client component. If the client and the server component reside in the same runtime environment, the virtual stub is initialized by the CM agent in such a way, that this virtual stub holds a local reference to the server component. Therefore, invocations between both components are local. If the client and the server component reside in different runtime environments, the virtual stub holds a Java RMI stub of the server component, thus invocations between both components are remote.

For example, if component *A* is migrated from location *L1* to location *L2*, the location relationships between *A* and other components are altered. The components in *L1* are remote components for *A* now, and the components in *L2* are now local components for it. After migrating *A*, *L1*'s CM agent must invoke the method *updateTargetRef(remoteA)* on *A*'s virtual stubs in *L1*, where *remoteA* is the remote reference to *A*. The CM agent in *L2* must invoke the method *updateTargetRef(localA)* on *A*'s virtual stubs in *L2*, where *localA* is the local reference to *A*. Thus, the invocations are automatically switched from local to remote and vice versa.

Measurement Results of the Local/Remote Invocations

To study the costs of method invocations, we conducted our experiments on two PCs: one is an Intel Pentium III 500MHz Desktop running Windows NT 4.0 and uses standard JDK 1.2 version of Java Virtual Machine; the other is an Intel Pentium III 700MHz Laptop running Windows 98 and uses standard JDK 1.2 version of Java Virtual Machine. These two machines were connected through a 100-Mbit Ethernet. To measure the time of one invocation, we performed 1000 invocations of a simple method in a cycle and repeated 10 times. This simple method receives a string from the caller and returns the same string to the caller. The measurements were carried out on an isolated network, and the reported times are the averages of these 10 measurements. Table 1 summarizes the performance measurements and compares the invocations in our component framework by the use of virtual stub to regular Java RMI.

Table 1. Comparative costs for a simple method invocation

Runtime environment	Middleware	Time in ms
The client and the server are in the same runtime environment on the desktop.	Java RMI	1.0114
	Our component framework	0.0623
The server runs on the laptop, and the client runs on the desktop.	Java RMI	2.7913
	Our component framework	2.8356

When a client and a server component are located in the same runtime environment, the invocation between both components in our component framework is significantly faster than in Java RMI, in spite of the overhead resulting from dependence management. By the use of Java RMI, even though both components are located in the same runtime environment, serialization must be executed. The computational costs of serialization, as shown in many papers [7, 11, 19], degrade the performance of RMI severely. As a rule of thumb, RMI's serialization takes at least 25% of the costs of a remote method invocation [12]. The costs of serialization rise with growing object structures. By the use of our component framework, the invocations between two components in the same runtime environment are actually local invocations, so that the system performance is improved.

When a client and a server component are located in different runtime environments, the remote invocations between both components in our component framework are a little slower than in Java RMI, because there are overhead costs of 0.0443 ms for supporting dependence management.

6   Conclusions and Future Work

This paper has presented a component framework that meets the demands of dynamic reconfiguration mentioned in Section 3. The component framework offers dependence management that analyzes the *dynamic dependencies* among components, and uses virtual stubs that not only realize location transparent invocations among components, but also dynamically monitor and manipulate interactions among components during a dynamic reconfiguration. In addition, the CM agent can automatically update an invalid reference to a component after its reconfiguration. In the component framework, not only a consistent reconfiguration is guaranteed, but also the disruption of the system is minimized, because only the actually affected interactions are blocked. Such a dynamic reconfiguration is carried out at the framework level, therefore, the burden of the reconfiguration on the component developers is minimal. Furthermore, the component framework can automatically switch invocations among components from local to remote and vice versa after the migration of a component. Remote invocation is used only if two components are really in different locations. This approach improves the system performance significantly.

At the present moment, our framework does not provide any support to guarantee that a group of reconfiguration actions is carried out as an atomic transaction. In the next step we will achieve this by using the Java transaction service. Furthermore, we believe QoS is also an important aspect of system consistency. If an application demands QoS, its QoS demands may not be guaranteed during a reconfiguration. For example, an application has a demand on latency. During a dynamic reconfiguration, it can happen that this demand is not fulfilled because of system interruption. In the future work, we will investigate what kind of support the component framework can provide to guarantee the QoS of the component-based system during a dynamic reconfiguration.

Acknowledgments

The authors thank Viktor Friesen and Alexander Leonhardi for their comments on earlier drafts of this paper. They also thank the anonymous reviewers for their helpful comments. The first author gratefully acknowledges the support of DaimlerChrysler AG.

Reference

1. Bachman, F. et al. Technical Concepts of Component-Based Software Engineering. Technical Report CMU/SEI-2000-TR-008, May 2000.
2. Bidan, Ch., Issarny, V., Saridakis, T., and Zarras, A. A Dynamic Reconfiguration Service for CORBA. In: Proceedings of the fourth International Conference on Configurable Distributed Systems, pages 35-42, Maryland, 1998.
3. Holder, O., Ben-Shaul, I. and Gazit, H. Dynamic Layout of Distributed Applications in FarGo. Proceedings of the 21st International Conference on Software Engineering (ICSE'99), Los Angeles, CA, USA, pages 163-173, 1999.
4. Holder, O., Ben-Shaul, I. and Gazit, H. System Support for Dynamic Layout of Distributed Applications. In: Proceedings of the 19th International Conference on Distributed Computing Systems (ICDCS'99), Austin, TX, USA, pages 403-411, 1999.
5. Kon, F. Automatic Configuration of Component-based Distributed Systems. PhD Thesis, University of Illinois at Urbana-Champaign, 2000.
6. Kon, F. and Campbell, R. Dependence Management in Component-Based Distributed Systems. IEEE Concurrency, 8(1), pp. 26-36, January-March, 2000.
7. Kono, K. and Masuda, T. Efficient RMI: Dynamic Specialization of Object Serialization. The 20th International Conference on Distributed Computing Systems, Taiwan, April, 2000.
8. Kramer, J. and Magee, J. The Evolving Philosophers Problem: Dynamic Change Management. IEEE Transactions on Software Engineering, SE-16, 11, pages 1293-1306, 1990.

9. Microsoft, COM, http://www.microsoft.com/com.
10. Milojicic, D. Middleware's role, today and tomorrow. IEEE Concurrency, pages 70-80, April-June 1999.
11. Muller, G., Marlet, R., Pu C., and Goel A. Fast, optimized Sun RPC using automatic program specialization. In Proc. of IEEE 18th International Conference on Distributed Computing Systems, pages 240-249, 1998.
12. Nester, Ch., Philippsen, M., and Haumacher, B. A More Efficient RMI for Java. ACM Java'99, pp.152-159, San Francisco, USA, 1999.
13. ObjectSpace. Voyager, http:www.objectspace.com, 2000.
14. OMG. CORBA, Object Management Group, http://www.omg.org, 1997
15. OMG. CORBA Component Model, Object Management Group, http://www.omg.org, 2000.
16. OSGi: Open Services Gateway Initiative. http://www.osgi.org, 2001.
17. Oueichek, I. and Rousset de P., S. Dynamic Configuration Management in the Guide Object-Oriented Distributed. In: Proceedings of the third International Conference on Configurable Distributed Systems, pages 28-35, Maryland, 1996
18. Rosenberry, W., Kenney, D., and Fischer, G. Understanding DCE, O'Reilly&Associates, Sebastopol, Calif., 1992.
19. Silva M., Atokinson M., and Black A. Semantics for parameter passing in a type-complete persistent RPC. In Proc. IEEE 16th International Conference on Distributed Computing Systems, pages 411-418, 1996.
20. Sun Microsystems. Enterprise JavaBeans, http://java.sun.com/products/ejb/index.html, 1999.
21. Sun Microsystems. Remote Method Invocation, http://java.sun.com/products/jdk/rmi/index.html, 1999.
22. Szyperski, C. Component Software - Beyond Object-Oriented Programming. Addison-Wesley / ACM Press, 1998.
23. Warren, I. and Sommerville, I. A Model for Dynamic Configuration which Preserves Application Integrity. In: Proceedings of the third International Conference on Configurable Distributed Systems, pages 28-35, Maryland, 1996.

Software Deployment Using Mobile Agents

Nils P. Sudmann and Dag Johansen*

Department of Computer Science, University of Tromsø, Norway,
nilss@cs.uit.no, dag@cs.uit.no

Abstract. In this paper we show how mobile agents can be applied
to software component updates in a distributed environment. One important aspect is that the control code for component updates can be
distributed at run time. Also, by selecting the right agent system one
gains flexibility in the choice of configuration languages.

1 Introduction

The principle of deploying web components over the Internet is currently touted
by key industrial players as *the* structuring approach for software systems. Com-
panies like, for instance, Microsoft (.NET), IBM (WebSpheres), Sun (JXTA), and
BEA (WebLogic) are all advocating web service architectures. The fundamental
idea is to download web service components over the network and install and
extend a core software base already running on the computers.

Fundamentally, this is not a new idea. Web components, application updates,
and similar extensibility techniques have been applied in, for instance, micro
kernel operating systems [Lie95,BSP+95], in Java environments with applets
and servlets, and in mobile agent technologies [GKCR98,AO98,BHRS98]. The
difference, though, is the massive focus this type of deployment architectures
currently gets.

In this paper, we present the latest in a series of middleware toolkits, which,
in principle, is similar to these emerging web services platforms. This is TACOMA
v2.2, a mobile agent system built to support software deployment over the network. In TACOMA, in contrast to all other early mobile agent systems, general
software installation has always been a key requirement to support. In this paper, we will show how to actually ship install logic along with the software
components to be installed.

The rest of this paper is organized as follows. In section 2, we introduce the
key concepts of TACOMA, the mobile agent system we use as infrastructure for
component deployment. In section 3, we discuss our software component deployment application. In section 4, we discuss various design options for component
deployment using mobile agents, and finally, section 5 concludes this paper.

* This work was supported by NSF (Norges forskningsråd), DITS program, Norway
grant no. 112578/431 and 126107/431.

J. Bishop (Ed.): CD 2002, LNCS 2370, pp. 97–107, 2002.

2   Concepts in TACOMA

Software component updates are inherently complex because components often are interdependent. Hence, care must be taken during maintenance to avoid breaking the system while it is in a inconsistent state. It is difficult and inflexible to build a generic software deployment system. Rather, we need support code that controls the actual update or install process and is supplied dynamically as the software component is updated. Mobile agents are computations that are able to relocate themselves from one host to another, and they are a convenient way to dynamically supply control code for the update process in a distributed setting.

In the TACOMA project [JvRS95,JLvR+02], we started out almost 10 years ago to build extensible servers with mobile code being deployed over the network. This was initially used to extend remote weather servers in the Arctic with client software [JH94]. We generalized and built several versions of our deployment middleware, but with focus on mobile agent support. However, in contrast to all other early mobile agent systems, our focus was on supporting agents written in multiple languages. A typical mobile agent in TACOMA was a simple Perl script that needed to be deployed throughout the network, or a C++ server extension that had to be added to a single remote server.

Hence, a TACOMA mobile agent is basically a software component that has to be deployed in a network of extensible servers. In principle, this is exactly the same as what emerging industrial web service infrastructures provide, where our mobile agent resembles a web service.

In TACOMA, a mobile agent collects initial state and state changes in a *briefcase*. Once an agent is ready to move, its briefcase should contain a sufficient snapshot of the state needed to pick up execution at another host. Briefcases are further divided into a set of named *folders*, which themselves consist of a list of *elements*. The element is the basic data type in this structure; it is interpreted by the TACOMA system as an sequence of bytes. By convention, actual interpretation beyond this is left to the application receiving it.

A *cabinet* is a persistent site-bound briefcase that a mobile agent may allocate and store data in for future visits to the host. Cabinets are used by our system as repositories to store software packages and information about them.

An agent *core* is a digitally signed immutable collection of initial state. It is used to authenticate an agent. Agents without a core are considered anonymous, and are severely restricted in what they are authorized to do in a general TACOMA configuration. In fact, in the configuration of TACOMA to general component deployment, agents are rejected if they are not signed by a trusted repository. The core is also used to validate the authenticity of the update control code and the software package. Only if the update control code is part of the core, is it allowed to execute with the needed permissions to perform software updates. This mechanism ensures that the code has not been modified while in transit. In effect, we turned a general mobile agent system into a safe installation toolkit. For more details, see [SJ00,SJ01].

An important aspect of TACOMA is the ability agents have to carry with them other agents. This is done by taking a briefcase representation of an agent, archiving it and incorporating it into the core of another agent. This agent may at a later point fetch the archive from its core and activate the initial agent.

3   The Software Deployment Application

Our infrastructure contains one or more repositories that contain the latest versions of software packages. These packages can be used to update or install new software at a number of hosts that are subscribing to the repository service. However, we do not require that all the subscribing hosts share the same software base after updates. That is, some hosts may be unavailable at update time, and may lag behind in updates. Furthermore, impatient host owners may update their software manually without waiting for a repository update. This implies that repositories cannot use their knowledge of previous package updates to determine future updates.

The repositories are TACOMA sites, containing software packages, and running a restricted version of our mobile agent system. A software package is a self contained archive with a version number. Each package is associated with a *probe agent* and a *update control agent*, which are package specific. In our system we currently use Redhat rpm packages, since most of our implementation has been centered around the Linux platform. These packages are stored in the TACOMA cabinet of the local repository. Furthermore, we store a list of hosts subscribing to the service.

Next, the software deployment application itself consists of two different agents, the state collector agent (State.Coll) and the installer agent (Pack.Install). The State.Coll agent travels in an itinerant style and collects information about hosts. The second type consists of several copies that work in parallel and does the actual software installation, see figure 1.

Like all TACOMA agents the snapshot of the State.Coll and Pack.Install agent consists of a core that is digitally signed by the repository. The core contains among others the command and control code and the list of nodes to visit. As mentioned, clients will only accept agents whose core is signed by parties they trust.

3.1   Step 1: The State.Coll Agent

The software update process starts at the repository. The repository regularly collects the list of packages available, and the list of hosts that are subscribing to its service. Next, the repository creates an agent core for the State.Coll agent containing the list of updates, the client host list, the State.Coll code, and a set of probe agents, one for each package, that determine the state of that particular software package at the client. The core is digitally signed by the repository with its key.

Now, the newly created State.Coll agent is activated. It examines its list of hosts that it has to investigate. It then tries to relocate itself to a host on

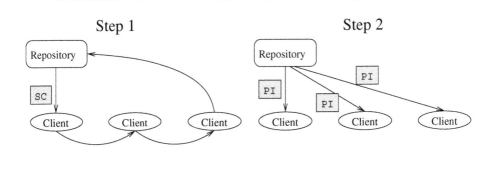

Fig. 1. TACOMA Software distribution Architecture. `SC` = `State.Coll`, `PI` = `Pack.Install`.

this list. Hosts unreachable at the moment will be re-tried later. Once it has been relocated to and authenticated by the receiving host, it is activated and the probe begins.

The `State.Coll` agent then activates each of the probe agents in sequence, supplying them with the package version available at the repository. The probe agent then determines the installed version of package it is designed for, and returns a simple binary answer to the question of whether an update to the `State.Coll` agent is needed or not.

Since all our updates currently come in the form of Red Hat rpm packages, all our probe agents are currently identical. In order to probe the clients installation, they simply execute the local rpm command to collect version numbers of installed packages. However, since the probe agent is dynamically supplied by the repository, it can equally well determine package versions using other methods. For instance, for packages not installed by rpm, it can locate a compiled binary by searching default installation paths for this package. Once a binary is found, it searches through it for a version string.

After the `State.Coll` agent has executed all of its probe agents, it creates a new entry in its briefcase that describes the the needed updates at the current host. From this list of needed updates, it subtracts packages that are locally cached, something which may happen because of unresolved dependencies, see section 3.3 below.

Finally, it picks a new unvisited host from its host list and repeats, until it has visited every host in its list. Hosts that are unreachable at any given time are rescheduled to the end of the host list. However, once three attempts have been made to reach a certain host, the `State.Coll` agent gives up, and deletes the host from its list. The reasoning behind this is that the host will probably be unavailable for some time, and will be caught by later runs of the `State.Coll` agent. When the host list is exhausted, the `State.Coll` agent returns to the repository.

3.2 Step 2: The `Pack.Install` Agent

The next step in our process is to disseminate the needed updates from the repository to clients. In this step, we need to allow the package supplier some control over the actual update process. This is achieved in the following way.

Once the `State.Coll` agent has returned to the repository, it compiles a list of hosts and packages, and generates one `Pack.Install` agent for each. These agents contain those packages that are needed at the host they are destined for. Furthermore, for each `Pack.Install` agent, the repository collects the software packages needed together with update control agents, one for each package. This is inserted into the `Pack.Install` core, and digitally signed by the repository.

Next the `State.Coll` agent launches the `Pack.Install` agents in parallel. Each `Pack.Install` agent travels to its host and begins installation. Once authenticated and activated, the `Pack.Install` agent activates the update control agents in sequence. These agents contain the actual control code that installs the software, and may be application specific or, as in our case, generic. Since we use the rpm package system, the update control agent simply executes the rpm tool locally and does some parsing of its output to detect unresolved dependencies.

However, if the package to be installed consists of, for instance, source code, the update control agent will be more complex, invoking compilers and linkers in the process of updating the installed software. The update control agent may even shut down running services, prior to updating them, and then restart them when the update process is completed.

Once all of the update control agents have finished executing, `Pack.Install` collects the results. However, to avoid flooding the repository, the `Pack.Install` agent does not report back success to the repository once it has finished. It does, however, respond to unresolved dependencies as discussed below.

3.3 Dependencies

Sometimes the `Pack.Install` agent may encounter unresolved dependencies during installation[1]. Such dependencies are duly noted and the installation aborted. However, to avoid transporting the payload twice over the network, the `Pack.Install` agent caches its payload in the local TACOMA cabinet. It then converts itself to a `State.Coll` agent and returns to the repository with a new list of packages that need to be collected.

If packages are needed but are unavailable in the repository, a human administrator is notified. Once the administrator has fetched the missing packages, he may manually start the probing process again, or simply wait until the repository does this at some later point.

---

[1] A new version of a package may require a new previously uninstalled package, or an update of a package on which it depends.

3.4 Privileges

The probe and update control agents all currently run with administrator privileges, since most software updates in our system require this. Our security framework is based on authentication using digital signatures, which in the end means that client administrators must trust the repositories they subscribe to.

The advantage to this approach is that it can be applied to existing systems, without the need for new security enforcement schemes. The disadvantage is that it has a coarse granularity, basically all or nothing is allowed, and does not follow the principle of least privilege advocated by security experts.

It is possible to extend our system to support a finer security granularity based on different user accounts. For instance, it is possible to map package suppliers to user accounts. This would require our system to authenticate the individual probe and update control agents that `State.Coll` and `Pack.Install` activates at the client. This modification is straightforward, since the probe and update control agents are full-fledged agents; they can be required to have a digitally signed core. Based upon this signature, which is the signature of the package supplier rather than the repository, one can map package suppliers to user accounts.

3.5 A Note on Performance

The `State.Coll` agent needs to do a full probe at clients of every package available at its repository. The reason for this is simple. There is no way to make sure that even the local TACOMA site has a correct view of the state of locally installed packages. Even if we cached earlier probes, a local administrator may have bypassed our system and made an update or downgrade manually.

Each package needs its own probe agent. Creating and activating an agent locally imposes an overhead of about 300 ms, not counting the computation of the probe agent itself. Once the number of packages becomes large, the overhead of creating and activating probe agents will reach unacceptable levels.

For this reason, we give local administrators the ability to turn caching of local probes on. This means that the probe agents will miss changes to the local packages done manually, but it greatly reduces the overhead of the `State.Coll` agent.

When caching is turned on, the results of local probes are stored in the local file cabinet. The cache lists the package name, the last version number probed, and whether an update is needed or not. The `State.Coll` then looks in the cache before activating a probe agent to determine if the probe is necessary. The probe is only launched when the package numbers differ or if the cache indicates that an update is necessary.

4   Design Options for Software Deployment

This section discusses some of the main design alternatives we were faced with when applying the mobile agent paradigm to software deployment problems. As such, it also constitutes our argument that mobile agents are well suited for software deployment.

4.1   Software Updates as Mobile Agents

One way to do software deployment using mobile agents is to select an appropriate mobile agent system, and deploy software components as mobile agents. The software components can then relocate themselves to another host as a mobile agent, and replace an already running agent there.

The problem with this approach is that software components have to be modeled and implemented as mobile agents. Most software components are not mobile agents, and redesigning a software package as a set of mobile agents still requires substantial work. Furthermore, most mobile agents systems execute their agents in a virtual machine, an execution layer providing safe code execution and a homogeneous environment in a heterogeneous network. This often conflicts with the needs of software upgrades that need to access the underlying operating system.

What we need is a mechanism that allows mobile agents to wrap generic software components, without modification of the software components themselves. In order to support this, the software components have to be separated from the update control and network code of the mobile agent. In this approach, the software component is added as a passive payload to the agent, while the update control and network code becomes the mobile agent.

The problem with this approach is that it requires some support from the agent system. The update control code needs to be granted privileges beyond those of a regular mobile agent in order to affect the system outside the safe sandbox of the agent environment. Either these privileges are granted indirectly through a service of the local agent system, or directly by running the update control code with all privileges needed to perform an update. In either case, some trust of the authenticity of the payload (the software component) and the update control code has to be achieved.

4.2   Single Itinerary Agent or Parallel Agents

The natural mobile agent approach to software installation is a single itinerant mobile agent. This agent is loaded with the software to be installed. It then travels to all the hosts which need to be updated in order, and installs its payload at them. The advantages are linked to the benefits of mobile agents. The update process puts little strain on network resources, since the agent updates one host at a time. The number of updates sent over the network is n, where n is the number of subscribing clients, with one additional status message sent back to the repository. Furthermore, since the mobile agent is autonomous, it operates asynchronously with no need for further control.

This approach has, however, its drawbacks. First, if hosts do not share exactly the same software base, parts of the payload might not be needed at a host. Furthermore, it is prone to failure, since the failure of a single host can potentially terminate the entire upgrade process. This is a common problem for mobile agents, and solutions have been developed [JMS+99,MvRSS96]. However, these solutions add to the complexity of the system, and are not always suited for our setting.

A second alternative is to perform the update in parallel, using n agents, one for each host that is to be updated. Now, each agent can configure its payload to the needs of the host it is going to update. This may potentially lower payload size, and thus network usage. The number of updates sent over the network is still equal to the number of hosts, n, while the number of status messages rises from 1 to n in this approach. The failure of one site no longer affects the agents updating other sites, so costly fault-tolerance mechanisms for mobile code need not be employed. However, since updates are performed in parallel, care must be taken not to stress the network when the agents are initially shipped, and status messages are sent back to the repository.

4.3   Global and Local Repositories

The second approach above scales poorly for truly large systems. In a setting with not only one local network, but thousands of local networks each containing several hundred hosts, the parallel update approach would need several hundred thousands of update agents that are shipped from a single repository. A supplier of software components may wish to spread this load between several different repositories.

Furthermore, local administrators would probably like additional control over updates emerging from a single global repository. For instance, if the global repository does aggressive updates (using its user base for cheap beta testing), local repositories may elect to delay updates until confidence in stability is achieved.

We used the following approach to solve these problems. Some hosts subscribing to a repository service may in fact act as repository services themselves. Any payload of an update agent from its parent repository is inserted into the local temporary repository. A system administrator may at his/her leisure move updates from the temporary repository to the local repository, making the update available to its local subscribers.

End users are able to subscribe to any repository, unless restricted by local policies. So end users may still live dangerously on the edge, by subscribing to an aggressive repository instead of a possibly more careful local repository.

4.4   Client State

Another problem is getting information about the clients of the repository. This includes what software components we need to update them. Having the clients themselves poll a server for updates is a common method today. The trouble with this approach is that the client has no idea about what updates are available and when. A client would need to get a list of all components available at the repository at frequent intervals, and compare it with the locally installed components. This wastes network bandwidth and puts additional strain on the repository.

Another approach is to have the repository probe all the clients subscribing to its service once a new component becomes available. Here the problem is that clients may be unavailable since they are disconnected or the network might be partitioned for a while. Clients that missed an update due to partition may not be aware of this fact. These clients will eventually become updated during the next regular repository probe.

We used a hybrid approach that combined the pull and push methods. Clients that are simply disconnected or turned off may issue a probe once the connection is re-established.

4.5   Mandatory and Optional Software

Basically, from a system administrators view, there are two types of software, optional software and mandatory software. Mandatory software consist of software the system operator deems necessary for the correct operation of the local network site. This includes things like security updates, virus checkers, and monitoring software. Other software packages are optional, and tailored toward the needs of the end user, which are not critical to the correct behavior of the target host.

To accommodate for these two classes of software, we have repository entries that are tagged as mandatory by the repository administrator. These are installed without interfering with the subscribing end user. Information about optional software is mailed to the end user, who may elect to include the software upon the next update. Once optional software is installed, further updates will be installed without user interference.

4.6   The Insecurity of Mobile Code

Another problem with the use of mobile agents is the safety requirements a generic mobile agent system must fulfill in order to execute foreign code. This is usually achieved by running the code on safe virtual machines that enforce safety [GM95,WLAG93]. These techniques isolate the system from the mobile agent, and the agent is then restricted to access the system through well defined services.

This voids our argument that mobile agents are useful in software deployment. We argued that the software that is to be deployed needs some control of the update process at a host. This control may be very system specific, and require access to the system beyond that provided by virtual environment offered.

Instead, we found that executing code based upon authentication and sufficient trust is much more suited in this setting. Thus, we have a closed set of virtual machines that are only available to agents whom we trust. Once access to these virtual machines is granted to a mobile agent, it may execute without further limitations. In our context, this means that our system is a closed agent system. Only mobile agents authenticated as repository agents gain access to the system while regular agents are denied access.

5   Conclusion

In this paper, we have shown how mobile agents can be used to do software component deployment. However, we have just demonstrated the potential in this technique. Currently, there is little reason for the `Pack.Install` agent to be a full-fledged mobile agent. Since the system currently uses only one type of software package (the Redhat rpm format), the agent can be replaced with a simple message from the repository to a service agent at the client. However, by using mobile agents, our model support arbitrary software packages, that may even be vendor specific, since the control code of the update is dynamically downloaded to the client.

The same argument goes for the `State.Coll` agent. The `State.Coll` agent benefits from several of the befits inherent in the mobile agent paradigm, such as asynchronous operation, preservation of bandwidth, and usefulness in disconnected environments. However, critics may say that the advantages gained by using mobile agents to collect state information about client hosts may not match the cost of having to deploy a mobile agent system in the first place. But, since the code that collects the state is supplied by the repository and dynamically uploaded to the client host, using mobile agents provides more flexibility. Thus, our approach demonstrates a fundamental principle in which mobile agents may be used to support application controlled updates.

The base agents are in place, and we are currently working on a tool set that allows repository administrators greater control over the deployment process. With this tool set, administrators can for instance schedule updates to happen at a specific time. Currently, administrators have to manually update repositories, even if the repository itself is a client to a parent repository. The administrator tool set will allow the administrator to automate this process, allowing for a tree of repositories where updates trickle down from a common root.

References

[AO98]   Y. Aridor and M. Oshima. Infrastructure for Mobile Agents: Requirements and Design. In *Proceedings of 2nd International Workshop on Mobile Agents (MA '98)*. Springer Verlag, September 1998.

[BHRS98]   J. Baumann, F. Hohl, K. Rothermel, and M. Straßer. Mole – Concepts of a Mobile Agent System. *World Wide Web*, 1(3):123–137, January 1998.

[BSP+95]   B. N. Bershad, S. Savage, P. Pardyak, E. G. Sirer, M. E Fiuczynski, D. Becker, C. Chambers, and S. Eggers. Extensibility, Safety and Performance in the *spin* Operating System. In *15th ACM Symposium on Operating System Principles*, December 1995.

[GKCR98]   R. S. Gray, D. Kotz, G. Cybenko, and D. Rus. D'Agents: Security in a multiple-language, mobile-agent system. In Giovanni Vigna, editor, *Mobile Agents and Security*, volume 1419 of *Lecture Notes in Computer Science*, pages 154–187. Springer-Verlag, 1998.

[GM95]   J. Gosling and H. McGilton. The java language environment: A white paper. Technical report, Sun Microsystems, Inc, May 1995.

[JH94]   D. Johansen and G. Hartvigsen. Architectural issues in the StormCast system. In *Prococeeding of the Dagstuhl Seminar on Distributed Systems*, number 938 in Lecture Notes in Computer Science, pages 1–16, Dagstuhl, Germany, 1994. Springer Verlag.

[JLvR+02]   D. Johansen, K. J. Lauvset, R. van Renesse, F. B. Schneider, N. P. Sudmann, and K. Jacobsen. A TACOMA Retrospective. *Software Practice & Experience, Wiley*, 2002. To be published.

[JMS+99]   D. Johansen, K. Marzullo, F. B. Schneider, K. Jacobsen, and D. Zagorodnov. NAP: Practical fault-tolerance for itinerant computations. In *Proceedings of the 19th IEEE International Conference on Distributed Computing Systems (ICDCS'99)*, pages 180–189, Austin, TX, June 1999. IEEE Computer Society.

[JvRS95]   D. Johansen, R. van Renesse, and F. B. Schneider. Operating System Support for Mobile Agents. In *Proceedings of the 5th Workshop on Hot Topics in Operating Systems (HOTOS-V)*, pages 42–45, Orcas Island, WA, May 1995. IEEE Computer Society.

[Lie95]   J. Liedtke. On μ-Kernel. In *15th ACM Symposium on Operating System Principles*, December 1995.

[MvRSS96]   Y. Minsky, R. van Renesse, F. B. Schneider, and S. Stoller. Cryptographic Support for Fault-Tolerant Distributed Computing. Unpublished technical report., February 1996.

[SJ00]   N. P. Sudmann and D. Johansen. Adding Mobility to Non-mobile Web Robots. In *Proceedings of the 20th International Conference on Distributed Computing Systems (ICDCS'00) Workshops*, pages F73–F79, 445 Hoes Lane, P.O. Box 1331, Piscataway, NJ 08855-1331, April 2000. IEEE Computer Society.

[SJ01]   N. P. Sudmann and D. Johansen. Supporting Mobile Agent Applications Using Wrappers. In *Proceedings of the 12th International Workshop on Database and Expert Systems Applications (DEXA'01)*, pages 689–695, Munich, Germany, September 2001. IEEE Computer Society.

[WLAG93]   R. Wahbe, S. Lucco, T. Anderson, and S. Graham. Efficient Software-Based Fault Isolation. In *Proceedings of the 14th ACM Symposium on Operating System Principles*, December 1993.

Packaging Predictable Assembly

Scott A. Hissam, Gabriel A. Moreno, Judith A. Stafford, and Kurt C. Wallnau*

Software Engineering Institute, Carnegie Mellon University, Pittsburgh, PA, 15213,
{shissam,gam,jas,kcw}@sei.cmu.edu, http://www.sei.cmu.edu/pacc

Abstract. Significant economic and technical benefits accrue from the use of pre-existing and commercially available software components to develop new systems. However, challenges remain that, if not adequately addressed, will slow the adoption of software component technology. Chief among these are a lack of consumer trust in the quality of components, and a lack of trust in the quality of assemblies of components without extensive and expensive testing. This paper describes prediction-enabled component technology (PECT). A PECT results from integrating component technology with analysis models. An analysis model permits analysis and prediction of assembly-level properties prior to component composition, and, perhaps, prior to component acquisition. Analysis models also identify required component properties and their certifiable descriptions. Component technology supports and enforces the assumptions underlying analysis models; it also provides the medium for deploying PECT instances and PECT-compliant software components. This paper describes the structure of PECT. It discusses the means of establishing the predictive powers of a PECT so that consumers may obtain measurably bounded trust in both components and design-time predictions based on the use of these components. We demonstrate these ideas in a simple but illustrative model problem: predicting average end-to-end latency of a 'soft' real time application built from off-the-shelf software components.

1 Introduction

Significant economic and technical benefits accrue from the use of pre-existing and commercially available software components to develop new systems. Variable component quality combined with their opacity require designers to rely upon extensive prototyping just to establish the feasibility of using a component in a particular assembly [1]. Many of the benefits of software component technology evaporate in the presence of high uncertainty and low consumer trust.

This paper describes a prototype prediction-enabled component technology (PECT). PECT is both a technology and a method for producing instances of the technology. A PECT instance results from integrating a software component technology with one or more analysis models. PECT is designed to enable predictable assembly from certifiable components. By this we mean:

---

* Corresponding Author

J. Bishop (Ed.): CD 2002, LNCS 2370, pp. 108–124, 2002.

- Assemblies of components are known, by construction, to be amenable to one or more analysis method for predicting their emergent (assembly level) properties.

- The component properties that are required to make these predictions are defined, certified, and trusted.

We therefore see component certification and predictable assembly as correlates.

Our underlying premise is that while it may be impossible to analyze, and thereby predict the runtime behavior of arbitrary designs, it is possible to restrict our designs to a subset that is analyzable. This premise has already been seen in the use of logical (formal) analysis and prediction [2][3], and it can also be applied to empirical analysis and prediction. It is a further premise of ours that software component technology is an effective way of packaging the design and implementation restrictions that yield analyzable designs, i.e., PECT.

Our research objective is to provide guidelines on how to construct PECT instances in different domains, and for different properties of interest. While research in component technology and software and system analysis continues, our focus is on how advances in these areas can be integrated and deployed. Our approach provides not only the architectural basis for this integration and deployment, but also criteria with which to empirically, statistically, and logically demonstrate the predictive effectiveness of PECT instances.

In the remainder of Sect. 1 we define the problem and our approach, and define key terminology used in this paper. In Sect. 2 we describe in some detail the PECT conceptual model. In Sect. 3 we give a brief illustration of these concepts using the COMTEK–λ prototype. Sect. 4 discusses related work, and Sect. 5 offers a few final thoughts.

1.1   Problem and Approach

Component technology, as it exists today, is more a marketplace phenomena than technology innovation. The major technical elements of component technology—for example, separate interfaces, multiple interfaces, encapsulation, and designed runtime environments—have been around for many years. What is significant about component technology is that IT producers and consumers have been rapidly adopting it in the form of Sun Microsystems' EJB™ and Microsoft's COM™ and many other "commercial off-the-shelf" component technologies [9].

Current generation component technologies address various syntactic and mechanistic aspects of component composition (*nee* integration), but more complex forms of behavioral composition have not been addressed. As software systems become more complex, and as their quality takes on greater social significance (safety, reliability, security, and so forth), the limitations of existing component technologies will (and already have) become manifest. Rely-guarantee reasoning is sufficient in a limited range of behavioral composition, but is not sufficiently expressive to be a general solution. And, of course, traditional testing has its own costs and limitations.

Our approach is to augment component technologies with sound analysis and prediction technologies. We refer to the resultant augmentation as a *prediction-enabled component technology* (PECT). Indeed, the marriage of component and analysis technology makes eminent sense:

- Analysis models are valid with respect to assumptions about the execution environment of an end application. For example, a performance model will likely depend upon assumptions pertaining to scheduling policy, process or thread priority, concurrency, resource management policies, and many other factors. These assumptions can be treated as design and implementation constraints, and made explicit, supported, and enforced by component technology. That is, assemblies of components can be rendered analyzable *by design and construction*.

- Analysis models refer to (are parameterized by) the properties of components being modeled. We refer to these as *analytic properties*, and the set of these as the component's *analytic interface*. An explicit, well-defined analytic interface provides an opportunity for certifying those component properties that support engineering analysis. This, in turn, provides a value proposition for certified, or *trusted*, component properties.

- Component technology is *par excellence* a means of packaging and deploying software technology. And, it is being adopted by industry. On a very practical level, we view component technology as a readily available distribution channel for packaging and deploying predictable assembly from certifiable components.

The last, and defining, element of our approach is that the packaging of a PECT is not complete until its predictive powers have been validated. Our objective is that each PECT be described by an objective, bounded confidence interval that is backed by mathematical and empirical evidence. We exclude from our purview any analysis technology that can not, in principle or practice, support such validation.

1.2   Assumed Terminology and Notation

We assume as background context for our research the existence of two distinct technologies: component technology and analysis technology. Here we define, without further elaboration, a number of terms that denote aspects of these technologies. We define only those terms most useful for our exposition; we make no effort at completeness. Our terminology is, in the main, consistent with that found in the software component technology literature [4][5][6]:

- *Software component*: An independently deployable and executable software implementation. Hereafter referred to as *component*.

- *Component model*: A specification of component types, allowable patterns of interactions among instances of these types (*components*), and between components and a component runtime environment.

- *Component runtime environment:* An execution environment that enforces aspects of the component model. The runtime plays a role analogous to that of an operating system, only at a higher level of abstraction.

- *Component assembly environment*: A development environment that provides services for component development, composition, and component and application deployment. The assembly environment may also provide assembly-time enforcement of the component model.

- *Component technology*: An integrated component model, component runtime environment, and component assembly environment.

- *Component assembly*: Noun—A set of components and their enabled interactions. Verb—To integrate a set of components, thereby enabling their runtime interaction.

- *Component property*: Something that is known and detectable about a component, denoted with 'dot' notation, e.g., c.p for component 'c' with property 'p'. Can be a measurable quantity or a behavioral model such as a state machine.

- *Assembly property*: Also known as *emergent property*. Something that is known about an assembly, also denoted using dot notation. Note that we reject the idea that *emergent property* is synonymous with *unpredictable property*.

Our terminology for analysis technology is of our own invention. It reflects the context in which we use analysis technology, i.e., component technology:

- *Analysis model*: A definition of terms and concepts pertinent to a particular emergent property. The language used by specialists in a particular property domain. An analysis model is analogous to a component model; it defines conceptual components and their relations to one another.

- *Property theory*: A theory, expressed in terms consistent with an analysis model, that can be used to predict the values of an emergent property. Can be, for example, a closed form formula or a formal theory such as used in model checking [7]. A property theory is analogous to a component assembly; it is a configuration of terms and concepts governed by an analysis model.

- *Analytic property*: A component property that is required by (is a parameter to) a property theory. The set of these properties for a property theory is the component's *analytic interface* for that theory.

- *Analytic assembly*: A component assembly interpreted in terms of a property theory. This could be a closed form formula, or some alternative view of the component assembly such as a state transition model or component and connector model.

- *Analysis environment*: An environment for computer-aided analysis of, and predictions about, analytic assemblies.

- *Analysis technology*: An integrated analysis model, analysis environment, and property theory(ies).

We use UML as our graphical notation, and UML object constraint language (OCL) to specify invariants. We assume the reader has some familiarity with this notation. We occasionally stray from the standard UML, but we do so only when limitations of UML require it; we are careful to highlight each such apostasy. References in the text to specific elements of diagrams are (*parenthesized and italicized*).

2   PECT Structure and Method

To give the reader an idea of what PECT is all about, we first describe the use of PECT instances from the perspective of an application assembler (Sect. 2.1). We then turn to the methodological aspects of producing PECT instances, first by concentrating on the structure of a PECT instance (Sect. 2.2), and then to the validation of PECT instances (Sect. 2.3).

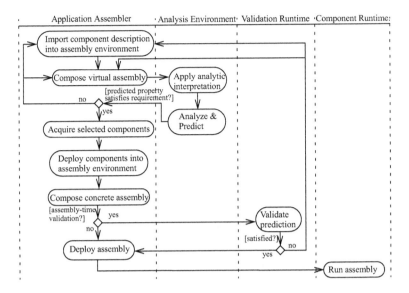

Fig. 1: The user-level workflow for PECT. Note that the (*Validate prediction*) step is distinct from the validation of the PECT itself. In this workflow, validation refers to a spot check of the assembly against a prediction. The terms (*virtual assembly*), (*concrete assembly*), and (*analytic assembly*) are found in the conceptual schema, in Fig. 2. We have taken liberties with UML by permitting multiple 'no' paths on conditional branches.

2.1 PECT User-Level Overview

A PECT is an infrastructure for predictable assembly and trusted components. But how is this infrastructure used in practice? The answer to this depends upon which user role is considered. Fig. 1 specifies a simple view from the perspective of the application assembler. The workflow is certainly optimistic, since all paths lead to a running assembly. A more realistic workflow would include exit paths on failure, and paths to modify the PECT, perhaps by using an alternative property theory.

A conceptual schema in Fig. 2 identifies and relates terms found in the above workflow and used in the following discussion. The key new terminology is:

- *Certified Component Description*: A component can be *described* by its interface. Analytic interfaces are descriptive not normative: they describe the properties of a component; they do not specify the values that components must achieve. An interface description of components that includes analytic interfaces can be imported into an assembly environment and used for the purpose of assembly-time analysis and prediction.

- *Virtual Assembly* and *Concrete Assembly*: An assembly of component descriptions is sufficient for analysis and prediction, but provides no runtime behavior. A concrete assembly, on the other hand, consists entirely of components, and therefore has runtime behavior; naturally, it is also sufficient for analysis and prediction. Virtual and concrete assemblies are mapped to analytic assemblies via analytic interpretations. Analytic interpretations are discussed in Sect. 2.3 under *Model Validity*.

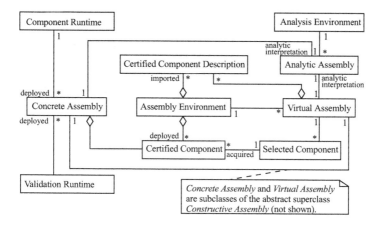

Fig. 2: The PECT conceptual schema identifies key terms and their relationships.

- *Validation Runtime*: The predictive power of a PECT is qualified by a statistical confidence interval or its formal equivalent. Nonetheless, an application engineer may wish to validate a PECT prediction. Doing so may require a specialized component infrastructure (i.e., a validation runtime) that is, for example, instrumented or based on an alternative runtime scheme. Assembly-time validation might be performed on a subset of assemblies, or as a 'sanity check' on a particular prediction.

2.2   Conceptual Structure of PECT Instances

A PECT arises from the association of an analysis technology with a component technology. Therefore, our description of the overall structure of PECT instances in Fig. 3 centers on the UML association class (*Predictable Assembly Model*).

The (*Constructive Model*) is the original component model plus any modifications that are required to specify the assumptions of a property theory. Component assemblies that are conformant to a constructive model are called *constructive assemblies*. The (*Concrete Assembly*) and (*Virtual Assembly*) in Fig. 2 are constructive assemblies. The OCL constraint (*Context p CT-t*) stipulates that each certifiable component property (*Theory Parameter*) is found in the analytic interface of the relevant constructive component types. An analogous constraint, not shown, is required for (*Other Theory Assumption*). These associations are confirmed during model validation (see Sect. 2.3).

2.3   Validation of PECT Instances

A technology that purports to enable predictable assembly would be meaningless if its predictions could not be validated. To paraphrase (and perhaps debauch) the wisdom of Wittgenstein: *A nothing will do as well as a something, that is, a prediction, about which nothing can be said.* The consumers of PECT will want to know ahead of time how much confidence to place in the predictive powers of the technology. This is provided by two distinct but related forms of validity: *model* and *empirical* validity.

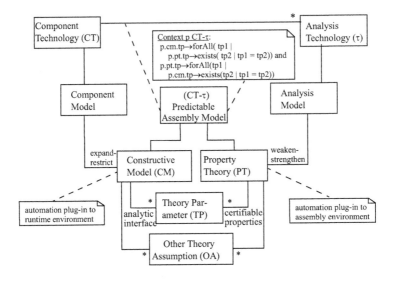

Fig. 3: The naming convention we use for PECT instances is to use the name of the component technology, e.g., *(CT)*, and one or more symbols to denote analysis models, e.g., (τ). In this figure, role cardinalities are 1 unless otherwise specified.

Model Validity. Our concern is to establish the validity of the *(Predictable Assembly Model)* depicted in Fig. 3. This consists in establishing that two conditions hold:

1. The mapping of assumptions from a *(Property Theory)* to elements of the *(Constructive Model)*, again, in Fig. 3, is consistent.

2. The analytic interpretation from *(Constructive Assembly)* to *(Analytic Assembly)* in Fig. 2 is both consistent *and* complete.

The first condition, which we refer to as *logical validity*, is analogous to establishing the validity of a theorem in formal logic. That is, *a theorem is valid if the conclusions follow from the premises.* In PECT, the theorem is a property theory; its assumptions are the theorem's premises; and its predictions are the theorem's conclusions. Establishing logical validity involves demonstrative (mathematical) reasoning.

The second condition, which we refer to as *interpretation validity*, demonstrates that each constructive assembly can be interpreted in terms of the property theory (completeness), and each constructive assembly has at most one interpretation (consistency). This last is a bit subtle. It is possible for a single constructive assembly to correspond to several analytic assemblies, but these analytic assemblies must form an equivalence class with respect to predictions made under the property theory.

Empirical Validity. Returning to logical validity, we said that a property theory is valid if its predictions follow from its assumptions (conclusions follow from premises). Continuing with the analogy to formal logic, a theorem is *sound* if, in addition to being valid, *the premises hold true.* In PECT, establishing that the assumptions hold true amounts to demonstrating that each theory assumption is enforced by the PECT runtime or assembly environments, *or by engineering practices.*

Unfortunately, the soundness of a property theory can almost never be formally established. Modern computing environments are complex, and one can never be absolutely certain that a property theory has adequately enumerated all its assumptions. In practice, then, empirical evidence is required. That is, we must treat predictions as falsifiable hypotheses, and each failure to falsify the prediction, within explicitly stated measurement tolerance, incrementally adds evidence that the theory is sound. That is, we do not *demonstrate* that the assumptions of the property theory hold true, we *infer* their truth inductively from experimental evidence.

Of course, this is no more than asserting the need for using traditional scientific method to demonstrate the soundness of property theories. It seems that Simon's thoughts on the application of scientific methods to artificial systems, and to engineering design of complex systems in particular, remain ahead of their time [10].

2.4   Integration by Co-refinement

There are many available component and analysis technologies in research and in the commercial marketplace. An important practical consideration for our research is to demonstrate that existing technologies can be integrated into viable PECT instances. However, since component and analysis technologies have developed independently, and to satisfy different objectives, their integration may not always be straightforward Where mismatches arise, either or both must be adjusted, as illustrated in Fig. 4.

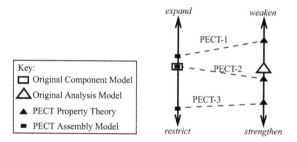

Fig. 4: Given a component model and analysis model, a PECT instance is produced through a process of co-refinement. Co-refinement (including a null refinement) transforms a component model to an assembly model, and an analysis model to a property theory.

Our idea of co-refinement is informal. Intuitively, expanding a component model removes or weakens design and implementation restrictions, and thus increases the set of allowable assemblies; restricting the component model has the opposite effect. Similarly, weakening an analysis model removes or weakens the assumptions (which can be thought of as preconditions) of property theories, again increasing the scope of the property theory to a larger set of assemblies, but perhaps at the cost of precision or reliability of predictions; strengthening an analysis model has the opposite effect. Three alternative co-refinements are depicted in Fig. 4, (*PECT-1*), (*PECT-2*) and (*PECT-3*). Each of these alternatives will exhibit different degrees of design freedom and expressiveness, and different degrees of predictive accuracy.

Of course, there are refinements of component and analysis models that do not fit neatly into the expand/restrict and weaken/strengthen dichotomies. For example, does modifying a component model to use asynchronous rather than synchronous communication expand or restrict set of assemblies that are conformant to the component model? At present, co-refinement appears to be the essential design problem of constructing a PECT instance—that is, it requires the use of judgment, experience, and taste on the part of the PECT designer to make the appropriate trade-off's that arise when associating an analysis model with a component model.

2.5   Refinement and Validation Taken Together

Co-refinement and validation are major activities in the development of PECT instances. Although we do not yet have a complete workflow to describe PECT development, one thing is clear: these two activities are mutually reinforcing, and the final workflow will almost certainly include an approximation of the fragment in Fig. 5.

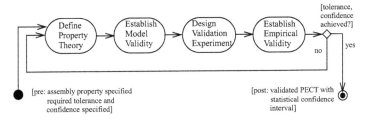

Fig. 5: A PECT development process will involve iteration among model validation, co-refinement, and empirical validation.

Although there are various intermediate steps missing in the workflow (such as implementing any required changes to the component runtime or assembly environments), the crucial point is that empirical validation is required to satisfy the guard condition for exiting the workflow. Our own experience suggests that empirical validation is effective at uncovering hidden, and therefore unsatisfied, assumptions of the property theory—that is, where these hidden assumptions are exposed by a violation of required measurement tolerance.

3   Illustration: COMTEK-λ

We now describe a prototype PECT, constructed from the COMTEK[1] component technology [11], and a widely known, if largely implicit, analysis model for predicting end-to-end latency. The objective of the prototype was to test the conceptual model of PECT and the PECT development process sketched in the previous section in a realistic but not overly complex problem setting.

---

1.   Formerly known as *WaterBeans*.

3.1   Component Technology: COMTEK

COMTEK was developed by the Software Engineering Institute (SEI) for the U.S. Environmental Protection Agency (EPA) Department of Water Quality to support end-user composition of water quality simulation from third-party simulation components. COMTEK runs on the Microsoft Windows-NT family of operating systems, and its components are deployed as Microsoft dynamic link libraries (DLL). Fig. 6 presents a screenshot of the COMTEK assembly environment. Despite its simplicity, the generality of COMTEK was demonstrated in several application domains.

The menu tabs above the assembly canvas in Fig. 6 display four families of components: Hydraulic Interfaces, Hydraulic Models, Wave Interfaces, and Test Interfaces. Fig. 6 shows an assembly built from components of the Wave Interface family. This and similar assemblies are the subject of the COMTEK-λ illustration. These assemblies implement audio signal sampling, manipulation, and playback functionality. We chose to develop a PECT for assembling audio playback applications since we could develop a simple performance analysis model to accommodate the relative simplicity of COMTEK.

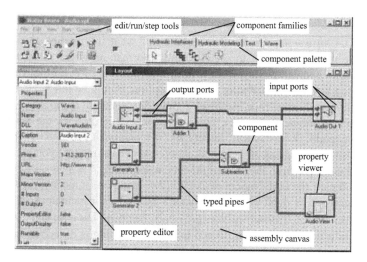

Fig. 6: COMTEK has the following high-level characteristics: a) it enforces a typed pipe-and-filter composition style; b) components may have multiple input and output ports, each of which may be connected by a pipe to other component ports; c) a round-robin schedule is calculated from component input/output dependencies; d) the execution of an assembly is sequential, and components are single-threaded and non-preemptive.

3.2   Analysis Technology: Latency Prediction

The problem we posed was to predict the end-to-end latency of an assembly, where latency is defined as the time interval beginning with the execution of the 'first' component executed in an assembly and ending with the return from the 'last' component in that assembly. We required that predicted assembly latency is, on average, within +/

-10% of observed assembly latency. We permitted ourselves such liberality because WindowsNT provides few performance guarantees. As will be seen, however, we did much better than a 10% margin of error, although this was never our goal.

The audio playback application lies in the domain of what is sometimes referred to as 'soft real-time' applications. In soft real-time applications, timely handling of events or other data is a critical element of the application, but an occasionally missed event is tolerable. In the audio playback application, audio signals received from an internal CD player must be sampled every 46 milliseconds for each 1,024 bytes of audio data. A failure to sample the input buffer, or to feed the output buffer within this time interval, will result in a lost signal. Too many lost signals will disrupt the quality of the audio playback; however, a few lost signals will not be noticeable to the untrained ear. Thus, audio playback has 'soft' real-time requirements.

3.3   COMTEK-λ Assembly Model

We begin with the more complex and extensive constructive model, and then turn to the property theory.

COMTEK-λ Constructive Model. The question of what information to include in a constructive model, and how to organize this information, is the same question we might ask of component models. We are not yet prepared to offer normative guidelines on either, and so the documentation we now describe should be interpreted as suggestive. With time and experience, we hope to propose a standard approach. For this relatively simple prototype, only a few views were needed to describe the essence of the constructive model. We use UML stereotypes (*<<component>>*) and (*<<analytic>>*) to distinguish those aspects of the specification that derive from the component model, and those that derive from the property theory, respectively.

Fig. 7 depicts the UML model of COMTEK-λ component metatypes. Instances of (*ComponentType*) are deployable units that are themselves instantiators—they provide runtime instances of themselves via (*getNewInstance()*). The property theory introduces two new component types, Φ and Θ, whose meaning is described later[1]. These types of components appear only in analytic assemblies, and have associated analytic constraints: they must possess specific properties that themselves are constrained, as specified in the pertinent OCL expressions.

Fig. 8 associates the definition of component latency used by the latency property theory with the COMTEK runtime[2]. Latency is defined as the time interval between two readings of a hypothetical, infinitely accurate clock. This definition was used for empirical validation. Fig. 8 also makes explicit the property theory assumptions relating to the execution schedule of components. Other assumptions, such as single threaded components and non-preemptive scheduling have been omitted for simplicity.

---

1.   These symbols were chosen for their mnemonic value, as will be seen.

2.   Some of the terms used in Fig. 8 are introduced in views of the constructive model not discussed in this paper.

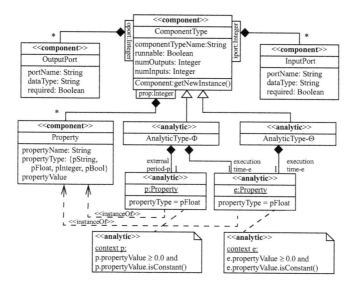

Fig. 7: COMTEK-λ Component Metatype Specification. The property theory introduces two analytic component types, (Φ) and (Θ). These subclasses of (*ComponentType*) have the additional constraint that their instances possess specific analytic component properties (*p*) and (*e*). This constraint is represented using non-standard UML.

Property Theory. The COMTEK-λ latency theory is summarized by the following open formula:

$$A.\lambda = f(A) = \max\left(\left(\sum_{\Phi_j \in A} \Phi_j.e + \sum_{\Theta_j \in A} \Theta_j.e\right), \max(\{\Phi_j \in A \mid \Phi_j.p\})\right) \qquad (1)$$

Assembly A is an enumerated set of components, and the kth component of A is denoted as either or Θ_k or Φ_k. These correspond to one of two analytic component types: Θ refers to components that only have dependencies that are internal to A, while Φ refers to components that also exhibit dependencies on external periodic events. A.λ is the end-to-end latency of an assembly. Each Φ component has two required properties that describe its latency information: '$\Phi.e$' and '$\Phi.p$,' while each Θ component has only the required property $\Theta.e$ (refer to Fig. 7); e and p are defined as:

- *e*: is the execution time of a component, exclusive of component blocking time.
- *p*: is the period of the external event on which a Φ depends and may block.

The function *max* returns the largest of its arguments. Note that this analytic model is not parameterized by invocation order or connections among components. Neither the summation nor *max* depend on the order of components of (*A*) in Eq. (1).

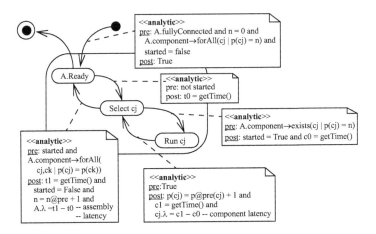

Fig. 8: Specification of Assembly Latency and Component Latency. The function $(p(ck))$ returns the number of times component ck has been run. The functions $(getTime())$ and $(setTime())$ read a hypothetical, infinitely accurate clock.

3.4   PECT Validity

The details of COMTEK-λ model and empirical validation are available in [12]. Here, we outline only the most important aspects of these validation exercises.

Model Validity. Our approach to constructing COMTEK-λ was driven by expediency. Accordingly, our strategy was to adopt as far as possible the design scheme represented by *(PECT-2)* in Fig. 4. To do so, we used the COMTEK component model as given assumptions for a custom fit latency theory. Following this approach was not especially demanding and worked well. Logical validity was demonstrated by a semirigorous derivation of the latency property theory from our knowledge of the internals of COMTEK. Interpretation validity was trivial to establish, mostly because the property theory was strengthened to deal just with steady state latency, and this, in turn, meant that order of component execution was irrelevant to latency prediction.

Nevertheless, our first "valid" property theory was falsified when we attempted to establish empirical validity. As detailed as our understanding of COMTEK was, we still manage to err by failing to appreciate the distinction between the Φ and Θ components of Eq. (1). In fact, this distinction never mattered until the latency property theory was introduced, which accounts for our error. We were pleased to discover the effectiveness of a combined model and empirical validation process, and at the same time confirm that property theories might impose constraints beyond those of an existing component technology, and that these constraints would be relevant *only* to that property theory.

Empirical Validity. Empirical validity consists in quantifying the accuracy and repeatability of predictions made using an analytic model by statistically comparing those predictions with actual measurements of assembly properties. The process of empirically validating a PECT can be summarized in the following steps:

1. Obtain analytic properties of components (for example, through measurement).
2. Design validation assemblies and predict the assembly property of interest.
3. Construct the assemblies and observe their properties.
4. Statistically analyze the difference between predicted and observed properties.

We constructed a component benchmarking environment for (1) and instrumented component runtime for (3). The first turned out to be non-trivial since it was required to simulate but not re-implement the COMTEK runtime. We used statistical methods for two different purposes: latency measurement (1) (3), and quantification of accuracy and repeatability of the predictions (4). The sources of our statistical approach are [13][14][15]. We consider a large sample of measured latencies and use their mean as the value to be used as inputs to the model.

For statistical analysis of the predicted latency (4) we used both descriptive and inferential statistics, namely correlation analysis, and confidence and tolerance intervals of the magnitude of relative error (MRE). We used thirty sample assemblies as the basis for statistical analysis of our latency theory (2). Thus, in the summary in Table 2, (N) refers to the number of distinct assemblies that we tested, i.e., ($N = 30$).

Correlation analysis allows us to assess the strength of the linear relation between two variables, in our case, predicted and observed latency. The result of this analysis is the coefficient of determination R^2, whose value ranges from 0 to 1; 0 meaning no relation at all, and 1 meaning perfect linear relation. In a perfect prediction model, one would expect to have all the predictions equal to the observed latency, therefore the goal is a linear relation. The results of the correlation analysis are shown in Table 1, and can be interpreted as the prediction model accounting for 99.99% of the variation in the observed latency. The significance level means that there is only a 1% probability of having obtained that correlation by chance.

Table 1: Correlation Analysis Results

Statistic	Meaning
$R^2 = 0.9999053$	Coefficient of determination
$\alpha = 0.01$	Significance level

For the statistical inference about the latency property theory, we are interested in the magnitude of relative error (MRE) between the predicted and the observed latency. To validate a property theory and draw statistical conclusions, we need a sample of MREs, based on a set of possible, and distinct, analytic assemblies. That is, for each assembly in the sample, we compute the MRE, obtaining in that way a sample of MREs. In doing this, we considered the mean of a sample of 15,000 measured assembly latencies to be the observed latency for each assembly.

We use tolerance intervals for statistical inference. Three types of questions are addressed by tolerance intervals [14]:

1. What interval will contain (p) percent of the population?
2. What interval guarantees that (p) percent of the population will not fall below a lower limit?

3. What interval guarantees that (p) percent of the population will not exceed an upper limit?

The first question applies to situations in which we want to control either the center or both tails of a distribution. In the case of MRE, because we are using the absolute value of the error, the predictions with MRE falling in the left tail of the distribution are even better than those in the center of the distribution. Therefore, it is better to use a one-sided tolerance interval, as in the case of the third question.

Table 2 is interpreted as saying that the MRE for 90% ($p = 0.90$) of assembly latency predictions will not exceed (*6.33%*); moreover, we have a confidence of 0.95 that the upper bound is correct. As can be seen, we achieved our goal of predicting with MREs no larger than 10%.

Table 2: Second MRE Tolerance Interval

N = 30	sample size
$\gamma = 0.95$	confidence level
p = 0.90	proportion
$\mu_{MRE} = 1.99\%$	over 30 assemblies
UB = 6.33 %	upper bound

4   Related Work

Related Work. Compositional reasoning techniques are a natural foundation upon which to build PECT property theories. Fisler and Sharygina exploit the idea of design restrictions to ameliorate the state space explosion associated with compositional model checking [17][3]. Neither of these approaches, however, address components as independently deployable implementations. Analysis algorithms that have been developed for architecture description languages (ADLs) are also relevant, not surprisingly given their use of "component and connector" abstractions. ADL based analysis models address liveness and safety [18][19], and performance [20][21]. However, ADLs treat components as abstractions, not implementations. The difference between interface specification and description causes difficulty in applying ADL-based results to component technology. Also related is work in component certification and trust. Representative is the use of pre/post conditions on component interfaces [22]. This approach does support compositional reasoning, but only about a restricted range of properties. Quality attributes, such as security, performance, availability, and so forth, are beyond the reach of these assertion languages. Commercial ventures in component certification, such as specified by Underwriter's Laboratory (UL), lack empirical validation or compositionality; but these may nonetheless prove influential [23]. Voas has defined rigorous mathematical models of component reliability derived from testing [24], but he does not provide an assembly model nor any means of demonstrating the empirical validity of the resultant reliability properties. Hamlet attacks the problem of empirical and compositional theories of reliability, but his approach is far too restricted and microscopic to be of practical utility [25].

5   Conclusion

We have described and illustrated the key ideas of prediction-enabled component technology. Our approach asserts that component certification and assembly-level prediction are correlates. PECT emphasizes the technical affinities between component technology and analysis technology to enforce design rules imposed by analysis models. This enforcement will lead to systems that are, by design and construction, analyzable and predictable, and to trusted components, where this trust is bound to specific engineering predictions. While we have only made initial and tentative steps to develop PECT ideas, the results are encouraging.

References

1. Wallnau, K., Hissam, S., Seacord, R., *Building Systems from Commercial Components*, Addison-Wesley, July, 2001.

2. Finkbeiner, B. & Kruger, I. "Using Message Sequence Charts for Component-Based Formal Verification," in Proceedings of the OOPSLA workshop on Specification and Verification of Component-Based Systems, Tampa, Florida, 2001.

3. Sharygina, N.; Browne, J.; & Kurshan, R. "A Formal Object-Oriented Analysis for Software Reliability: Design for Verification," in Proceedings of the ACM European Conferences on Theory and Practice in Software, Fundamental Approaches to Software Engineering (FACE), Genova, Italy, April 2-6, 2001. URL: <http://st72095.inf.tu-dresden.de:8080/fase2001> (2001).

4. Bachmann, F., Bass, L., Buhman, C., Comella-Dorda, S., Long, F., Robert, J., Seacord, R., & Wallnau, K.; Volume II: Technical Concepts of Component-Based Software Engineering (CMU/SEI-2000-TR-008), Pittsburgh, PA: Software Engineering Institute, Carnegie Mellon University. URL: <http://www.sei.cmu.edu/publications/documents/00.reports/00tr008.html> (2000).

5. Heineman, G. & Council, W. Component-Based Software Engineering Putting the Pieces Together, Reading, MA: Addison-Wesley, 2001.

6. Szyperski, C. Component Software Beyond Object-Oriented Programming, New York, Reading, MA: ACM Press, Addison-Wesley, 1997.

7. E. M. Clarke, E.A. Emerson, and A.P. Sistla, "Automatic Verification of Finite-State Concurrent Systems Using Temporal Logic Specifications," ACM Transactions on Programming Languages and Systems, Vol. 8, No. 2, April 1986, pp. 244-263.

8. Klein, M., Ralya, T., Pollak, W., Obenza, R., A Practitioner's Handbook for Real-Time Analysis, Boston, MA: Kluwer Academic Publishers, 1993.

9. Len Bass, Charles Buhman, Santiago Comella-Dorda, Fred Long, John Robert, Robert Seacord, and Kurt Wallnau, Volume I: Market Assessment of Component-Based Software Engineering Assessments (CMU/SEI-2001-TN-007), Pittsburgh, PA: Software Engineering Institute, Carnegie Mellon University. URL: <http://www.sei.cmu.edu/publications/documents/01.reports/01tn007.html> (2001).

10. H. Simon. The Sciences of the Artificial, 3rd ed, Cambridge, MA: MIT Press 1996.

11. D. Plakosh, D. Smith and K. Wallnau. Builder's Guide for WaterBeans Components (CMU/SEI-99-TR-024, ADA373154). Pittsburgh, PA: Software Engineering Institute, Carnegie Mellon University. URL: <http://www.sei.cmu.edu/publications/documents/99.reports/99tr024/99tr024abstract.html> (1999).

12. S. Hissam, G. Moreno, J. Stafford, K.Wallnau,.Packaging Predictable Assembly with Prediction-Enabled Component Technology (CMU/SEI-2001-TR-024). Pittsburgh, PA: Software Engineering Institute, Carnegie Mellon University. URL: <http://www.sei.cmu.edu/publications/documents/01.reports/01tr024.html> (2001)

13. C.F. Kemerer. "An Empirical Validation of Software Cost Estimation Models," in Communications of the ACM 30, 5, May 1987: 416-429.

14. NIST, NIST/SEMATECH Engineering Statistics Internet Handbook, National Institute of Standards and Technology (NIST), online at <http://www.itl.nist.gov/div898/handbook/>.

15. R.E. Walpole and R. H. Myers. Probability and Statistics for Engineers and Scientists. New York: MacMillan Publishing Company, 1989

16. Astley, M., Sturman, D., and Agha, G., "Customizable Middleware for Modular Distributed Software," in Communications of the ACM, Vol. 44, No. 5, May 2001, pp. 99-107.

17. K. Fisler, S. Krishnamurthi and D. Batory. "Verifying Component-Based Collaboration Designs," in Proceedings of the Fifth ICSE Workshop on Component-Based Software Engineering, Toronto, Canada, May 2001: 84-87

18. R. Allen and D. Garlan. "A Formal Basis for Architectural Connection," ACM Transactions on Software Engineering and Methodology, Vol. 6, No. 3, Jul. 1997, pp. 213-249.

19. J. Magee, J. Kramer, and D. Giannakopoulou, "Analysing the Behaviour of Distributed Software Architectures: A Case Study," Proceedings, Fifth IEEE Workshop on Future Trends of Distributed Computing Systems, Oct. 1997, 240-247.

20. S. Balsamo, P. Inverardi and C. Mangano, "An Approach to Performance Evaluation of Software Architectures", Proceedings of the 1998 Workshop on Software and Performance, Oct. 1998, 77—84.

21. B. Spitznagel, D. Garlan, "Architecture-Based Performance Analysis," Proceedings of the 1998 Conference on Software Engineering and Knowledge Engineering, San Francisco, California, 1998.

22. B. Meyer, Object-Oriented Software Construction, Second Edition, Prentice Hall, London, 1997.

23. Underwriter Laboratories, UL-1998, UL Standard for Safety for Software in Programmable Components, Northbrook, IL, 1998.

24. Jeffrey Voas, Jeffery Payne, "Dependability certification of software components," in the Journal of Systems and Software, no. 52, 165-172, 2000

25. D. Hamlet, D. Mason and D. Woit. "Theory of Software Reliability Based on Components," in Proceedings of the 23rd International Conference on Software Engineering, Toronto, Canada, 2001: 361-370.

Dynamic Replacement of Active Objects in the Gilgul Programming Language

Pascal Costanza

University of Bonn, Institute of Computer Science III,
Römerstr. 164, D-53117 Bonn, Germany,
costanza@cs.uni-bonn.de, http://www.pascalcostanza.de

Abstract. GILGUL is an extension of the Java programming language
that allows for dynamic object replacement without consistency problems. This is possible in a semantically clean way because its model
strictly separates the notions of reference and comparison that are usually subsumed in the concept of object identity. This paper sketches
problems that occur in attempts at replacements of active objects and
presents some solutions, including both variants that preserve consistency and those that trade consistency for timeliness. The latter are
enabled by means of the new *recall* construct that even allows for the
replacement of objects with non-terminating loops.

1 The TAILOR Project

Unanticipated Software Evolution. Software requirements are in a constant flux.
Some changes in requirements can be anticipated by software developers, so that
the necessary adaptations can be prepared for, for example by suitable parameterization or by application of appropriate design patterns. However, unanticipated changes of requirements occur repeatedly in practice, and by definition
the above suggested techniques cannot tackle them.

To obviate such problems, programming languages and runtime systems
should incorporate features that allow for manipulations of program internals
without destructively modifying their source code. This leads to an increase in
the number of options for unanticipated evolution as well as a decrease in the
pressure to prepare for anticipated variability.

In order to provide for this significant simplification of software development,
the goal of the TAILOR Project at the Institute of Computer Science III of the
University of Bonn [19] is to explore several approaches that enhance programming languages and runtime systems in order to allow for unanticipated software
evolution. In doing so, special attention is paid to the following issues.

Component Orientation. The focus on Component-Oriented Software compli-
cates the requirements even further, since components are usually deployed using a compiled format, and their source code is not available for modifications.
Even if the source code can be accessed in some cases, destructive modifications
are still not feasible, since they would lapse in the presence of new versions of a
component.

J. Bishop (Ed.): CD 2002, LNCS 2370, pp. 125–140, 2002.
© Springer-Verlag Berlin Heidelberg 2002

Reduction of Downtime. Essentially, unanticipated software evolution can take place at two points in time. They can be performed before a program is being linked into its final form, or they can happen during runtime. Changes to software that are carried out before linktime can be made effective only by stopping an old version of a program and starting the new one. This results in downtimes that induce high costs and possibly determine an application's success or failure. Alternatively, runtime systems should be provided with features that allow for subsequent unanticipated evolution of an already active program.

Challenges. Accordingly, the TAILOR Project deals with enhancements of programming languages and runtime systems that allow for unanticipated software evolution on the stringent condition that components are to be included whose source code is not available, and that modifications can still be made on already active programs. This paper presents one of the approaches of the TAILOR Project that rests on the simple idea of dynamic object replacement.

2   Dynamic Object Replacement

In principle, unanticipated evolution can always be dealt with by manual redirection of references. If one knows the reference to an object and wants to add or replace a method or change its class, one can simply assign a new object with the desired properties. The new object can even reuse the old object by some form of delegation [12], so that a recovery of the old state is not needed.

On the conceptual level, however, there are two consistency problems involved in this approach. Firstly, if there is more than one reference to an object, they all must be known to the programmer in order to consistently redirect them. Secondly, even if all references are known, they have to be redirected to the new object one by one. This approach is likely to lead to an inconsistent state of the objects involved if message are sent via these references during the course of the redirections (for example within another thread; see figure 1).

It would be straightforward if we could simply "replace" an object by another one without changing the references involved. Such a replacement would be an atomic operation and hence, would avoid the consistency problems shown above. We have discussed this subject previously on the basis of a specific example in [4].

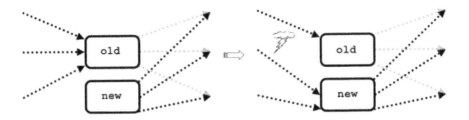

Fig. 1. If an object is replaced by manual redirection of references, messages may be sent to both objects during the replacement, probably leading to an inconsistent state.

In that paper we have also shown that a dissection of the concept of object identity and a strict separation of the included notions of reference and comparison is needed in order to introduce means for dynamic object replacement.

This can be illustrated with an implementation technique called "Identity Through Indirection" in [11]. Here, a reference to an object is realised as an object-oriented pointer (OOP). An OOP points to an entry in an object table which holds the actual memory addresses. Since we do not want to restrict our model to this implementation technique, we abstract from this terminology and say that object references point to entries which hold *referents* that represent the actual objects (see figure 2). Note that an actual implementation of this model does not have to resemble the illustration given here.

In our approach, references are never compared. To be able to compare objects we combine "Identity Through Indirection" with "Identity Through Surrogates" [11]. Each object is supplemented with an attribute that stores a *comparand*. Comparands are system-generated, globally unique values that cannot be manipulated directly by a programmer. The comparison of objects (o1 == o2) then means the comparison of their comparands (o1.comparand == o2.comparand), but they are never used for referencing.[1] Based on this scheme, we outline the programming language GILGUL, a compatible extension of Java, in the following sections. (More details can be found in [2].)

There are four levels that can be manipulated when dealing with variables in GILGUL: the reference and the object level that already exist in Java, and the referent and the comparand level that are new in GILGUL. A class instance

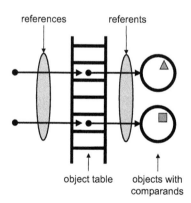

Fig. 2. GILGUL's model: references point to entries in an object table, and each object stores a comparand.

---

[1] In [11] this attribute is named *surrogate*. Elsewhere, names like "key", "identifier" and "OID" are used for this concept. However, these and other terms found throughout the literature might raise the wrong associations. In our approach, we have coined the artificial word *comparand* to stress that this attribute is a passive entity that is never used for referencing, but strictly within comparison operations only.

creation expression (new MyClass(...)) results not only in the creation of a new object, but also in the creation of a new reference, a new referent and a new comparand. The class instance creation expression returns the reference to the object's referent, which in turn has the comparand among its attributes.

Operations on Referents. In GILGUL, the *referent assignment operator* #= is introduced to enable the proposed replacement of objects.[2] The referent assignment expression o1 #= o2 lets the referent of the variable o1 refer to the object o2 without actually changing any references. Effectively, this means that all other variables which hold the same reference as o1 refer to the object o2, too. This can be realised simply by copying the referent of o2 to the entry of o1 in the object table. Consider the following statement sequence.

```
o1 = new MyClass();
o2 = o1;
o2 #= o3;
```

After execution of the referent assignment, all three variables are guaranteed to refer to the same object o3, since after the second assignment, o1 and o2 hold the same reference (see figure 3).

Figure 3 also illustrates why a strict separation of reference and comparison is needed in order to allow for this kind of manipulations. Assume that you want to compare o2 and o3 after execution of the statement sequence given above, resulting in the scenario on the right-hand side of figure 3. In this situation, comparison of variables without the use of comparands is ambiguous on the conceptual level, since comparison of the references would yield false, whereas comparison of the referents would yield true. The decision for one or the other option would be arbitrary and cannot be justified other than by technical considerations only. Therefore, we opt for comparison of properties stored inside of the objects involved and thus make comparison of variables unambiguous.

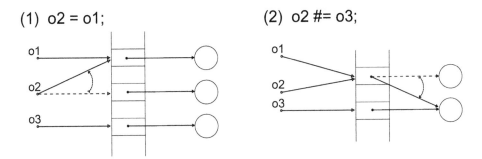

(1) o2 = o1;   (2) o2 #= o3;

Fig. 3. Referent Assignment: After execution of o2 #= o3, all three variables refer to the same object. Since o1 holds the same reference as o2, it is also affected by this operation.

---

[2] The hash symbol # is meant to resemble the graphical illustration of an object table.

Note that the referent assignment operator #= is a reasonable language extension due to the fact that the standard assignment operator = copies the reference from the right-hand operand to the left-hand variable, but not the referent stored in the respective entry in the object table.

Since null does not refer to any object, the referent assignment is prevented from being executed on null, by means of both compile-time and runtime checks.

Operations on Comparands. Technically, it is clear that comparands may be copied freely between objects. There are, in fact, good reasons on the conceptual level to allow the copying of comparands. For example, decorator objects usually have to "take over" the comparand of the decorated object so that comparison operations that involve "direct" references to a wrapped object yield the correct result. Other usage scenarios are given in [3].

Comparands are introduced in GILGUL by means of a new basic type comparandtype which can be used to create new comparands via comparand creation expressions (new comparand). By default, the definition of java.lang.Object, and therefore all objects include an instance variable named comparand of this type.

The equality operators == and != that are already defined on references in Java are redefined in GILGUL to operate on comparands, such that o1 == o2 means the same as o1.comparand == o2.comparand, and o1 != o2 means the same as o1.comparand != o2.comparand.

Given these prerequisites, we can let a wrapper "take over" the comparand of a wrapped object in order to make them become equal by simply copying it as follows: wrapper.comparand = wrapped.comparand.

Ensuring the uniqueness of a single object is always possible by assigning a freshly created comparand as follows: o1.comparand = new comparand.

In Java, the equality operator == is only applicable if one operand can be cast to the type of the other, thereby excluding meaningless comparisons of arbitrarily-typed references [8]. Consequently, a comparand assignment of the form expr1.comparand = expr2.comparand is only accepted if expr2 can (possibly) be cast to the type of expr1. This restriction can be lifted by an explicit cast as follows: expr1.comparand = ((Object)expr2).comparand. Other forms of comparand assignment are always accepted.

Since null does not have a comparand it is prevented from being accessed by a combination of both compile-time and runtime checks. This ensures that testing equality against null is guaranteed to be unambiguous.

The actual implementation of comparands is hidden from programmers. In particular, GILGUL prevents comparands from being arbitrarily cast and, for example, does not allow arithmetic operators to be executed on comparands.

Since comparands cannot be manipulated directly, there are no limitations on how they are implemented in a concrete virtual machine. The only requirement they have to fulfil is that if o1.comparand and o2.comparand have been generated by the same (different) class instance or comparand creation expression, then o1.comparand == o2.comparand yields true (false), and o1.comparand != o2.comparand yields false (true). A reasonable and efficient implementation scheme is outlined in [2].

Example of Use. Returning to our given problem, we are now able to apply the new operations to achieve the desired replacement of an object atomically. We can apply oldObject #= newObject to let newObject replace oldObject consistently for all clients that have references to oldObject.

However, one has to be careful when newObject wants to refer to oldObject in order to delegate messages that it cannot handle by itself. In order to avoid unwanted cycles, one must take care to use a fresh temporary variable for forwarding purposes, as follows (see figure 4; refer to [2,4] for more details).

```
// let a new reference refer to oldObject
   tmp #= oldObject;

// use tmp for forwarding
   newObject.orgObject = tmp;

// ensure that equality behaves well
   newObject.comparand = oldObject.comparand;

// tmp, and so newObject.orgObject remain unchanged
   oldObject #= newObject;
```

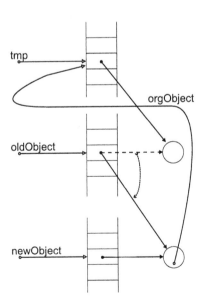

Fig. 4. Application of oldObject #= newObject: When newObject.orgObject holds a different reference to the same object as oldObject beforehand, it will still refer to the former oldObject afterwards, since the temporary reference is not affected. In this way, the state of replaced objects can smoothly be reused.

The actual "replacement" of oldObject is initiated by the last operation, and thus is indeed atomic. Further note that the temporary variable can be used to revert the replacement by application of oldObject #= tmp.

However, this idiom is only needed when newObject needs to reuse oldObject. Otherwise, a "simple" replacement is sufficient. In this case, reversal of a replacement can also be achieved by the use of an additional reference, but it is not needed for forwarding purposes.

As we can see, GILGUL's new operations give the programmer the possibility of "replacing" the former object atomically and thereby relieves him/her from having to deal with any consistency problems that result from many, perhaps unknown, references to the target object. Furthermore, the objects involved need not anticipate such modifications, reducing the complexity of the development of actual components to a great extent.

3   Replacement of Active Objects

Although quite powerful, GILGUL's new operations face a problem when dealing with active objects. Consider figure 5 that depicts an attempt at replacement of object1 that still has a method m() executing on it. After an attempt at replacement of obect1, it is unclear what object the active method m() should continue to execute on afterwards. There are only two options – either it continues to execute on the old object that has been replaced, or it chooses the new object. Both options have serious drawbacks. If m() continues to execute on the old object, it does not reflect the programmer's intention to have the object replaced. If it chooses the new object, this may lead to severe consistency problems, for example, if m() is implemented differently in the class of the new object. This example also illustrates why in the general case, such attempts cannot be detected statically since they might be issued in other objects and especially in totally different source code.

In order to ensure consistency, the default semantics of GILGUL are defined as follows. If the active method m() and the attempt at object replacement are

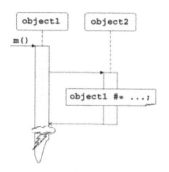

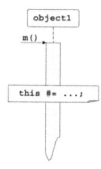

Fig. 5. Replacement of object1 – what object should m() continue to execute on?

Fig. 6. Replacement of this – method m() is active by definition.

executed by different threads the referent assignment operation blocks until m() (and all other methods that are active on the target object) complete. If they are executed by the same thread (that is, on the same execution stack) the referent assignment operation throws an (unchecked) ReferentAssignmentException.

Replacement of this There are several situations when an object knows best when to be replaced. For example, the State pattern [6] gives the advice "to let the State subclasses themselves specify their successor state and when to make the transition". However, a referent assignment this #= *expression* implies that the method that currently executes on this is active in the same thread by definition (see figure 6).

GILGUL relaxes its restrictions for this case and does not throw a ReferentAssignmentException if it is ensured (by a combination of static and dynamic checks) that after the replacement of this, code will no longer be executed on this. For example, in the case of a void method this can be accomplished by just placing the replacement of this at the end of the method. For non-void methods a new construct is introduced as follows.

```
int m() {
    . . .
    return expression with this #= replacement;
}
```

The semantics are as follows. First, the return expression is evaluated. Then, the replacement of this is carried out. Last, the method completes and returns the result of the evaluation in the first step. Together, these steps ensure that the replacement of this is indeed the last statement that gets executed on this.[3]

Another variation of this construct occurs in combination with the throw statement: throw *expression* with this #= *replacement*. The semantics are defined accordingly.[4]

Advanced Requirements. So far, GILGUL does not offer a completely satisfactory solution for replacements of active objects. For the default case, our main goal was to ensure consistency, and consequently, this precludes solutions for the following issues.

 - The rule that replacements block until active methods in other threads complete does not by itself handle the situation when the active method consists of a non-terminating loop (for example, in the case of daemon threads).

---

[3] Possibly, there are still other methods active on the current object. In this case, the rules hold that are given in the previous section.

[4] In previous versions of GILGUL, we have allowed replacements of this to be placed inside of the finally block of a try statement. This would ensure roughly the same semantics (both for return and throw statements). However, the finally block is meant to be used for code that should always execute, even when an exception is thrown. It is more likely that replacements of this should not occur in this case, so we have added the with construct to our design with these slightly different semantics.

– More often than not, administrators might be willing to trade timeliness for (temporary) inconsistency and so want to have an object replaced immediately rather than having to wait for the completion of other methods.

In GILGUL, the concept of *recalls* is introduced to provide support for these cases. In the following sections, we first outline the concept of recalls and afterwards show how they can be combined with referent assignments in order to provide a feasible means to deal with these cases.

Recalls. Exceptions in Java are a means to step out of the standard flow of control, and they can be caught by dedicated exception handlers, possibly at a higher level in the call stack, to revert to a corrected flow. In other words, the current call stack is *unwound* until a matching exception handler is found [8].

A *recall* in GILGUL mimics the behaviour of Java's exceptions, but instead of relying on the definition of dedicated exception handlers, a return to the standard flow takes place as soon as the call stack is clear of a particular receiver during the process of unwinding. For example, assume the throw of a recall on object2 in figure 7. The current call stack is unwound up to the first method call on object2, and then this particular method is called again on object2.

Note that a recall guarantees that immediately before the point of return to the standard flow of control, the current call stack does not contain any method calls to the specified object. So by definition, there is no method active on this object at this point in time (at the marked spot in figure 7).[5]

Just as in the case of exceptions in Java, Recall is a plain class in GILGULand instances thereof can be thrown and caught. It is unchecked, like java.lang.RuntimeException, in order to have it smoothly integrated into existing Java code.

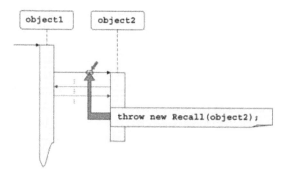

Fig. 7. A *recall* on object2 unwinds the current stack up to the first method call on object2, and then calls this method again. Just before reexecution of this method call (at the marked spot), the call stack is guaranteed to be clear of object2 as a receiver.

---

[5] If there is no method active on the target object at the moment of the throw of a respective recall, this recall is simply ignored and evaluates to a non-operation.

The catch of a recall can be employed in order to set corresponding objects to a consistent state. However, the respective recall should be rethrown in order to guarantee its effective completion, as follows.

```
try {
    ...                        // do your standard stuff here
} catch (Recall recall) {
    ...                        // reset your object(s)
    throw recall;              // and rethrow the recall
}
```

Since GILGUL's recalls are not exceptions in the strict sense to indicate that something has gone wrong, Recall is not defined as a subclass of java.lang.Exception, but as a subclass of the more general class java.lang.Throwable. This ensures that a general catch of all exceptions does not accidentally catch a recall as well.

Further note that in the presence of parameters to the method call that gets reexecuted by a recall, the (possibly complex) parameter expressions are not reevaluated, but the previously evaluated values are simply reused.[6]

Combination with Referent Assignments. Given these prerequisites, GILGUL's referent assignment can be amended by recalls in order to replace even active objects. This is accomplished by annotating the application of the referent assignment operator accordingly, for example as follows.

```
expression1 #= expression2 with global recall;
```

The options are as follows: a *local recall* throws the recall only for the current thread; a *global recall* throws it for all other threads that have a method executing on the target object, but not the current thread. These options can be combined, as in *expr1* #= *expr2* with local recall, global recall. Then the recall is thrown for both the current thread and other threads. The combination of a local and a global recall can be be abbreviated, as in *expr1* #= *expr2* with total recall.

The actual Recall instance that is thrown in this case takes the left-hand side of the referent assignment expression as a parameter. This means that the respective call stacks are unwound up to the first method call on the object referred to by the left-hand side. The actual replacement of this object is deferred to this point in time, when the call stack is guaranteed to be clear of methods that are active on this object (as a receiver), and just before the reexecution of the respective method call (at the marked spot in figure 7).

As a consequence, by means of the recall construct, the replacement takes place at a point in time when it is safe to carry it out. Afterwards, the standard flow of control is reentered and for example, can return to a thus temporarily terminated loop. Since recalls may be caught during the unwinding of the call

---

[6] In Java bytecode, the call of a method consists of pushing parameters on the operand stack, and then, as a distinct step, execute an invocation of the respective method. It is only this last step that gets reexecuted by a recall, and the invocation merely reuses the old state of the operand stack.

stack, it is possible to reset the target object (and possibly dependent objects) to a reasonable, consistent state. However, it is not required to provide for such clearance code because recalls are unchecked. Therefore, they can still be thrown even in unanticipated contexts. In the latter case, it is the task of the programmer who wants to replace a specific object to decide if clearance is needed or not and to take the necessary steps.

Relation to Java's Thread Model. There is a close relation of GILGUL's recalls to Java's *interrupts* that are used in order to signal that a specific thread should terminate. In the latter case, no automatic steps are taken by the runtime system to actively stop the thread, but instead all threads are required to regularly check their own interrupt flags and terminate eventually. In order to help programmers to remember to check for interrupts, some standard thread-oriented methods in Java, like wait(...) or Thread.sleep(...), may throw a (checked) InterruptedException when the corresponding flag is set.[7]

Essentially, global recalls in GILGUL mimic this behaviour. Instead of directly throwing recalls in other threads, a global recall merely sets a corresponding flag in each thread. This recall flag is checked in the well-known methods that already check for the interrupt status, namely wait(...), Thread.sleep(...) and so on, and they may throw recalls accordingly. Additionally, the recall flag is checked in the equally well-known Thread.yield(). Since platform independent components are expected to at least occasionally call Thread.yield() for compatibility reasons, and generally make use of the other methods mentioned as well, the recall mechanism will most likely be already applicable in most cases without change of existing components.[8]

A Template for Long-Running Methods. As a preliminary summary, we now give a code template for long-running methods.

```
void longRunningMethod() {
  try {
    for (aVeryLongTime) {
      Thread.yield(); // implicitly check for global recalls
      doYourActualStuff();
    }
  } catch (Recall r) {
    resetToConsistentState();
```

---

[7] Note that this is the only default means in Java to support the termination of threads. Up to JDK 1.2, the class java.lang.Thread has included methods stop(...) and suspend(...) for explicit termination, but they have since been deprecated for safety reasons [18].

[8] In Java, the method Thread.yield() is used as a hint to the runtime system to indicate where switches between thread contexts may occur, and is essentially a Thread.sleep(0). The occasional call of Thread.yield() is optional in pre-emptive implementations of Java's thread model, but is required in cooperative ones. See [13] for more details on Thread.yield().

```
    throw r; // rethrow the recall
  }
}
```

Please note the following.

- The try-catch block is only required if there is a need for clearance in the presence of recalls. Otherwise, Java's standard exception handling mechanism guarantees the propagation of recalls to higher levels.
- If the longRunningMethod() is the topmost method that has been called for the respective object on the call stack, the throw of a recall is guaranteed to reexecute this method (after object replacement, if thrown in conjunction with a referent assignment). There is no need for the programmer to take explicit steps in order to achieve this behaviour.
- The only requirement that is currently placed on the programmer is to occasionally insert checks for recalls, for example by calling Thread.yield().[9]

State of Implementation. A beta-quality implementation of the complete GILGUL programming language can be freely downloaded as a compiler and runtime system from the GILGUL homepage [7]. The software includes a working implementation of the recall mechanism and its combination with the referent assignment operator, as described in the previous sections.

The GILGUL runtime system is a modification of the Kaffe virtual machine [10], both released under the Gnu Public License. We have put our main focus on providing a stable proof of concept in a manageable amount of time, and not on topnotch industrial-strength performance, given the manpower of just one programmer for the compiler and one for the runtime system. Therefore we have chosen to only modify the pure interpreter part of the Kaffe virtual machine, and have not yet addressed issues of just-in-time or dynamic compilation.

We have also completed a detailed analysis of GILGUL's runtime performance in order to determine the relative speed in comparison to the pure Kaffe virtual machine. We have used standard benchmarks for this purpose, for example VolanoMark [20], and they report an average penalty of less than 5 percent. This is mainly due to some clever optimisations for the general case and, for example, the avoidance of a centralized object table, but instead the use of implementation techniques that make double indirection nearly as fast as direct pointers. Details will be presented in a forthcoming diploma thesis [16].

4 Related Work

Object Identity. GILGUL is the first approach known to the author that strictly and cleanly separates the notions of reference and comparison at the level of a

---

[9] A programmer may also choose to explicitly check for global recalls by inspection of the respective recall flag. However, we expect programmers to want to do this seldomly, so we have not presented the details here.

programming language. An overview of related work centered around the theme of object identity is given in [4].

Note that this separation of object identity concerns is orthogonal to the usual distinction between reference semantics and value semantics that is found for example in Smalltalk [17], Eiffel [15], and Java [8]. These languages allow programmers to choose from these semantics when comparing variables, but they all still rely on comparison of references in order to establish object identity.[10] For this reason, object identity usually coincides with reference semantics. In contrast, our approach relies on comparands to determine (logical) identity, and this opens up new degrees of flexibility.

Microsoft's component object model COM [1] separates object identity and references to the degree that it generally allows components to return different references for repeated requests of the same interface. However, the special IUn-known reference is required to never change as an exceptional case for comparison purposes. Again, object identity and reference semantics coincide and therefore COM components cannot be dynamically replaced unless prepared for. COM's *monikers* provide an alternative mechanism of object identification, targeted at linking and persistence, that allows the physical implementation of objects to change occasionally. However, it is not used as a general reference mechanism.

Dynamic Object Replacement. The programming language Smalltalk provides an operation become: that enables the programmer to (symmetrically) "swap" two objects without actually changing their references. Early Smalltalk implementations were based on object tables, and so this operation was straightforward to implement. Modern Smalltalk implementations that use direct pointers either take considerable effort to implement become: correctly, or reduce become: to an asymmetrical operation [17]. However, there are still some serious drawbacks. Smalltalk's become: is not type-safe because it does not check for compatible storage layouts of the objects involved. Furthermore, it does not pay any attention to methods currently executing on the objects, but just lets them continue to execute on the "swapped" objects. In contrast, GILGUL's referent assignment respects Java's type system without sacrificing flexibility (as shown in [2]), and introduces means to correctly and explicitly deal with active objects.

Replacement of Active Objects. We are aware of only one approach that allows for dynamic software evolution and tries to deal with non-terminating loops without stopping them, but rather by letting the programmer define states of a loop that allow for quasi-"morphing" to another loop [14].

Another more recent approach for unanticipated software evolution is [5]. That paper describes an extension of the Java Platform Debugging Architecture that is included in version 1.4 of the Java Development Kit. That approach works on a different level of granularity, since it aims at replacements of classes

---

[10] Whether the actual semantics of comparison is defined in the respective classes or must be determined by choosing from different comparison operators/methods varies from language to language. A thorough examination of these issues is given in [9].

at runtime, not objects as in GILGUL. Furthermore, the issue of replacement in the presence of active objects has not yet been addressed. For the time being, that approach relies on completion of active methods.

5   Conclusions and Future Work

We have designed the programming language GILGUL, a compatible extension to Java. It introduces the new basic type **comparandtype** and the referent assignment operator #=. It also changes the definition of the existing equality operators == and != according to the GILGUL model. We have shown an example of how to apply GILGUL's new operations for the purpose of dynamic object replacement without the need to deal with consistency problems.

This model is a generalization of what can be expressed in terms of object identity in current object-oriented programming languages. GILGUL offers flexible means for declaring restrictions on which operations are valid on specific referents and comparands, for example in order to prevent the replacement of sensible objects. These restrictions can range from the unrestricted applicability of GILGUL's new operations to the reduction to the traditional stringent restrictions placed on object identity. More details are given in [2].

In this paper, we have also sketched the problems with which dynamic object replacement is faced in the presence of active objects, both in multi-threaded and single-threaded contexts. By default, GILGUL offers means to deal with these situations in a way that preserves consistency. If programmers are willing to trade consistency for timeliness, or even need to break consistency in order to be able to replace objects at all in the case of non-terminating loops, they can take advantage of GILGUL's advanced facilities for these cases.

We have outlined the concept of *recalls* that has been introduced in GILGUL. Like exceptions, recalls unwind the call stack, and can be thrown and caught. Unlike exceptions, the return to the standard flow of control is guaranteed as soon as the call stack is clear of a specific object as a receiver of a method call. At this point in time, the very first call to the specified object is simply reexecuted.

The referent assignment operator can be annotated with several variants of recalls, which means that the actual replacement is deferred until the corresponding call stack is clear of the object to be replaced. Just before reexecution of the first method call to this object, the actual replacement takes place.

Although this combination of the referent assignment operator and a recall might break consistency, target objects are still able to react to the throw of recalls by providing recall handlers for clearance purposes, just like exception handlers in Java. However, even if recall handlers have not been provided, replacements can still be carried out ensuring timeliness, and replaceability in the presence of non-terminating loops. This might sometimes be the last resort before a system shut-down becomes inevitable.

The implementation of the GILGUL compiler and runtime system has just been completed, and we have briefly sketched some of its properties.

Acknowledgements

The author thanks Tom Arbuckle, Michael Austermann, Ferrucio Damiani, Paola Giannini, Peter Grogono, Arno Haase, Günter Kniesel, Thomas Kühne, Sven Müller, James Noble, Markku Sakkinen, Oliver Stiemerling, Clemens Szyperski, Dirk Theisen, Kris De Volder and many anonymous reviewers for their critical comments on earlier drafts and related publications, which led to substantial improvements.

This work is located in the TAILOR Project at the Institute of Computer Science III of the University of Bonn. The TAILOR Project is directed by Armin B. Cremers and supported by Deutsche Forschungsgemeinschaft (DFG) under grant CR 65/13.

References

1. D. Box. *Essential COM*. Addison-Wesley, 1998.
2. P. Costanza *Dynamic Object Replacement and Implementation-Only Classes*. 6th International Workshop on Component-Oriented Programming (WCOP 2001) at ECOOP 2001, Budapest, Hungary.
3. P. Costanza and A. Haase. *The Comparand Pattern*. EuroPLoP 2001, Irsee, Germany.
4. P. Costanza, O. Stiemerling, and A. B. Cremers. *Object Identity and Dynamic Recomposition of Components*. in: *TOOLS Europe 2001*. Proceedings, IEEE Computer Society Press.
5. M. Dmitriev. *Towards Flexible and Safe Technology for Runtime Evolution of Java Language Applications*. Workshop on Engineering Complex Object-Oriented Systems for Evolution (ECOOSE) at OOPSLA 2001, Tampa, Florida, USA.
6. E. Gamma, R. Helm, R. Johnson, and J. Vlissides. *Design Patterns*. Addison-Wesley, 1995.
7. The GILGUL homepage. http://javalab.cs.uni-bonn.de/research/gilgul/
8. J. Gosling, B. Joy, G. Steele, and G. Bracha. *The Java Language Specification, Second Edition*. Addison-Wesley, 2000.
9. P. Grogono and M. Sakkinen. *Copying and Comparing: Problems and Solutions*. in: *ECOOP 2000*. Proceedings, Springer.
10. The Kaffe homepage. http://www.kaffe.org/
11. S. N. Khoshafian and G. P. Copeland. *Object Identity*. in: *OOPSLA '86*. Proceedings, ACM Press.
12. G. Kniesel. *Type-Safe Delegation for Run-Time Component Adaptation*. in: *ECOOP '99*. Proceedings, Springer.
13. D. Lea. *Concurrent Programming in Java, Second Edition*. Addison-Wesley, 1999.
14. I. Lee. *DYMOS: A Dynamic Modification System*. Dissertation, University of Wisconsin-Madison, USA, 1983.
15. B. Meyer. *Eiffel: The Language*. Prentice Hall, 1992.
16. S. Müller. *Transmigration von Objektidentitäten – Integration der Spracherweiterung Gilgul in eine Java-Laufzeitumgebung* (in German). University of Bonn, Insitute of Computer Science III, diploma thesis, 2002. (in preparation)

17. D. N. Smith. *Smalltalk FAQ*. http://www.dnsmith.com/SmallFAQ/, 1995.
18. Sun Microsystems, Inc. *Java 2 SDK, Standard Edition Documentation, Version 1.3.1.* http://java.sun.com/j2se/1.3/docs/
19. The Tailor Project. http://javalab.cs.uni-bonn.de/research/tailor/
20. VolanoMark Java Benchmarks. http://www.volano.com/benchmarks.html

Beyond Generic Component Parameters

Uwe Aßmann

Research Center for Integrational Software Engineering (RISE),
PELAB, IDA, Linköpings Universitet, Sweden,
http://www.ida.liu.se/~rise, uweas@ida.liu.se

Abstract. For flexible use in application contexts, software components should be parameterized, but also extended appropriately. Until now, there is no language mechanism to solve both problems *uniformly*. This paper presents a new concept, *component hooks*. Hooks are similar to generic component parameters but go some steps beyond. Firstly, they allow genericity on arbitrary program elements, leading to *generic program elements*. Secondly, they introduce an abstraction layer on generic parameters, allowing for structured generic parameters that bind several program elements together. Thirdly, if they are abstract set or sequence values, they can also be used to *extend* components. Lastly, since they only rely on a meta model they are a language independent concept which can be applied to all languages.

Hooks form a basic parameterization concept for components written in languages with a meta model. For such languages, hooks generalize many well known generic language mechanisms, such as macros, semantic macros, generic type parameters, or nested generics. They also provide a basic concept to realize simple forms of aspect weavers and other advanced software engineering concepts.

1 Introduction

Over time, various generic parameters concepts have appeared in programming languages and component systems. Mainly, they allow for parameterizations of classes, types, or packages with other classes and types. A generic parameter marks one or several program elements in a component which should be replaced consistently by a valid type. Spoken in more abstract terms, the *substitution* or *bind operation* substitutes every reference of a generic parameter type to a reference of a type.

This paper introduces *hooks*, an abstraction concept for generic parameters which generalizes them in several directions.[1] Firstly, hooks provide genericity for arbitrary program elements, not only types (Section 2). Secondly, hooks

---

[1] Hooks enable us to attach things to other things. In the literature, the metaphor has been used several times to denote parameterizations of components, e.g., of parameterization of classes [Pre95] or extensions of components such as procedure extensions in emacs Lisp [LLStGMG98]. Here, we use the word in a similar way, but relate it to arbitrary meta objects of the component language.

J. Bishop (Ed.): CD 2002, LNCS 2370, pp. 141–154, 2002.
© Springer-Verlag Berlin Heidelberg 2002

may be structured. This allows for structured parameter values that parameterize component parts which are not directly related (Section 3). Thirdly, hooks generalize generic parameters to sets and sequences of program elements. Then, hooks can be *extended* to enrich a component with additional functionality (Section 4). Fourth, many hooks can be regarded as being *implicitly defined* by the programming language (Section 5). This simplifies component extensions. Since the component language can easily be varied, also to XML or binary languages (Section 6), hooks provide a general parameterization and extension mechanism for every language with a meta model.

In essence, the concept of hooks introduces an indirection between the program elements of a component and the actual generic parameter. Hence, hooks introduce a new abstraction level for generic parameters; generic parameters are no longer directly tied to program elements.

2   Generic Program Elements

For this paper, we assume that components are programmed in a strongly typed programming language with a compile-time meta model. Such languages are called *open languages* [CM93] [Aßm98] since they originally are designed for language extension. They support *static meta-programming*, execute the meta programs during compilation, and remove them afterwards. In contrast, modern object oriented languages support a run time meta model (Java, C#) which is not available at compile time (*dynamic meta programming, reflection*).

We start with some basic definitions. Every element of a program corresponds to a language concept. In an open language, the concepts are represented on the meta level, i.e., as types in the language's meta model. Hence, every element of the program is related to a meta object, a type in the language's meta model.[2]

Definition 1 (Principle of Type Safe Substitution). *In a language with a meta model, if a program element should be substituted by another, it can be checked whether the meta model type of the replacing program element is equal to that of the replaced program element.*

We assume that a component is a set of arbitrary program elements.

Definition 2 (Component). *A component is a set of program elements.*

This definition of a component is rather general. It covers many cases of static parameterization and static composition of components. Any kind of source code units, such as classes, methods, packages, even aspects may be regarded as components. However, the definition does not cover run time composition.

Definition 3 (Hook). *A hook is a set of program elements or positions in a component, being marked-up as generic.*

---

[2] The literature uses these terms rather loosely; actually it is the language's model and the program's meta model. However, even UML's model is called *UML meta model* although it is a meta model for UML specifications, and a model for UML.

Hooks generalize generic parameters. Their definition will be explained and elaborated on in the paper. As a base language for components, we use Java, although any other language can be used. As a notation for hooks, we use XML markup: Appendix 1 contains an XML schema. Other markup techniques, such as language extensions, can also be employed. In this scenario, hooks are sets of program elements which are marked-up as generic. For instance, a hook that marks up a generic super class looks as follows:

---

class Chicken **extends**
    <generic name="Super" type="Type"> Animal </generic> { .. }

Alternatively, a markup may be *empty* which means that it marks a position in the component. A hook that marks up a super class position looks as follows, using the abbreviation syntax for XML closing tags:

---

class Chicken **extends** <generic name="Super" type="Type" /> { .. }

Figure 1 illustrates that hooks provide an *indirection* mechanism for denoting generic parameters and positions of components. It displays a method component with three hooks: a generic type parameter, a hook for the entry point of the method, and a hook for the exit points of the method. In the case of the generic parameter T, the hook T marks up a position for a type reference. In the case of the method entry, the hook points to the entry position of the method. This hook is predefined by the programming language and marked up implicitly (Section 5). In the case of the method exit, the hook refers to the two exit positions where control flow returns from the method. Hooks describe generic parts of components in a more abstract way than generic parameters do since they abstract from the concrete representations of the component.

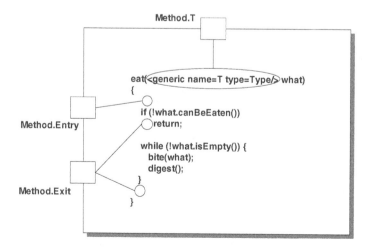

Fig. 1. A method component **Method** with three hooks, a generic type parameter, a hook for the entry point of the method, and a hook for the exit points of the method.

We use XML mainly for presentation purposes. Actually, XML markup has a major deficiency since its substitution mechanism is not type-safe, and hence too weak for our purpose. Standard methods for XML transformation, e.g., languages such as XSLT, replace markup with context free pattern matching and disregard the context and *semantic constraints*. Here, we require a type-safe rewriting machinery: a *bind* operation for a generic hook must check whether the value it substitutes for the markup fits into context. Such checks are typically performed by a template expander in a compiler, or by the evaluator of the static meta programs. Here, they are assumed to be a given underlying mechanism.

Example 1. Generic modifiers are generic program elements. For instance, the **synchronized** modifier in Java ensures exclusive execution of a Java method. When they are marked up as being generic several methods can be consistently instantiated for a parallel context:

```
class Chicken extends Animal {
    <generic name="Synch" type="SynchModifier" /> eat() { .. }
    <generic name="Synch" type="SynchModifier" /> drink() { .. }
}
```

Here, **Synch** is the name of the generic modifier hook. During parameter-ization, its markup can be replaced by the **synchronized** modifier. Suppose, several chickens live in parallel and nurture from a shared food and water re-source. Then, this resource should have its access synchronized. In the following example [[ ]] is an operator to read a component from a file, and << >> is an operator to produce program elements from strings:

```
[["Chicken"]].findHook("Synch").bind(<<"synchronized">>);
```

This expression expands the component to:

```
class Chicken extends Animal {
    synchronized eat() { .. }
    synchronized drink() { .. }
}
```

Hence, generic modifiers instantiate several methods consistently to the same synchronization behavior. Also, due to type safety, it can be enforced that generic synchronization modifiers are replaced by synchronization modifiers. In general, generic program elements introduce consistent behavior for different components beyond the purposes which can be modeled by inheritance.

Related Work That Uses Generic Program Elements. To our knowledge, the first language that provided generic parameters was CLU [LAB+79]. Similarly, type parameters were employed in Ada83 [Ada83]. Ada95 generalized the generic type concept to generic packages, packages to which classes can be passed as pa-rameters [Ada95]. This concept allows for easy construction of frameworks since large subsystems can be parameterized by classes. From Ada83, there also leads a trace to C++ templates [Str97]. They are more flexible since parameter values can be concatenated to identifiers. For instance, this allows for the renaming of methods:

```
template class Chicken<class Color> {
   eat<Color>() {...}
}
```

which then is expanded to `eatBrown` if `Color` is bound to `Brown`.

Template Metaprogramming employs C++ templates for more sophisticated purposes, e.g., for static control flow constructs [CE00]. These are control flow constructs which are evaluated at compile time, resembling the `#ifdef` statements of the C preprocessor. However, they are evaluated by the standard template mechanism and provide type-safety. On the other hand, this mechanism represents all generic program elements with generic types, and that might be the wrong way of abstraction.

PARIS provides *program schemes* which can be parameterized by all kinds of program elements [KRT87]. It supports a form of type-safety although it does not yet provide an explicit meta model. Instead, it guesses the type of a generic parameter from its position in the template. Beyond simple substitution, PARIS proposes an parameterization process which is guided by a rule base and produces a software artifact automatically. From the papers, it is unclear how successful this automatic parameterization process has been in practice.

BETA *slots* are generic program elements which may be substituted by *code fragments* [BNS⁺91] [LKLLMM94]. The substitution is guided by the language's grammar. Only strings that are produced from a certain non-terminal (fragments) may be substituted for the non-terminal. The BETA meta-programming system enforces correct substitution and allows reuse of fragments because they are stored in files. Fragments can even be compiled separately. Hence, BETA slots and fragments are one of the most advanced genericity concepts available.

Semantic Macros extend standard macro processors by letting the macro access results of the semantic analysis of the compiler [Mad89] [KFD99]. Then, macro substitution can be made type safe. Every macro has a result type in terms of the meta model (or, in the types of the abstract syntax tree, if a meta model is not available). Since the context of a macro reference may query the type which is required to be substituted, macro references are rejected if they do not substitute to the right meta model type. Hence, Semantic Macros simplify the use of type-safe substitution and they provide a simple implementation technique for component parameterization. They can even serve as language extensions for hooks, i.e., can embed the hook concept in a component language. However, Semantic Macros are *unstructured* and cannot deal with the structured parameterizations in the next section.

3   Structured Generic Parameters

Since hooks introduce an indirection concept for generic parameters, the parameterizations become more flexible. Furthermore, hooks can be structured to represent *structured generic parameters*. Structured generic parameters provide another degree of freedom for parameterization. Every part of the structured parameter substitutes a different value. Hence, in one go several parameterizations can be performed together, and a component may be parameterized much more flexibly than with unstructured simple generic parameters.

Example 2. As an example, consider a communication between two partners, obeying a communication protocol. Such a protocol must be initialized, usually in a constructor, and finalized, usually in a destructor (we assume for this example that Java contains destructors with the usual syntax of C++ or C#).

We extend the definition of our `Chicken` component (Figure 2). As the XML schema in the appendix indicates, a structured hook can be compared to a record. Every part of a structured hook must name the structured hook (`sname`), must indicate a `feature`, and a `type`. For our component, the following class for the value of the structured hook can be defined:

```
class ProtocolValue { Statement init; Call call; Statement destr; }
```

We can write the following extension program that binds the structured generic parameter with a structured value

```
[["Chicken"]].findHook("SendEggs").bind(new ProtocolValue(
    <<"egg.initialize()">>,<<"human.receive()">>,<<"egg.finalize()">>));
```

To simplify the example, we omit the sub-hooks for the definition of the objects `egg` and `human`. Then the following class results:

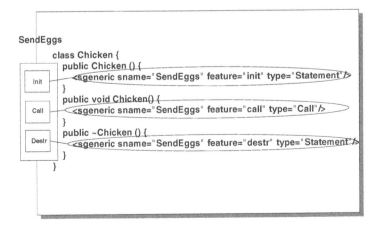

Fig. 2. A structured hook. It can be replaced in one go with a structured value of parameters. It parameterizes disconnected component parts.

```
class Chicken {
   public Chicken () {
      <sgeneric sname="SendEggs" feature="init" type="Statement">
         egg.initalize();
      </sgeneric>
   }
   public void produce() {
      <sgeneric sname="SendEggs" feature="call" type="Call">
         human.receive(egg);
      </sgeneric>/>
   }    public ~Chicken () {
      <sgeneric sname="SendEggs" feature="destr" type="Statement">
         egg.finalize();
      </sgeneric>/>
   }
}
```

For the moment, we leave the hook markup in the component, it is to be extended again in Section 4.

Nested hooks provide one advantage over standard parameterization mechanisms such as polymorphic hot spots [Pre95]. The above example can only be expressed by subclassing and polymorphism if all inserted calls go to the same object. If, as in the example, different objects are called, subclassing is not sufficient. However, a structured generic value can provide different values for all of the three sub-hooks.

With structured hooks, several generic parameters of sets of components can be parameterized together in a consistent way. Hence, they lend themselves to generic frameworks. Since we have used a very general component notion these frameworks may be generic over any type of program unit.

Related Work. Program scheme approaches such as PARIS allow to parameterize program parts with several parameters, however do not support structured generic parameters for binding several generic parameters together. One approach with structured generic parameters is GenVoca [BST+94]. GenVoca expresses structuring by nesting and describes nested values with a context free language over the possible values. On the other hand, GenVoca does not allow to markup components, and requires that all subvalues of a structured parameter are substituted to one position in the component. Hence, it does not support parameterization of disconnected program parts.

The only available fully-fledged nested generic parameter mechanism is BETA slots and fragments [LKLLMM94], although it has not been recognized as such. BETA slots (the hooks) are instantiated with BETA fragments (the values), and these may contain slots so that a fragment can nest slots. However, nested fragments must be created as a sequence of parameterizations; a closed form for a parameter value cannot be created. However, this differs only marginally from our approach.

Different program parts can only be parameterized together if the generic parameter *points to* the parts, but is not *identical* to the parts. And structured hooks provide this indirection.

4   Set Hooks for Component Extension

In this section, we consider the case when a hook refers to program elements or positions found in a set or list of equally typed program elements. Many language elements appear in lists or sets, e.g., fields in classes, parameters in parameter lists, or modifiers in modifier sets. With such *set hooks*, it is possible to generalize the notion of a generic parameter to component extensions. If we allow that a hook is bound several times, i.e., if it may be *extended* with additional program element values, a component can be extended step by step by extending of its hooks (Figure 3). We assume a suitable *extend* operation for this purpose which also should be type safe.

Hook extension is useful for many purposes. It goes beyond standard binding of generic parameters because it does not only allow for parameterization, but for extension. Thus it is important for all those situations in component based software engineering when a component based system needs to be extended with new functionality. These situations often occur in software evolution or incremental software processes such as XP [Bec99]. Also, adding a new member to a class is equivalent to the extending the hook of its members. Hence, hook extension can model class extensions in inheritance, as well as merge operations in record and class calculi [Bra92]. However, this only holds for pure extensions without overriding old members. To mimick the full effect of extension and merge oper-

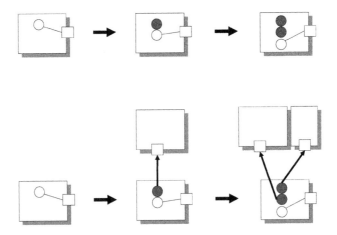

Fig. 3. Extending a hook for component extension. Above: adding more and more program elements to the hook. Down: Adding program elements that relate the component to other components, e.g., communication statements.

ations, the extensions must be checked whether they override existing members.

Example 3. Extensions of hooks can also model simple aspect oriented extensions. In aspect-oriented programming, *aspects extend* a *system core* with additional features [KLM+97]. For instance, an animation aspect can be specified separately and weaved by an extension into the core.

Suppose, we extend the hooks in Example 2 a second time with the following operation

```
[["Chicken"]].findHook("SendEggs").extend( new ProtocolValue(
    <<"initEvents()">>,<<"fireEvent()">>,<<"finalizeEvents()">>));
```

then this example provides a simple form of aspect weaving. The extension operation can be thought of as adding an animation aspect to the core of the component. It introduces new statements which send an event to an animation object, and this additional object animates that the chicken has produced an egg and sent it to the waiting human. This extension can be repeated for other components to be animated, and in this way a useful animation aspect can be added to a system core.

Aspect weavings can be modeled as extensions of hooks if the aspects depend on the core but not vice versa. Spoken in terms of program analysis, there should be forward data dependencies from the core to the aspect, but not vice versa. When extending the core with such forward dependencies, the semantics of the core is not changed, but the aspect receives all necessary data from the core so that it can execute. Clearly, hook extension works for the animation aspect and other ones, for instance debugging or communication aspects. Of course, extension of set hooks has the usual problems of Aspect Oriented Programming, e.g., the aspect interaction problem. Whenever two extensions conflict with each other semantically, the order in which they are applied is important. It is future work to develop precise criteria when these problems occur, how they can be detected, and how they can be remedied.

A generic mechanism that supports aspect orientation must provide nested parameterization. Since an aspect is defined as a concern that *cross-cuts* a core, weaving requires that many parts of the core are extended with different values *consistently*. Until now, no generic mechanism for such extensions was known. Our hope is that aspect weavers can be simplified with extensions of structured hooks, at least for aspects which only depend on the core.

5   Implicit Hooks

So far we only allowed generic parameters which were declared to have a name and a type in the meta model. However, the block structuring rules of a language aid in identifying many *implicit positions* which have standard names. These can be regarded as generic parameters which are *implicitly defined* by the language report. For instance, Figure 1 contains two hooks which have been implicitly defined by the semantics of a method: every method has an entry point, and one or several exit points.

For such *implicit hooks*, we can introduce default names that need not be declared by the component writer, but can be inserted automatically from a component analyzer. Such a tool can mark up implicit hooks without human intervention. Compare Figure 4 with Figure 1. Its markup can be derived automatically if default names for method entry and exit are given.

Example 4. If extensions can address implicit hooks with their default names aspect weavings become simpler. Consider the following extension which extends Example 2 with a debugging aspect. In our simple case, the aspect wraps all methods of the **Chicken** class with additional entry and exit code that prints debugging output:

```
[["Chicken"]].findHook("Chicken.<method>.Entry").extend(
    <<"System.err.println("enterMethod <method>");">>);
```

which results in the following component, still being generic:

```
class Chicken {
    public Chicken () {
        System.err.println("enterMethod_Chicken()");

        <sgeneric sname="SendEggs" feature="init" type="Statement">
            egg.initalize();
        </sgeneric>
    }

    public void produce() {
        System.err.println("enterMethod_produce()");
        <sgeneric sname="SendEggs" feature="call" type="Call">
            human.receive(egg);
        </sgeneric>/>
    }

    public ~Chicken () {
        System.err.println("enterMethod_~Chicken()");
        <sgeneric sname="SendEggs" feature="destr" type="Statement">
            initalize();
        </sgeneric>/>
    }
}
```

If a component system has a component reader that recognizes and marks up implicit hooks automatically, transformations like the above are possible but component writers need not declare hooks. Since an implicit hook is similar to a join point in Aspect Oriented Programming which is immediately useful for

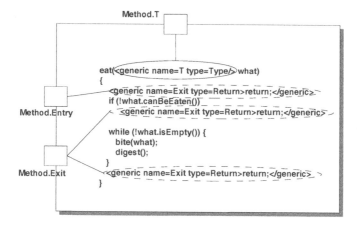

Fig. 4. Knowing the programming language semantics and naming conventions, implicit hooks can be derived by a component reader.

aspect weaving. However, it also opens up the component to a larger extent, and sacrifices information hiding. Hence, implicit hooks provide a very weak interface notion, namely the default positions in a component that have been defined by the programming language report. Of course, a component system need not use implicit hooks, or can forbid them for particular components or extensions.

6 Extension to Other Component Languages

Since a markup language treats the underlying language as text the latter can be exchanged. Of course, it can also be exchanged with XML languages. Then, the markup XML schema becomes an XML name space that extends another XML language naturally. What still has to be ensured is type safety, i.e., the transformation facility has to know about the meta model of the XML language and ensure type safe substitution and extension.

Also binary components can be made generic with our approach. A machine language also has a meta model. Of course, this model is semantically not as rich as that of its corresponding source language but lends itself to type-safe substitution, markup, and hook abstraction. All concepts can be transfered: parameterization of all meta objects of the machine language, markup with XML or other mechanisms, grouping of several program parts into structured hooks, set hooks, and finally, implicit hooks. It is obvious that a substitution machinery is required which can handle binary representations.

This insight paves the way for a generic parameterization technology that is independent of the underlying component language. If the substitution machinery and the markup technology is chosen appropriately with the component language, the parameterization machinery does not depend on them and can work for different languages. It may very well be the case that we can build *parameterization frameworks* which work for all programming and specification languages, and which are parameterized with a markup technology, a meta-model, and a type-safe substitution machinery.

7   Implementation

The COMPOST library realizes the component model of this paper for Java. COMPOST consists of two layers. The lower layer is a Java transformation and refactoring engine which can read java components, transform them, and pretty print them again [ALN00]. It also ensures type safe substitution and extension. In the upper layer called *boxology,* components, hooks, and simple bind and extension operations are reified as objects. Components are called *fragment boxes* and provide generalized genericity as outlined in this paper. Since COMPOST is a standard Java library it can be used to write parameterization and extension programs similar to those shown in this paper.

At the moment, COMPOST uses a different markup technology to XML. *Hungarian notation* defines naming schemes for identifiers that convey additional semantics [SH91]. Hungarian notation is also used in other component approaches, e.g., in Java Beans. Using these naming conventions for identifiers, the COMPOST component reader finds declarations of hooks, automatically marks up implicit hooks, and finally checks type-safe substitution with regard to its Java meta model. At the moment, we are extending the concepts to XML as a component language. The goal of this work is to provide a component model for XML documents, and to unify software and document composition in a uniform mechanism (*uniform composition*).

8   Conclusion

This paper has introduced, step by step, several extensions of generic type parameters. Once an indirection concept between the program elements of a component and the generic parameter is introduced (*hooks*), components can be parameterized more flexibly and also extended (generic program elements, structured generic parameters for grouping of parameter values, extension of implicit hooks). As applications, protocol parameterizations, unforeseen extensions and aspect weavings have been shown. Since the parameterization and extension model is independent of the component language, it shows the way towards a general genericity and extension framework.

References

[Ada83]   International Organization for Standardization. *Ada 83 Reference Manual. The Language. The Standard Libraries*, 1983.

[Ada95]   International Organization for Standardization.   *Ada 95 Reference Manual. The Language. The Standard Libraries*, January 1995. ANSI/ISO/IEC-8652:1995.

[ALN00]   Uwe Aßmann, Andreas Ludwig, and Rainer Neumann. COMPOST home page. http://i44w3.info.uni-karlsruhe.de/~compost, March 2000.

[Aßm98]   Uwe Aßmann. Meta-programming Composers In Second-Generation Component Systems. In J. Bishop and N. Horspool, editors, *Systems Implementation 2000 - Working Conference IFIP WG 2.4*, Berlin, February 1998. Chapman and Hall.

[Bec99]   Kent Beck. *Extreme Programming Explained: Embracing Change.* Addison-Wesley, 1999.

[BNS⁺91]   Lars Bak, Claus Nörgaad, Elmer Sandvad, Jörgen Linkskov Knudsen, and Ole Lehrmann Madsen. *Software Engineering Environments*, volume 3, chapter "An Overview of the Mjölner BETA System", pages 331–362. Ellis Horwood, 1991.

[Bra92]   Gilad Bracha. *The Programming Language Jigsaw: Mixins, Modularity and Multiple Inheritance.* PhD thesis, University of Utah, 1992.

[BST⁺94]   Don Batory, Vivek Singhal, Jeff Thomas, Sankar Dasari, Bart Geraci, and Marty Sirkin. The GenVoca model of software-system generation. *IEEE Software*, 11(5):89–94, September 1994.

[CE00]   Krzysztof Czarnecki and Ulrich Eisenecker. *Generative Programming: Methods, Techniques, and Applications.* Addision-Wesley, 2000.

[CM93]   Shigeru Chiba and Takashi Masuda. Designing an Extensible Distributed Language with a Meta-Level Architecture. In O. Nierstrasz, editor, *Proceedings of the ECOOP '93 European Conference on Object-oriented Programming*, LNCS 707, pages 483–502, Kaiserslautern, Germany, July 1993. Springer-Verlag.

[KFD99]   Shiram Krishnamurthi, Matthias Felleisen, and Bruce F. Duba. From Macros to Reusable Generative Programming. In U. W. Eisenecker and K. Czarnecki, editors, *Generative Component-based Software Engineering (GCSE)*, number 1799 in Lecture Notes in Computer Science, Erfurt, October 1999.

[KLM⁺97]   Gregor Kiczales, John Lamping, Anurag Mendhekar, Chris Maeda, Cristina Lopez, Jean-Marc Loingtier, and John Irwin. Aspect-oriented programming. In *ECOOP 97*, volume 1241 of *Lecture Notes in Computer Science*, pages 220–242. Springer-Verlag, 1997.

[KRT87]   S. Katz, C. A. Richter, and K.-S. The. PARIS: A system for reusing partially interpreted schemas. In *Proceedings of the 9th International Conference on Software Engineering*, pages 377–385. IEEE Computer Society Press, 1987.

[LAB⁺79]   B. Liskov, R. R. Atkinson, T. Bloom, E. B. Moss, R. Schaffert, and A. Snyder. CLU reference manual. Technical Report MIT/LCS/TR-225, Massachusetts Institute of Technology, October 1979.

[LKLLMM94]   J. Lindskov Knudsen, M Löfgren, O Lehrmann Madsen, and B. Magnusson. *Object-Oriented Environments - The Mjolner Approach.* Prentice Hall, 1994.

[LLStGMG98] Bil Lewis, Dan LaLiberte, Richard Stallman, and the GNU Manual Group. *GNU Emacs Lisp Reference Manual.* GNU Free Software Foundation, for emacs version 20.3, revision 2.5 edition, May 1998.

[Mad89]   William Maddox. Semantically-sensitive macroprocessing. Technical Report CSD-89-545, University of California, Berkeley, 1989.

[Pre95]   Wolfgang Pree. *Design patterns for object-oriented software development.* Addison-Wesley, New York, ACM press, 1995.

[SH91]   C. Simonyi and M. Heller. The Hungarian revolution: A developing standard for naming program variables. *Byte Magazine*, 16(8):131–132, 134–138, August 1991.

[Str97]   Bjyrne Stroustrup. *The C++ Programming Language: Third Edition.* Addison-Wesley Publishing Co., Reading, Mass., 1997.

Appendix 1: XML Schema for Hook Markup

```
<schema xmlns="http://www.w3.org/2000/10/XMLSchema"
    elementFormDefault="unqualified" attributeFormDefault="unqualified">
<element name="generic" type="Hook"/>
<element name="sgeneric" type="StructuredHook"/>
<complexType name="Hook">
  <sequence>
    <element name="name" type="string" minOccurs="1" maxOccurs="1"/>
    <element name="type" type="JavaType" minOccurs="1" maxOccurs="1"/>
  </sequence>
</complexType>
<complexType name="StructuredHook">
  <sequence>
    <element name="sname" type="string" minOccurs="1" maxOccurs="1"/>
    <element name="type" type="JavaType" minOccurs="1" maxOccurs="1"/>
    <element name="feature" type="string" minOccurs="1" maxOccurs="1"/>
  </sequence>
</complexType>
<!------ The used fragment of the meta model of Java ---------!>
<complexType name="Type"/>
<complexType name="Statement"/>
<complexType name="Call"/>
<complexType name="SynchModifier"/>
</schema>
```

CC4J – Code Coverage for Java
A Load-Time Adaptation Success Story

Günter Kniesel[1] and Michael Austermann[2]

[1] University of Bonn, Institute of Computer Science III,
Römerstr. 164, D-53117 Bonn, Germany,
gk@cs.uni-bonn.de
[2] SCOOP Software GmbH, Am Kielshof 29, D-51105 Köln, Germany,
maustermann@scoop-gmbh.de

Abstract. Code coverage and tracing are extremely important for quality assurance in large scale software projects. When Java components are required to be deployed in distributed dynamic environments, e.g. as a part of an application server, load-time adaptation is the only practicable method capable of instrumenting these facilities. Load-time adaptation is, however, a relatively new technology whose scalability in industrial strength projects is so far unproven.

This paper reports on the development of a quality assurance tool, CC4J, which has been implemented using novel load-time adaptation techniques. Our evaluation, performed in the context of a large-scale, deployed, Java software project, shows that this is a resoundingly successful approach. The system's core has been implemented by one person in less than two weeks. Within less than four weeks after its first use CC4J was adopted by the entire project and the quality assurance department recommends adopting the tool in other projects.

1 Introduction

The work reported in this paper has been carried out in a large scale software project. The goal of the project is the development of a distributed system in the domain of electronic payment transactions, known for its extremely high quality and safety-requirements. These are reflected in the contract with the customer, which imposes, as a key quality measure, 100% *code coverage* during testing. This means that all unit tests together must exercise every line of code. Another important quality assurance aspect is the *tracing* of system activity at different levels of detail. This makes the overall flow of control comprehensible and verifiable during functional testing *and* deployment.

Code coverage and tracing functionality is needed in different combinations in different versions of the system. For instance, realistic performance tests require that no code coverage data is collected but tracing is still enabled at the same level as in the final system. Therefore, different versions of the functional components, instrumented for different purposes, are required. In general, the number of possible variants grows exponentially with the number of different

J. Bishop (Ed.): CD 2002, LNCS 2370, pp. 155–169, 2002.

available adaptations. Generating these statically would be prohibitive. Even worse, many of these variants might be used just once since after the test had been performed, changes in the code would automatically render them invalid.

For these reasons, we need means of instrumenting the code base "on the fly" depending on the current suite of tests and the current quality assurance measure (code coverage, tracing at different levels, etc.).

The system is currently being developed by a team of more than 100 software engineers at T-Systems[1]. Its component-based J2EE architecture makes it a good candidate for the evaluation of component adaptation techniques in a realistic environment.

Summary In the context of component-based development load-time adaptation of byte code can be regarded as a key technology. Components are delivered in binary format – so *adaptation of byte code* is ultimately required. This can be performed statically or dynamically, at load-time. Static adaptation has the advantage of adding no load-time penalty to a program's execution. However, static instrumentation might become impractical if many different adaptation variants are to be managed. Moreover, it is inapplicable if dynamic component loading is possible and the name of dynamically loaded classes is determined at run-time, via reflection. Then the only point where it is feasible to determine and adapt all components that are actually used by a program is *during the class loading process*.

The paper is structured as follows. In section 2 we review the state of the art of code coverage and tracing solutions. In section 3, we give a short introduction to JMangler, the employed tool for load-time adapation of Java class files. In section 4 we introduce the developed code coverage tool. Its implementation by load-time adaptation is described in section 5. The experience from the deployment of CC4J in the project is reported in section 6. Section 7 comments on the related work before concluding in section 8.

2   State of the Art

It is common practice to manually insert log statements into code. However, logging the execution of *every line of code* this way is prohibitively expensive and prone to common programming errors. In addition, the temporary nature of unit tests prohibits the integration of test code and related logging statements into the code that is being tested because in the deployed code bases all test code should be removed. On the other hand, unit tests contained in separate modules cannot be aware of every line of code that they test nor can they report on individual lines of code. In other words, there is no alternative but to keep instrumentation separate from the underlying system. This is particularly the case in the context of components, whose source code is unavailable.

In the following we first state the practical requirements of the project and then review the three categories of basic approaches that might be applicable:

---

[1] T-Systems is the information technology division of Deutsche Telekom.

- commercial off-the-shelf systems
- aspect-oriented languages
- aspect-oriented tools

2.1   Application Requirements

The following specific requirements were the main criteria for choosing one particular solution to be applied in the project.

Platform Independence. The system must run on any Java 1.3 compliant virtual machine, at least on Windows NT/2000 and SUN Solaris platforms.

Arbitrary Modifications. Implementing tracing and logging requires the ability to add new helper classes, extend existing classes by new methods and fields and – most importantly – to modify the *byte code* of existing methods.

General Applicability. The adaptation tool must be applicable to any legal Java program.

Component Based Architecture. Tracing and logging are orthogonal aspects of adaptation which should be implemented as independent components.

Easy Configuration. Application of different adaptations to the same classes should be possible without any changes in program code.

2.2   Commercial Off-the-Shelf Tools

The need for a solution available at short notice suggested an evaluation of commercial off-the-shelf tools in the first place. However, the choice of code coverage tools for Java is quite limited, with *Rational PureCoverage* and *Tangent JProbe Coverage* being the only realistic alternatives. Rational's tool is inapplicable, because it only supports Java applications on Windows platforms. JProbe Coverage is platform-independent and available as part of the JProbe Suite.

Neither tool provides tracing support. Even if they had done so, the related licence fees would still have been prohibitive given that tracing must also be available during deployment (in thousands of installed devices). We know of no other commercial tools that support incremental automatic instrumentation of code for tracing purposes.

Obviously, existing tools are unsuitable in the context of our project and the only way to achieve our goals was to implement our own load-time adaptation applications using a suitable language or tool.

2.3   Aspect-Oriented Languages

Novel aspect-oriented programming language extensions for Java [Asp01] are platform independent and enable modifications of existing method code. However, their high abstraction level does not allow them to refer to concepts such as the individual lines or statements of a program. Without this ability, we cannot insert instrumentation code that logs the execution of control flow statements (if, while, ...).

2.4   Aspect-Oriented Tools

The required level of detail can be addressed by aspect-oriented tools that support a lower level of abstraction. In particular, tools for the load-time transformation of Java class files come to be regarded. We are aware of only four approaches that go beyond the mere representation of Java class files by providing complete solutions for the integration into the class loading and linking process of the Java platform:

- Binary Component Adaptation [KH98]
- Java Object Instrumentation Environment [CCK98]
- Javassist [Chi00]
- JMangler [KCA01], [Aus00]

A detailed comparison of these tools can be found in [KCA01]. It shows that only JMangler is applicable in the context of the requirements listed above. In particular,

- BCA has been integrated into the implementation of the Java Virtual Machine of JDK 1.1 for Solaris, and therefore cannot be used with other JVMs. Furthermore, it does not allow adaptation at the level of individual statements.
- JOIE and Javassist cannot adapt applications that employ their own class loader, thus violating the general applicability requirement.

JMangler was therefore the obvious candidate for our evaluation. An introduction to JMangler is given in the next section.

3   JMangler

JMangler[2] is a Java framework for transformation of class files at load-time. Programmers can write their own *transformer components* that analyse the classes on target and decide which concrete transformations are to be carried out. Multiple transformer components, or simply *transformers*, can be deployed simultaneously. JMangler provides the ability to combine their transformations and to perform these transformations on all classes of a program (Figure 1). All transformations that respect binary compatibility [GJSB00] are supported, including arbitrary modifications of method bodies.

JMangler plugs neatly into any Java 1.3 platform being able to run on any compliant JVM and to work with any legal Java program. It is configured by an XML file that includes information on the actual transformer components that are to be applied.

In the following sections we outline JMangler's basic concepts, and describe how JMangler is integrated into the Java platform. For more detailed descriptions we refer to [KCA01], [Aus00]

---

[2] See `http://javalab.cs.uni-bonn.de/research/jmangler/`

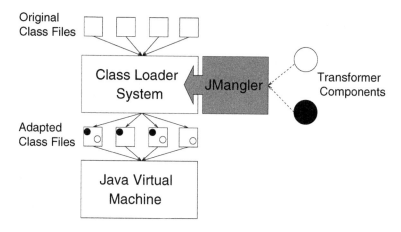

Fig. 1. Architecture of the JMangler Framework

3.1 Basics

JMangler supports all transformation of class files that do not violate binary compatibility [LY99]. In particular, it supports:

- addition of classes, interfaces, fields and methods;
- changes to a method's `throws` clause;
- changes to a class's `extends` clause that do not reduce the set of direct and indirect superclasses;
- changes to a class's `implements` clause that do not reduce the set of direct and indirect superinterfaces;
- the addition and modification of annotations that respect binary compatibility;
- changes to method code.

All transformations mentioned in the first five items of this list are called *interface transformations*. The addition of a method including an initial method body is still regarded as an interface transformation. Changes to method code are called *code transformations*.

Transformers are Java classes that implement specific interfaces (`Interface-Transformer` and `CodeTransformer`). Implementation of these interfaces can be performed using JMangler's API. It supports three types of operations:

- analysis of class files, in order to determine whether a specific transformation is applicable,
- interface transformations and
- code transformations.

A transformer component that implements the operations of the `Interface-Transformer` interface can perform one or many related interface transformations. The same is true for code transformations. A transformer can play both roles by implementing both interfaces. Thus it is possible for one component to provide a consistent set of related interface and code transformations.

3.2 Composition of Transformers

JMangler enables composition of independently developed transformers in the sense that multiple transformers can be jointly applied to the same program. A user who wants to transform a program at load-time can specify this easily in a configuration file. This file has a simple XML-based syntax describing:

- the set of interface and code transformers to be applied;
- parameters to be passed to the transformers;
- the ordering of code transformers;
- and some other options (debugging, etc.).

Different application-specific transformers can be easily composed from the same set of basic transformers. Each composition specification can be stored in a different XML file. Switching between different configurations simply requires providing a different file name as a parameter to the invocation of JMangler:

```
jmangler <configFile> <main> <parameters>
```

This invocation starts the JVM, loads JMangler and the transformers specified in the configuration file and then initiates execution of the program to be adapted.

In the context of the electronic payment transactions project, this open architecture makes it possible to develop transformers for code coverage and tracing separately. Further transformers, even from third parties, can be integrated later, when needed. This approach protects the coding resources already invested while still providing options for further code evolution and extension.

Last, but not least, JMangler is freely available under the terms of the GNU LGPL (http://www.gnu.org/copyleft/lesser.html), which explicitly allows for the development of commercial applications.

4 CC4J

It is not the purpose of this paper to describe all the applications that have been developed using JMangler but to focus on one representative case that proves the applicability of load-time transformation in a commercial context. Therefore we will concentrate henceforth on one application, Code Coverage for Java (CC4J).

CC4J's main responsibility is to determine which lines of code have or have not been executed during one run of an application. *We define, that a line of code has been executed, if the flow of control has reached the line at least once.* It does not matter if the execution has failed to complete successfully or if an exception has been raised.

CC4J consists of the following subcomponents:

Core. The CC4J backend is implemented as a load time transformer. It instruments classes to collect coverage data for one test run. The code coverage data is stored in a *Code Coverage File (CCF)*.

Merger. This component combines the CCFs of different test runs into one file in the same format. This is needed to gain an overview of the total coverage achieved by all test runs.

Object	Unused	Used	Used (%)
All classes	101	17	86.0
de.scoopgmbh.figures.BaseFigure	9	0	100.0
de.scoopgmbh.figures.Circle	13	2	87.0
Circle()	3	0	100.0
computeArea()	2	0	100.0
computePerimeter()	2	0	100.0
getParameters()	6	2	75.0
de.scoopgmbh.figures.FigureTest	22	5	81.0
de.scoopgmbh.figures.Hexagon - Error: Class not present in :	13	2	87.0
de.scoopgmbh.figures.InvalidFigureParameterException	2	2	50.0
de.scoopgmbh.figures.Rectangle	18	2	90.0
de.scoopgmbh.figures.Triangle	24	4	86.0

Fig. 2. Screenshot of the CC4J GUI

Report Generator. The report generator transforms CCFs into human-readable reports (for instance, in HTML format for the project intranet or as postscript for printing).

GUI. The graphical user interface (Figure 2) visualizes code coverage and highlights unexecuted lines in the sourcecode.

These components and their interactions are depicted in Figure 3. By default, the core collects coverage data for every loaded class. Collection of coverage data for test classes can be prevented by specifying them in an exclusion list. This is done in the configuration file which is passed as parameter to the invocation of CC4J.

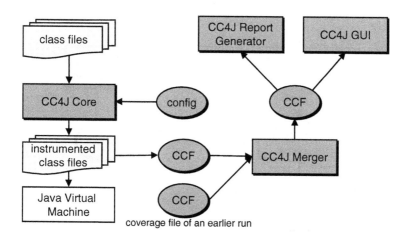

Fig. 3. Architecture of CC4J

For the code coverage files, CC4J uses a simple XML based format, which can be further processed by standard tools. This promotes easy extensibility. Appendix B shows the coverage file generated by CC4J when executing the ubiquitous "Hello World" application (Appendix A).

5   Implementation Using JMangler

Taking advantage of JMangler's component architecture, CC4J has been realised in the form of implemented as a combined interface and code transformer component (Figure 4). In the following, we will focus on two main aspects of its implementation:

– Determination of log points
– Efficient storage of logging data

5.1   Determination of Logging Points

Since CC4J adapts classes at load-time, one has to determine where to insert logging code into the *byte code sequence* of methods. Those points within byte code sequences at which logging data has to be collected, we name *logging points*.

Fortunately Java's class file format [LY99] helps in determining logging points. By default, Java compilers generate line number and source file information for each class. They store it in the *source file attribute* and *line number table attributes* of class files. This information is intended to be used by debuggers for mapping a method's byte code to the corresponding lines of code in the source file (Figure 5).

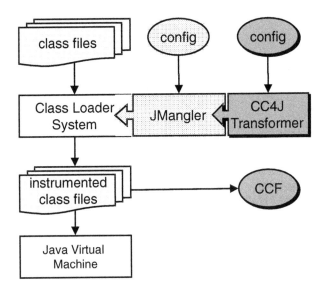

Fig. 4. Implementation of CC4J with JMangler

Source file	Byte code

```
1 public class Sample {
2   void sayHello() {
3     System.out.println("Hello");
4     return;
5   }
6 }
```

```
Method void sayHello()
  0 getstatic #8
  3 ldc #1
  5 invokevirtual #9
  8 return
```

LINE NUMBER	PROGRAM COUNTER
3	0
4	8

Fig. 5. Method (left) that prints "Hello", with its byte code (right) and line number table (bottom).

For the determination of logging points the CC4J transformer analyses the line number table of each method in a class file. The logging point for a given (source code) line number is the corresponding program counter value in the line number table. For instance, in Figure 5, the logging point for line 3 is at program counter value 0.

Discussion. Since line number information is generated by default, the solution described above is sufficient in most cases. In the project for which CC4J has been developed initially, it suffices always. Still, one could argue that the line number information might not be available if explicitly turned off. Determining code coverage in such cases requires a transformer component that logs the execution of every byte code instruction or statement. Detecting individual source code statements in byte code is a more complex task than the line number based logging, which could be realized if required.

One could also ask why it is necessary to instrument every statement if the goal is to test whether all statements have been executed. Consider a basic block containing several statements. If control reaches the last statement, then all previous statements must have been executed. Control can exit in the middle of a basic block only if an exception is thrown. It might appear that a big improvement in performance could have been obtained by using this property. However, to determine whether an exception has occurred each basic block has to be wrapped with a try-catch statement. We implemented and compared both approaches and found out that the apparent optimization results in a more than double increase of execution time. This is because the inserted try-catch statement inhibits standard optimisations of the HotSpot JVM.

5.2   Efficient Storage of Logging Data

At each logging point some logging data has to be stored. The overall runtime overhead of determining code coverage is almost exclusively determined by the costs of storing the logging data. Therefore, this task must be highly optimized to keep the runtime overhead small.

One option is to provide a central logging object. Calls to this object could result either in immediate writing to a log file or could be buffered in a data structure, e.g. a hashtable, for the subsequent writing of the log file. This approach has the advantage of simplicity and makes it easy to change the policy governing the writing of the log file. However, it has the disadvantage of adding one avoidable level of indirection to every logging operation. This would affect every line of code to be executed.

Another possibility is to let every class manage its logging data itself. For this distributed approach, every class is adapted to contain a buffer whose size corresponds exactly to the number of logging points for methods of this class. Logging can access this data structure without any indirection. Every log point writes to exactly one entry in this buffer.

CC4J is implemented using the distributed approach because it saves storage and minimises the increase in running time.

The logging data is saved to secondary storage in CCF format when the virtual machine begins its shutdown sequence. This avoids the high costs of continuous output to secondary storage and also prevents long-running applications from writing endless log files with mostly redundant entries.

For environments that are extremely constrained in memory we also experimented with a data structure that reduces the memory costs to the 32nd part. However, this results in increased run-time costs since thread synchronisation, required to prevent race conditions, is involved in the execution of every line of code.

6   Evaluation

When the suggestion to implement code coverage and tracing by load-time transformation of Java byte code was first put forward in the project, it received much skepticism. It was doubted that a novel technique and its implementation as a recently available research tool could be applied successfully in an industrial environment. In particular, the responsible project officers required proof of:

- feasibility,
- timeliness of delivery,
- cost-effectiveness,
- smooth integration into the development cycle and
- efficiency.

To this end, it was decided to create CC4J as a proof of concept on condition that it had to be done with minimal resources (in terms of manpower). In the following, we report on the required manpower (which determines the timeliness of delivery and cost-effectiveness), performance measurements, and the current use of CC4J within the project development cycle.

6.1   Implementation Effort

The system's core, consisting of the JMangler transformer component described above, has been implemented by one person in less than two weeks.

6.2   Application

Evaluation of CC4J in the project was first conducted by a single programmer, who used the tool to perform automated nightly unit tests of his code including full coverage data collection. At the end of all test runs, the collected coverage data was automatically merged. The results were inspected with the CC4J GUI on the following day to identify additional tests that would include previously uncovered code.

This approach was so successful that it was adopted by the entire project within less than four weeks after the first use of CC4J. Currently, the CC4J suite is being deployed as the official code coverage tool of the project for all developed Java code, including components that run within application servers. The quality assurance department of T-Systems recommends adopting the tool in other projects.

6.3   Run-Time Performance

The run-time impact of class file instrumentation is illustrated by an example employing SUN's Java compiler and different project subsystems running on Oracle's IAS Application Server.

Javac. The javac compiler contained in the JDK 1.3 consists of 143 classes that compile to 582 KB of byte code. We measured the performance of javac when compiling itself on an AMD Athlon 1GHz processor with 384 MB of main memory, running under Windows 2000. During the measurement no other user processes were active.

The non-instrumented version of javac compiled its own source within 3.2 seconds. Enabling the collection of code coverage data, the compilation time was 7.3 seconds, which is an increase of 128%. This includes the overhead resulting from the load-time adaptation (in this case the determination and insertion of logging points).

To determine the overhead resulting exclusively from the collection of code coverage data, we used a JMangler option to dump the transformed classes. Executing these dumped classes, it is possible to measure the pure run-time overhead without the influence of the adaptation process itself. For these dumped – already adapted – classes the compilation time was 4.0 seconds. This is an increase of just 25%, which is remarkable, given that the instrumented application executes additional instructions for *every line of the original code.*

Another remarkable experience was that it is more important to generate code that does not inhibit standard optimisations of the HotSpot JVM than to reduce the number of inserted instructions (see 5.1).

Applications on Oracle IAS. The results reported above were compared to a typical regression testing scenario of the project. We tested a subsystem with 412 classes that compiled to 1,3 MB of byte code. Automatic unit testing of the whole system took 503 seconds without instrumentation and 887 seconds with CC4J. This is an increase of 76%.

We were also interested in the influence of CC4J on I/O-intensive server applications and found out that it is negligible. There was no measurable difference in the throughput of instrumented applications compared to the original ones.

The relatively low impact on run-time performance contributed to the acceptance of CC4J and to its fast adoption in the project.

7   Related Work

In addition to the tools and technologies discussed in section 2 there are several existing and emerging Java APIs that are related to our project: reflection, JVMPI and JPDA.

For a portable and generally applicable implementation of CC4J's core functionality the *reflective capabilities* of Java promote no assistance because they do not allow programmatic modification of existing method code.

The information that can be gained by using the *Java Virtual Machine Profiler Interface (JVMPI)*[3] is too coarse grained to be used for coverage or tracing. Due to restrictions in JVMPI, one cannot record information about the execution of statements other than class instantiation, method entries, and method calls.

The *Java Debug Interface (JDI)* [4] allows more detailed examination of running programs but does not allow for customization of the gathered information. For instance, tracing should ideally provide application-specific semantic information (e.g. reporting "Missing payment." instead of "Return from method m in class C of package P"). Furthermore, permanently running deployed applications in debug mode in order to gather relevant tracing information is no practical option, given the performance impact of the debug mode in JDK 1.3.

Last, but not least, the recent implementation of dynamic class exchange [Dmi01] as an extension of the Java Platform Debugger Architecture (JPDA) is a powerful complement to JMangler's capabilities but no replacement. Support for dynamic class redefinition, when in a new class version only method bodies are allowed to change, is available in the HotSpot JVM, which is included in

---

[3] See http://java.sun.com/j2se/1.4/docs/guide/jvmpi/index.html)
[4] See http://java.sun.com/j2se/1.4/docs/guide/jpda/)

the JDK 1.4 release[5]. However, HotSwap is just for redefinition of classes that have already been loaded. Its `RedefineClasses()` method takes just old and new class versions, and it is the programmer's responsibility to prepare the new version (in the form of a complete `.class` file). Interception of loaded classes and their modification is not a part of the HotSwap API.

8   Conclusions and Future Work

In this paper we have reported on the development and evaluation of a commercial code coverage tool, CC4J, which is implemented using the JMangler load-time adaptation framework.

Our evaluation has shown that load-time adaptation is a mature technology. Its applicability for the timely and cost-effective implementation of quality assurance measures has been proven within a large scale industrial project.

Load-time transformation of byte code has the potential to support arbitrary adaptations beyond those required for quality assurance during software development. In the context of component-based development this can even be regarded as a key technology because components are delivered in binary format and often deployed in dynamic environments like application servers.

Our run-time performance evaluations indicate that JMangler is immediately useful in scenarios where adaptation is performed before deployment at the customer (like in our quality assurance task) and during deployment of long-running applications. In the first case, the time spent on adapting classes is not an issue at all. In the second case, it just accounts for a small percentage increase of overall run-time.

In contrast, use of JMangler for adaptation of short-running and time-critical applications would require further optimization of the framework. The goal must be to lower the fixed costs of system startup and tune the API for class file analysis and modification. Corresponding improvements of JMangler are subject of ongoing work. An interesting option for future work is to take advantage of the current and upcoming ability of Java to perform dynamic class replacement [Dmi01]. This would allow instrumented byte code to be added just when needed and to be removed again later on. Regarding CC4J, a possible future enhancement might be the support of a finer grained notion of code coverage. For example, a single source line may sometimes contain a number of statements. Therefore, logging the entry point to individual statements might be technically more adequate. However, this would require significantly more sophisticated analysis of byte code.

Acknowledgements

Misha Dmitriev helped us understand the relation of JMangler to the HotSwap project at Sun Microsystems and contributed many insightful comments on technical aspects and writing style. We are further indebted to Tom Arbuckle Pascal

---

[5] See http://java.sun.com/j2se/1.4/docs/guide/jpda/enhancements.html)

Costanza and the anonymous reviewers for careful proofreading and numerous suggestions that significantly improved the paper and the quality of our English writing.

References

[Asp01]   Aspect oriented software development home page. http://aosd.net, 2001.

[Aus00]   Michael Austermann. Ladezeittransformation von Java-Programmen. Master's thesis, Universität Bonn, Institut für Informatik III, 2000.

[CCK98]   Geoff A. Cohen, Jeffrey S. Chase, and David L. Kaminsky. Automatic program transformation with JOIE. In *Proceedings of the USENIX 1998 Annual Technical Conference*, pages 167–178, Berkeley, USA, 1998. USENIX Association.

[Chi00]   Shigeru Chiba. Load-Time Structural Reflection in Java. In Elisa Bertino, editor, *Proceedings of ECOOP2000*, LNCS 1850. Springer, 2000.

[Dmi01]   Mikhail Dmitriev. Towards flexible and safe technology for runtime evolution of java language applications, 2001. In proceedings of Workshop on Engineering Complex Object-Oriented Systems for Evolution (ECOOSE) at OOPSLA 2001, http://www.dsg.cs.tcd.ie/ecoose/oopsla2001/papers.shtml.

[GJSB00] James Gosling, Bill Joy, Guy Steele, and Gilad Bracha. *The Java Language Specification Second Edition*. Addison-Wesley, 2000.

[KCA01]   Günter Kniesel, Pascal Costanza, and Michael Austermann. JMangler - A Framework for Load-Time Transformation of Java Class Files. In *Proceedings of International Workshop on Source Code Analysis and Manipulation (SCAM)*. IEEE Computer Society Press, 2001.

[KH98]   Ralph Keller and Urs Hölzle. Binary Component Adaptation. In Eric Jul, editor, *Proceedings ECOOP '98*, LNCS 1445, 1998.

[LY99]   Tim Lindholm and Frank Yellin. *The Java Virtual Machine Specification (2nd Ed)*. Java Series. Addison Wesley, 1999.

A   The Hello World Application

```
public class HelloWorld {
  public HelloWorld() {
    super();
    return;
  }
  public static void main(String[] args) {
    System.out.println("Hello World!");
    return;
  }
}
```

B   Sample Code Coverage File

This section shows the coverage file generated by CC4J when executing the "Hello World" application printed in Appendix A.

```
<?xml version="1.0" encoding="US-ASCII" ?>
<SCOOP_CC4J>
 <SEQUENCE_OF_CLASSES>
  <CLASS name="HelloWorld" sourcefile="HelloWorld.java">
   <METHOD name="HelloWorld()">
    <LN l="3" s="n"/>
    <LN l="4" s="n"/>
   </METHOD>
   <METHOD name="main([Ljava/lang/String;)V">
    <LN l="7" s="e"/>
    <LN l="8" s="e"/>
   </METHOD>
  </CLASS>
 </SEQUENCE_OF_CLASSES>
 <ERRORLOG/>
</SCOOP_CC4J>
```

Each line of code in the source of a method results in a LN-tag in the coverage file. The l attribute contains the corresponding line number, the s attribute contains the status of this line. The value e represents *executed*, n represents *not executed*.

Scenario-Based Connector Optimization
An XML Approach

Welf Löwe[1] and Markus Noga[2]

[1] Växjö universitet, MSI, Software Tech. Group, 351-95 Växjö, Sweden,
welf.lowe@msi.vxu.se
[2] Universität Karlsruhe, Program Structures Group,
Adenauerring 20a, 76133 Karlsruhe, Germany,
noga@ipd.info.uni-karlsruhe.de

Abstract. Software components can be connected by XML process-ing pipelines, which may perform adaptations. In our model, individual pipeline stages serialize source data structures to XML, perform one or multiple XSL transformations, transport the message to its destination and finally deserialize it to target data structures. Implementation of this model is open to optimizations. The present paper discusses two such optimizations: symbolic execution and lazy evaluation.

1 Introduction

With new problems at hand, management used to ask, "Build or Buy" a solu-tion? Today, this question only applies to smallish problems. For entire systems, "Buy, Build and Integrate" has become the method of choice. That is, suitable components are bought, the missing remainder is built and the entire system is subsequently integrated.

This strategy separates system integration spatially and temporally from component design. Mismatches between components from different vendors, and between bought and custom-built components inevitably result. Thus, adapta-tion of components has become essential.

In [8], we presented a lightweight XML middleware architecture that explic-itly addresses the adaptation problem. We also described basic optimizations like generator usage and intermediate structure omission. This article covers major new optimizations for the system, symbolic execution and lazy evaluation. Both are scenario-based: the former depends on the adaptation scenario, the latter on the communication scenario at hand.

The next section briefly revisits the middleware architecture in [8] and basic technologies it employs. Section 3 covers symbolic execution, while section 4 deals with lazy evaluation. Section 5 summarizes our results and outlines directions for future work.

J. Bishop (Ed.): CD 2002, LNCS 2370, pp. 170–184, 2002.
© Springer-Verlag Berlin Heidelberg 2002

2   Related Work

The first subsection summarizes basic XML technologies, most prominently XPath [17] and XSLT [20]. The second subsection briefly revisits our middleware architecture [8].

2.1   Basic Technologies

XML is a well-known storage format for depth-first preorder traversals of trees [16]. There are various type description languages for XML tree nodes, among them DTDs and the more expressive XML Schemas [18,19].

The Document Object Model, or DOM, provides an abstract, non-typed interface to XML tree nodes [15]. Its operations realize basic tree traversal and manipulation operations. E.g., child, parent and sibling nodes can be accessed, as well as attributes.

XPath is a query language for XML document trees [17]. It is inspired by the concept of path languages. XPath expressions are sequences of steps. Each step projects a set of source nodes onto a new set, which is subsequently filtered.

Syntactically, steps consist of an optional axis, a selection and optional additional filters. Axes determine the projection direction: onto child nodes, parent nodes, siblings, descendants, ancestors etc. If an axis is not specified, the child axis applies by default. Selection filters the projected set by node name or type. E.g., the Xpath expression $parent{:}A/B/C$ selects C-children of B-children of A-parents of the current node. The optional additional filters can be arbitrarily complex predicates. Additionally, there are wildcards for element names "*" and entire path fragments "//".

XSL transformations, or XSLTs, perform maps on XML trees [20]. They are inspired by rewrite systems: an XSLT is an ordered set of rules. They consist of an applicability test, called match expression, and a body, which may contain output statements, recursive rule applications and some additional elements of functional programming.

Rules operate on a current node. They are checked for applicability in order of their definition. The body of the first matching rule is executed. At points of recursive rule applications, a sequence of new current nodes is selected according to a select expression. These new nodes are processed in the same manner. The transformation is initiated by applying the rules to the tree root.

In practice, the match expression is an XPath expression without axes. For a positive match, it must return the current node if applied to the current node or any ancestors thereof. Select expressions in recursive rule applications are also specified as XPath expressions. In this paper, we simplify the rule body to output statements and a single recursive rule application. We disregard the inner structure of output statements.

2.2   Connection and Adaptation

For the purpose of this paper, we define components to be software artifacts with typed input and output ports linked by communication channels called connectors. The notions of ports and connectors are known from architecture systems [13,3]. The problems solved by connectors are wide spread in general; [10] gives an overview. They may be as complex as most components, and thus require the same amount of consideration in design and implementation, cf. [14]. On the design level, we have explicit connector entities with a formal semantic allowing for consistency checking, cf. [1]. On the implementation level, connectors are executable first class entities allowing for reuse and composition, cf. [4].

However, we focus on special connectors with limited problems to solve. We assume connectors to be

- point-to-point data paths with in- and out ports known at compile time,
- executable in the sense that they implement stateless data transformation functions (adaptations) also known at compile time, and
- language independent as they do not require sender and receiver component to be implemented in the same programming language.

In this limited scenario, there is no need for explicit connector objects in the production code. Instead, we try to eliminate them to increase the system performance. Therefore, connector code fragments can be generated from the connector specification and merged into the sender and receiver component code. This meta-programming technique is known as "grey-box-connection", cf. [2] where it is used to adapt method calls. It is generalized in [6]. That work shows the generation of connectors adapting the synchronization and activity of components using abstract specifications. The generated adapter fragments are woven into the sender and receiver components and thus disappear from the production code as first class objects.

In the present paper, we use a similar approach for connectors adapting the exchanged data. The required and provided parameters of a communication are specified with XML Schema specifications, the adaptation with XSLT scripts. The specific runtime environment and the generator tools are described below.

2.3   Middleware Architecture and Generator Tools

The middleware architecture in [8] builds on the above model. Components are software artifacts with typed input and output ports. Connectors can perform adaptations. The system is strongly typed and statically type safe.

At runtime, our middleware serializes output port data to an XML wire format. Adapting connectors perform XSLTs on the wire format. Input ports parse the wire format and reconstruct the corresponding object graphs. Fig. 1 shows adapted communication between two components at runtime.

The wire format is not generic, but derived from the port types using one of the schemes in [7] or [11], which map data types to DTDs and XML Schema, respectively. This approach preserves strong typing and static type safety in the XML representation.

As types are known at deployment time, our middleware analyzes the component sources at that point. Using a metaprogramming system, we generate

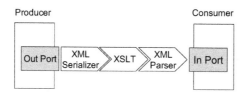

Fig. 1. Adapted communication between components.

specific wire format descriptions, as well as serializers, transformers and deserializers optimized for these formats. These fragments are woven into the component sources. [9] discusses code analysis and generation in detail.

3   Symbolic Execution

Symbolic execution jointly preprocesses transformations and document types given as DTDs or Schemas. If static analysis can guarantee that parts of the document type are never visited by a transformation, serialization may safely omit those parts of the document. Conversely, if static analysis detects that a rule cannot match on documents of the given type, that rule test can safely be omitted. The efficacy of these omissions depends on the adaptation scenario. Their impact is obviously the largest for filtering adaptations which omit large amounts of data.

We start with an overall view. Static preprocessing initially clones generic programmatic representations of the rules for each node type and possible grammatical context. We then eliminate inapplicable rules based on match expressions. Using tight conservative approximations with regular grammars, the select statements are then refined to precisely defined document traversals. Invocations of locally inapplicable match rules are removed. Together, this yields a conservative approximation of the document type parts actually visited.

Now, we are ready to discuss the process in more detail. Given routines implementing the XSLT **match** and **select** operations described in 2.1, each rule r with match m_r, output o_r and select expression s_r can be expressed as in Algorithm 1, which operates on a current node **n**. The **main** routine performs the entire XSL transformation when invoked on the document root node **d**.

If our document nodes are typed, unlike DOM, we can clone these algorithms with respect to node types. For each node type E we define a class class_E. In object-oriented terms, the **transform** m_r functions become methods operating on the current object **this** instead of a parameter node **n**, cf. Algorithm 2. Note that the recursive invocation of **transform** is now restricted to transform methods actually defined in the class of the target node **n'**, cf. the **inner** loop.

Now we are ready to specialize the class_E. We initially analyze match expressions. As stated in 2.1, a match expression matches a given node if the corresponding XPath expression returns the node when applied to the node or any of its ancestors. Thus, based on the node type, we can determine whether

Algorithm 1 (XSL Transformation Schema)

```
boolean transform_r(Node n){
    if match(n,m_r){
        output(n,o_r);
        NodeList nl := select(n,s_r);
        for (Node n' in nl) {
            inner: for (r' in rules) {
                if transform_r'(n') break inner;
            }
        }
        return true;
    }
    return false;
}
void main(Document d){
    for (r' in rules) {
        if transform_r'(d.rootNode) break;
    }
}
```

Algorithm 2 (Specialized XSL Transformation Schema)

```
class_E is
    boolean transform_r() {
        if this.match(m_r) {
            this.output(o_r);
            NodeList nl := new NodeList := this.select(s_r);
            outer: for (Node n' in nl) {
                inner: for (r' in n'.rules) {
                    if n'.transform_r'() break inner;
                }
            }
            return true;
        }
        return false;
    }
    boolean transform_r2(){ ...
```

a given match expression must, may, or must not match. Algorithm 5 in the appendix defines this analysis. As they are guaranteed not to be invoked, we can safely eliminate the transformation methods for all must not matches. Similarly, all rules defined later than a must match can be eliminated.

If we clone a class for different document type contexts, may matches can turn into must or must not matches. This reduces the number of methods. We clone as long as the method count decreases. This procedure terminates even for recursive transformations due to the bounded size of match expressions and the bounded number of methods per class.

We turn our attention to the select expressions. The `select` routine implements the selection of nodes for a given XPath expression and context node. It proceeds by steps, projecting the current node sequence along the given axis, e.g., to children, and filtering down the projection by name, type and additional criteria. `select` returns a sequence of nodes `ns` ordered in document order, to which recursive transformations are applied.

We conservatively approximate `ns` for each context node type E and all contexts of E with a set of formal languages, one per context. If the select expression contains only *this*, *child* and *descendants* axes, our approximation is context *in*sensitive and the set contains exactly one langauge.

First, we consider individual axes. Let E be a node type and a be an axis. Let $approx(E, a)$ be the context-free language that conservatively approximates the mapping of E along a given the information in the document type. For the default axis *this*, e.g., $approx(E, this) = \{r \rightarrow E\}$ with starting symbol r. The algorithms 4 in the appendix compute approximations for nontrivial axes.

A step consists of an axis, a select expression and optional filters. If the select expression specifies a concrete element type E, we can specialize the above axis approximation for this step by replacing all terminals for element types $E' \neq E$ with ϵ. If filters are present, we similarly replace all terminals E with $E \mid \epsilon$ as they may be filtered out.

A select expression consists of multiple steps. We combine step approximations into select expression approximations by successively replacing element type terminals with the grammar rules for the respective next step. If that grammar defines the empty language, we effectively remove the corresponding terminals completely. Algorithm 6 in the appendix defines the approximation of steps and select expressions precisely.

If the approximation for a select expression is the empty language, recursive invocations of `transform` are not required. We may skip the `for` loops in Algorithm 2. In general, we could replace the `outer: for` loop by an acceptor for the selection sequence language and specialize the recursive invocations in the `inner: for` loop according to the rule set of the accepted element node type. However, the efficacy of these optimizations is quite low. Experience with database systems teaches that selection is by far the most expensive operation. We will therefore use the above approximations to optimize select operations.

The bigger the node set generated by projection on an axis, the more expensive it is to compute. Thus, *ancestor, descending, preceding, following* are generally more expensive than *parent, child, sibling*. We will attempt to replace expensive axes with cheaper operations.

A node can only be part of a selection path if its approximation language is non-empty. Otherwise, the final step in a selection cannot match, although intermediate steps may generate large node sets. With our analyses, we can safely skip their computation. Algorithm 7 in the appendix defines iterators searching only those nodes that are potentially selected. The sequence `ns` is replaced by such an iterator. The final result of all optimizations defined in this section is sketched in Algorithm 3.

Algorithm 3 (Optimized XSL Transformation Schema)

```
class_E is
   boolean transform_r(){
      if this.match(m_r){
         this.output(o_r);
         Iterator a := new AxesIterator(axis(s_r)); //Algorithms 7
         a.init(this);
         Iterator ns := new SelectionIterator(); //Algorithm 7
         ns.init(a, selection path set(s_r));
         while ((n':=ns.next()) != null){
            for (r' in n'.rules){
               if n'.transform_r'() break this loop;
            }
         }
         return true;
      }
      return false;
   }
   boolean transform_r_2(){ ...
```

4 Lazy Evaluation

If only stochastic data about access profiles are available, static analysis fails. Consider a common case: a component transfers documents to a viewer and requires adaptation. A human navigating the transformed document visits only fractions of it. However, we cannot statically determine *which* fractions.

In these stochastic cases, lazy evaluation is an alternative to eagerly transforming and transmitting all outgoing data. The producing component is lazy and transmits only a handle to the consumer. Upon actual access, the consumer requests the required fragments from the producer, who partially transforms the source and transmits the results.

The performance of this approach hinges on hardware scenarios and application profiles. Before we consider how the XML transformation pipeline allows for partial processing, we estimate the potential of the lazy approach with a model.

When comparing one large with many smaller messages, we must account for the lag l of a transmission in seconds and the throughput t of the channel in kBit/s. A message of size m kBits requires τ seconds where:

$$\tau(m) = \tau_{l,t}(m) = l + \frac{m}{t} \qquad (1)$$

The application determines the data size m in kBits, the fraction f of the data required on the remote side and the number n of unique accesses, i.e. the number of fragments to transmit. With (1), we determine lazy and eager processing times

$$\tau_{\text{lazy}}(m, f, n) = n\tau\left(\left\lceil \frac{mf}{n} \right\rceil\right) \qquad (2)$$

$$\tau_{\text{eager}}(m) = \tau(m) = \tau_{\text{lazy}}(m, 1, 1) \qquad (3)$$

for a given hardware scenario (l, t).

Perhaps surprisingly, the tradeoff between eager and lazy processing is almost independent of the hardware scenario for a given data size. Solving $\tau_{\text{lazy}}(m, f, n) = \tau_{\text{eager}}(m)$ for a given m, we realize that only the product lt is relevant, which varies little between LAN, WAN and modem scenarios. In short, what counts is the amount of data that can be transmitted instead of waiting for the network.

Now that lazy evaluation is demonstrated to be effective, we still have to show that it applies to the XML processing pipeline. Let us initially assume simple connectors without transformation. Then, processing is limited to serialization, transport and reification of an object graph.

Let d_s and d_t, resp., of class D be the root of the source and target data graphs in question. On the remote side, D and recursively all depending classes are extended by a private attribute c_a and an access method m_a per attribute a of a class. c_a indicates complete transmission and reification of a. m_a checks c_a before access and triggers transport and reification of the object if necessary. Additionally, we add remote access stubs to the producing side.

Initially, we serialize a shallow of d_s, transport it to the consuming component and reify it to d_t. Whenever we initially access an attribute of d_t, transport and reification are triggered. Subsequent accesses are local.

Depending on the memory consistency model and on the communication semantics, we may have to deep copy d_s or block the execution of the source component. Those requirements are independent of the communication optimization, but outside our current focus. For a discussion, we refer to [6,5].

Objects accessed via different paths should be transported only once. This is guaranteed by the same bookkeeping approach used in complete depth-first transmission: the producer component maintains a hash table of serialized objects for the active session. The initial stub access (on the consumer side) retrieves an object o by triggering serialization of o (on the producer side). The producer retains an id, the XML mapping of the shallow of o and a hash table entry. The receiver maintains an array of deserialized objects by id.

Whenever the receiver accesses an object o' containing an alias to o, we find the the corresponding id in our hash table. Together with the shallow of o' we transmit the id of o. An receiver side access $o'.o$ does not trigger a communication as o has been reified already. A simple lookup in the array of deserialized objects with the id gets the required object. Figure 2 sketches this bookkeeping.

As our initial performance estimate shows, there are minimum transmission sizes for any given hardware scenario. Thus, instead of transmitting a single object shallow, we serialize and deserialize a copy of some level.

Finally, we consider the general case with transformations. For the sender component, very little changes – it is irrelevant if a remote component access or a transformation access triggers the serialization and transmission of some parts of the data structure in question. We only transmit the id together with the first serialization of an object.

Initially, we serialize a shallow of the root object d_s, and start the transformation until the remote root object d_t can be reified by the consumer. Depending

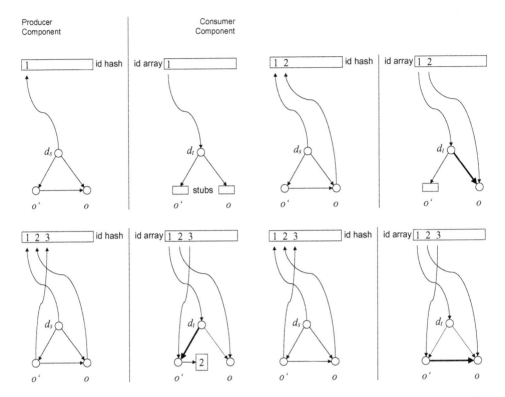

Fig. 2. Initial situation after root object transmission (top, left): d_s is serialized and refers to id 1, d_t is deserialized and accessible by id 1. After the first access to $d_t.o$ (top, right): o (id 2) is serialized and deserialized, respectively. After the first access to $d_t.o'$ (bottom, left): o' (id 3) is serialized and deserialized, respectively. Instead of a stub for the access to o, o' contains already the id of o (id 2). After the first access to $d_t.o'.o$, i.e. the second access to o (bottom, right): with a look up in the id array, id 2 is replaced by the actual reference to o.

on the transformation script, this may already trigger the serialization of some further parts of the sender side data structure.

Three observations lead to the lazy evaluation of the transformation: (i) XSL transformations are functional. Invocations of the **transform** method, cf. Algorithm 2 in the previous section, are free of side effects except output. (ii) XSL may traverse the input document in an arbitrary fashion, although depth-first is an important special case. They may cache intermediate results of any size, but the output document is written in depth-first order. (iii) Our mapping of data structures to XML traverses the data structures in depth-first order.

When we access an object o the first time, we trigger the transformations to reify it. The next accesses to o are local (as discussed above). The transformation is performed only partially: the recursive call to **transform** is stopped (and stored as a bound routine for later resume), whenever the **output**, cf.in

Algorithm 2, indicates that we do not generate the shallow of o but some descendants. We stop the main transformation process and store it as a bound method if the shallow of o is complete.

Observation (i) guarantees we can postpone the recursive decent, observations (ii) and (iii) ensure a transformation will produce few other objects than o. The candidates are objects accessible by an attribute of the current object (siblings of o) and objects accessible by an attribute of o (children of o). For those objects, we captured a bound routine that can be resumed to get the actual object if accessed the first time. If we try to access an object for which a bound routine was not captured, we resume the main transformation process.

5   Perspectives

Symbolic execution and lazy evaluation are highly promising optimizations. They both eliminate transmission overheads. In a sense, the approaches are complimentary: Symbolic execution applies to scenarios with static overhead, whereas lazy evaluation applies to scenarios with stochastic overhead.

We have started to implement lazy evaluation. Although transformations are not fully realized yet, initial measurements for lazy deserialization are highly promising. We are confident that benefits will continue to unfold.

Symbolic execution is still pending implementation. Measurements on our early XSLT compilers indicate that bookkeeping for node sets alone accounts for some 40% of total execution time. Replacing them with simple iterators and eliminating superfluous match tests should increase transformation performance by a factor of two [12].

Future work will focus on implementation and full evaluation of our optimizations. Moreover, we aim to determine worthwhile optimizations by automatic analysis of access profiles. Finally, we want to combine both approaches: lazy evaluation could benefit from splitting the global adaptation into a sequence of partial ones. To determine effective splits, we have to analyze the access profile as well. Each partial adaptation could again be optimized with a more precise approximation of the data structures and transformation rules involved.

References

1. Robert Allen and David Garlan. A formal basis for architectural connection. *ACM Transactions on Software Engineering and Methodology*, July 1997.
2. U. Aßmann, T. Genßler, and H. Bär. Meta-programming Grey-box Connectors. In *Proceedings of the 33rd TOOLS (Europe) conference*, 2000.
3. Len Bass, Paul Clement, and Rick Kazman. *Software Architecture in Practice*. Addison Wesley, 1998.
4. Stéphane Ducasse and Tamar Richner. Executable Connectors: Towards Reusable Design Elements. *ACM SIGSOFT*, 22(6):483 – 499, November 1997.
5. Dirk Heuzeroth, Thomas Holl, and Welf Löwe. Combining static and dynamic analyses to detect interaction patterns. In *IDPT*, 2002. (submitted to).

6. Dirk Heuzeroth, Welf Löwe, Andreas Ludwig, and Uwe Aßmann. Aspect-oriented configuration and adaptation of component communication. In Jan Bosch, editor, *Third International Conference on Generative and Component-Based Software Engineering, GCSE*, page 58 ff. Springer, LNCS 2186, 2001.
7. W. Löwe and M. Noga. Component communication and data adaptation. In *IDPT*, 2002.
8. W. Löwe and M. Noga. A lightweight xml-based middleware architecture. In *20th International Multi-Conference Applied Informatics, AI*. IASTED, 2002.
9. W. Löwe and M. Noga. Metaprogramming applied to web component deployment. In *ETAPS Workshop on Software Composition*, 2002.
10. Nikunj R. Mehta, Nenad Medvidovic, and Sandeep Phadke. Towards a Taxonomy of Software Connectors. In *International Conference on Software Engineering, ICSE 2000*. ACM, 2000.
11. M. Noga and W. Löwe. Data types and XML schema. *Journal of Markup Languages - Theory and Practice (to appear)*, 2002.
12. Tobias Schmitt-Lechner. *Entwicklung eines XSLT–Übersetzers*. Universität Karlsruhe, IPD Goos, May 2001.
13. M. Shaw and D. Garlan. *Software Architecture in Practice – Perspectives on an Emerging Discipline*. Prentice Hall, 1996.
14. Mary Shaw. Procedure calls are the assembly language of software interconnection: Connectors deserve first-class status. In D.A. Lamb, editor, *Studies of Software Design, Proceedings of a 1993 Workshop*, pages 17–32. Springer, LNCS 1078, 1996.
15. *Document Object Model*. W3C, http://www.w3.org/DOM/, 2000.
16. *Extensible Markup Language (XML) 1.0*. W3C Recommandation, http://www.w3.org/TR/1998/REC-xml-19980210, 1998.
17. *XML Path Language*. W3C Rec., http://www.w3.org/TR/xpath, 1999.
18. *XML Schema Part 1: Structures*. W3C Recommendation 2 May 2001, http://www.w3.org/TR/2001/REC-xmlschema-1-20010502, 2001.
19. *XML Schema Part 2: Datatypes*. W3C Recommendation 2 May 2001, http://www.w3.org/TR/2001/REC-xmlschema-2-220010502, 2001.
20. *XSL Transformations (XSLT)*. W3C Rec., http://www.w3.org/TR/xslt, 1999.

A   Appendix with Algorithms

The following algorithms compute context free grammar rules that conservatively approximate the result of mapping E along the axis. We denote terminals representing element node types with capital letters.

The *child* axis of a node contains all its children in document order. Let cm be the content model for E, and $G(cm)$ the grammar rules generating cm, then:

$$approx(E, child) := G(cm) \tag{4}$$

Let $D ::= cm(\ldots, E, \ldots)$ denote a DTD rule defining D whose content model contains E. Then, the *parent* sequence is given by the following set productions with start symbol r:

$$approx(E, parent) := \{r \rightarrow D \mid \text{``}D ::= cm(\ldots, E, \ldots)\text{''} \in DTD - rules\} \tag{5}$$

Let $F(cm)$ be the finite acceptor for a regular context model cm and $G(F)$ the corresponding grammar productions. The *preceding-sibling (following-sibling)* axis contains siblings of the current node occurring before (after) in the document. The *ancestor* (*descendant*) axis of a node contains all transitive parents up to the root (transitive children). Algorithm 4 computes their approximations. More complex axes can be built from these simple ones.

Algorithm 5 conservatively estimates the matches for individual transformation rules. It symbolically executes the matches on the DTD, traversing the path expressions step by step starting with the last step e. $e.sel$ denotes the selection of this step, $e.axis$ the axis and $e.filter$ the presence of optional filter operations. The algorithm simultaneously traverses the DTD from the element node type E of the context node up to the root R. It checks if a certain path must, may or cannot match in a document conforming to the DTD.

Algorithm 6 approximates possible element node sequences of selections s_r relatively to a sequence of root nodes defined by some axes. In- and output sequences are given as grammar productions. The algorithm symbolically executes selection on the DTD, traversing the selection path step by step starting with the first step e. For each step, the productions R are updated. Node types filtered out by $e.sel$ are removed. If $e.filter$ marks the step as optional, all productions are marked as optional. Now, the grammar reflects the sequence of selections up to this step. If there are no steps left, we are done. Otherwise, we have to execute the next step symbolically on this sequence. Therefore, we compute a new root sequence by applying the next axis on each element. This is done by replacing the each remaining node types E with the axiom r_E of productions R_E corresponding to the next axis. Then we enter recursion.

If we hit a node of type E in the actual selection process at runtime, we can stop further searching if the symbolic execution of selection on the DTD indicates future selection steps will fail. I.e., we simply check if the sequence S_E generated by R_E is empty. This idea is exploited in the iterators defined in Algorithms 7. They select the root node sequences for the *ancestor* and *descendant* axes, respectively. Other axes iterators are computed analogously. Both algorithms compute the sequence in an initialization phase and store it in an internal container. Thereby they skip those element nodes n that can be excluded by the observations above, i.e. elements with a type $E = Type(n)$ where $S_E = \varepsilon$.

The finally iterator in Algorithm 7 computes a selection s_r composed of multiple steps and a given current node set. It proceeds step by step, starting with the first step e. For each step, nodes n in the current set are checked for conformance with $e.sel$. Also, nodes that failed the static execution, e.g., whose $S_{Type}(n) = \varepsilon$, are eliminated. If there are no steps left, the current set is the result of the selection and the algorithm terminates. Otherwise, each node is replaced with the result of iterating over it according to the next axis. Then we enter recursion.

Algorithm 4 (Axis approximations)
```
preceedingSibling( element node type E ) is
```
   compute $F = \{F(cm(\ldots, E, \ldots)) \mid \text{“}D ::= cm(\ldots, E, \ldots)\text{”} \in DTD\text{-}rules\}$
   forall $f \in F$ {
      mark all states with outgoing E transition as E states;
      delete all states not reaching an E state and their transitions;
      set all E states final;
      delete unreachable states and their transitions;
   }
   return $G(\bigcup F)$

```
followingSibling( element node type E ) is
```
   compute $F = \{F(cm(\ldots, E, \ldots)) \mid \text{“}D ::= cm(\ldots, E, \ldots)\text{”} \in DTD\text{-}rules\}$
   forall $f \in F$ {
      mark all states with incoming E transition as E states;
      create a new starting state and add ε transitions to all E states;
      delete unreachable states and their transitions;
   }
   return $G(\bigcup F)$

```
ancestorOrSelf( element node type E ) is
```
   nodeTypes := $\{E\}$
   rules := $\{r_E \rightarrow \varepsilon\}$
   loop
      forall $X \in$ nodeTypes {
         add D to nodeTypes if $"D ::= cm(\ldots, X, \ldots)" \in DTD\text{-}rules$
         add $r_D \rightarrow X \, r_X$ to rules
      }
   until nodeTypes stable;
   return rules $\cup \{r \rightarrow R \, r_R\}$ where R is the document root element type

```
descendantOrSelf( element node type E ) is
```
   nodeTypes := $\{E\}$
   rules := $\{r \rightarrow E \, r_E\}$
   loop
      forall $X \in$ nodeTypes {
         add $r_X \rightarrow \varepsilon$ to rules if $"X ::= EMPTY" \in DTD\text{-}rules$
         add $E_1, \ldots, E_n$ to nodeTypes if $"X ::= cm(E_1, \ldots, E_n)" \in DTD\text{-}rules$
         compute $G(cm(E_1, \ldots, E_n))$ and rename its axiom r_X
         in the result, replace E_i by $(E_i \, r_{E_i})$
         add the result to rules
      }
   until nodeTypes stable;
   return rules

Algorithm 5 (Approximate Matches)

```
approximateMatches( element node type E, DTD root node type R,
                    match expression m) is
  class:= "must match"
  e := last step of m
  a := remainder of m
  if (e.filter) class:= "may match"
  if (e.sel ≠ "*" ∧ e.sel ≠ E) return "no match"
  nodeTypes := approx(E, e.axis)
  if (a empty) {
     if (m absolut ∧R ∉ nodeTypes) class:= "no match"
     return class;
  }
  for all E' in nodeTypes {
     class(E') := approximateMatches(E', R, a);
  }
  if (for all E' in nodeTypes: class(E')="no match") return "no match"
  if (for all E' in nodeTypes: class(E')="must match") return class
  return "may match"
```

Algorithm 6 (Approximate Selections)

```
typedef Rules = grammar rules for sequences of element node types;

// Input  Rules define the sequence of relative root element node types
// Output Rules define the sequence of selected element node types

Rules approximateSelections( Rules R, selection path expression s_r) is
  e := first step of s_r
  m := remainder of s_r
  if (e.sel = A) replace occurrences of E ≠ A in R by ε;
  if (e.filter) replace occurrences of E in R by (E|ε);
  if (m empty) return R;
  else {
     replace occurrences of element node types E in R by a unique r_E;
     for all replaced element node types E {
        R_E = approx(E, m.axis);
        replace axiom of R_E by r_E;
     }
     return approximateSelections(⋃ R_E ∪ R,  m);
  }
```

Algorithm 7 (Iterators)

```
class ChildIterator  extends Iterator is
   Queue Node nodes := new Queue();
   void init(Node n){
      for cn in children(n) if (S_{Type(cn)} ≠ ε) nodes.enqueue(cn);
   }
   Node next(){if (nodes.empty) return null; else return nodes.dequeue();

class AncestorOrSelfIterator  extends Iterator is
   Stack [Node] nodes := new Stack();
   void init(Node n){
      while (n ≠ R){
         if (S_{Type(n)} ≠ ε) nodes.push(n);
         n := parent(n);
      }
   }
   Node next(){if (nodes.empty) return null; else return nodes.pop();}

class DescendantOrSelfIterator extends Iterator is
   Queue [Node] nodes := new Queue();
   void init(Node n){
      if (S_{Type(n)} ≠ ε) nodes.enqueue(n);
      for cn in children(n) init(cn);
   }
   Node next(){if (nodes.empty) return null; else return nodes.dequeue();}

class SelectionIterator is
   Iterator [Node] nodes;
   void init(Iterator a, SelectionPath s_r){
      nodes := new Iterator();
      e := first step of s_r
      m := remainder of s_r
      while ((n := a.next()) != null)
         if ( conforms(n,e) ∧ S_{Type(n)} ≠ ε ) nodes.add(n);
      if (m empty) return;
      else {
         Iterator [Node] newNodes:= new Iterator();
         for ( n in nodes ) {
            generate iterator i for axis of e and initialize over n
            newNodes.concat(i);
         }
         init(newNodes, m);
      }
   }
   Node next(){if (nodes.empty) return null; else return nodes.next();}
```

Adapting Components
with Mismatching Behaviours

Andrea Bracciali[1], Antonio Brogi[1], and Carlos Canal[2]

[1] Dipartimento di Informatica, Università di Pisa, Italia
[2] Depto. Lenguajes y Ciencias de la Computación, Universidad de Málaga, Spain

Abstract. Component adaptation is widely recognised to be one of the crucial problems in Component-Based Software Engineering. We present a formal methodology for adapting components with mismatching interaction behaviours. The three main ingredients of the methodology are: (1) The inclusion of behaviour specifications in component interfaces, (2) a simple, high-level notation for expressing adaptor specifications, and (3) a fully automated procedure to derive a concrete adaptor from a given specification.

1 Introduction

Component adaptation is widely recognised to be one of the crucial problems in Component-Based Software Engineering (CBSE) [5,17,15]. The possibility for application builders to easily adapt off-the-shelf software components to work properly within their application is a must for the creation of a true component marketplace and for component deployment in general [4].

Available component-oriented platforms (e.g., CORBA [27], COM [8], Java-Beans [29], VisualStudio .NET [21]) address software interoperability by using Interface Description Languages (IDLs). The provision of an IDL interface defining the signature of the methods offered (and possibly required) by a component is an important step towards software integration. IDL interfaces highlight signature mismatches between components in the perspective of adapting or wrapping them to overcome such differences.

However, even if all signature problems may be overcome, there is no guarantee that the components will suitably interoperate. Indeed, mismatches may also occur at the protocol level, because of the ordering of exchanged messages and of blocking conditions [30], that is, because of differences in component behaviours. While case-based testing can be performed to check the compatibility of the behaviour of components, more rigorous techniques are needed to lift component integration from hand-crafting to an engineering activity.

The availability of a formal description of the interaction behaviour of software components is necessary in order to rigorously verify properties of systems consisting of large numbers of components that dynamically interact one another [10]. For instance, an application builder would like to be able to determine beforehand whether the inclusion of a third-party component may introduce a deadlock possibility into her application.

J. Bishop (Ed.): CD 2002, LNCS 2370, pp. 185–199, 2002.
© Springer-Verlag Berlin Heidelberg 2002

In this paper, we focus on the problem of adapting components that exhibit mismatching behaviour. As we already pointed out, available component platforms do not provide suitable means for describing the interaction behaviour of a component. Consequently, behaviour mismatches can be only manually adapted.

The problem of component adaptation has been the subject of intensive attention in the last few years. A number of practice-oriented studies have been devoted to analyse different issues to be faced when adapting a third-party component for a (possibly radically) different use (e.g., see [14,12,18]). A formal foundation for component adaptation was set by Yellin and Strom in their seminal paper [31]. They used finite state machines (FSM) for specifying component behaviour, and introduced the notion of *adaptor* as a software entity capable of letting two components with mismatching behaviours interoperate.

The objective of this paper is to present a formal methodology for adapting components with possibly mismatching interaction behaviours. The three main aspects of the methodology are the following:

1. *Component interfaces.* We extend traditional IDL with a description of component behaviours. A component interface therefore consists of two parts: A signature definition (describing the functionalities offered and required by the component), and a behaviour specification (describing the interaction protocol followed by the component). Syntactically, signatures are expressed in the style of traditional IDLs, while behaviours are expressed by using a subset of π-calculus [23] — a process algebra which has proved to be particularly well suited for the specification of dynamic and evolving systems.

2. *Adaptor specification.* We present a simple notation for expressing a specification of an adaptor intended to feature the interoperation of two components with mismatching behaviours. The adaptor specification is given by simply stating a set of correspondences between actions and parameters of the two components. The distinguishing aspect the notation is to allow a high-level, partial specification of the adaptor.

3. *Adaptor derivation.* A concrete adaptor component is then automatically generated, given its partial specification and the interfaces of two components. This fully automated process exhaustively tries to build an adaptor that will allow the components to interoperate while satisfying the given specification. The advantage of separating adaptor specification and derivation is to automate the error-prone, time-consuming task of generating a detailed implementation of a correct adaptor, while simplifying the task of the (human) software developer.

In the rest of this paper, extended component interfaces are introduced in Sect. 2, the notation for adaptor specifications is described in Sect. 3, while Sect. 4 illustrates the automatic generation of adaptors from specifications. The applicability of the whole methodology is exemplified in Sect. 5, where a realistic case of adaptation between two components employing different file transmission protocols is analysed. Finally, Sect.6 is devoted to discuss related work and to draw some concluding remarks.

2   Component Interfaces

Components interfaces will be described in terms of *roles*. Typically, a role is an abstract description of the interaction of a component with any other component it is related to. Hence, a component interface will be represented by a set of roles, each one devoted to a specific facet of the behaviour of the component.

The specification of a role is divided into two parts. The first one describes the component at the signature level, and it is similar to traditional IDL descriptions. Instead, the second part will describe the behavior related with the role signature using a notation derived from process algebras:

> role *roleName* = {
>   **signature** *input and output actions*
>   **behaviour** *interaction pattern* }

The signature interface of a component role declares a set of input and output actions. These actions can be seen as the set of messages sent and received by the role (representing the methods that the component offers and invokes, the values or exceptions returned, etc.). Notice that typically IDLs represent only the services that the component *offers* to its environment (that is, the set of its output actions), while we explicitly represent also the services *required* by the component, as a set of input actions.

Both input and output actions may have parameters, representing the data interchanged in the communication. Parameters can be typed in order to allow for type-checking. For our purposes it is enough to distinguish between just two types: `Link` –representing channels through which messages can be sent and received– and `Data` representing any other data value.

With respect to the behaviour interface, it is described by means of what we call an *interaction pattern* [3]. Intuitively speaking, an interaction pattern describes the essential aspects of the finite interactive behaviour that a component may (repeatedly) show to the external environment.

The language we use for describing these patterns is a variant of the synchronous π-calculus. Since the calculus allows link names to be sent and received as values, it has proved to be a very expressive notation for describing applications with changing topologies, such as open systems. In particular, we use a sugared subset the polyadic π-calculus [22], a generalized version the basic π-calculus in which tuples, and not only single names, can be sent along links. The set of behaviour expressions formally defined as follows:

> E ::= 0 | a. E | (x)E | $[x = y]$ E | E || E | E + E
>
> a ::= tau | x?(d) | x!(d)

The special process 0 represents inaction, while internal actions are denoted by `tau`. Input and output actions are respectively represented by `x?(d)` and `x!(d)`, where `x` is the link along which the actions are performed and `d` is a tuple of names (either links or data), sent or received along `x`. Restrictions, like `(x)E`, represent the creation of a new link name `x` in an expression `E`.

There is also a matching operator, used for specifying conditional behavior. Thus, the pattern `[x=y]` E behaves as E if x=y, otherwise as 0. Finally, also non-

deterministic choice (+) and parallel (||) operators are defined. The summation
E + E' may proceed either to E or to E'. On the other hand, communication will
only be allowed between expressions belonging to different components. Hence,
E || E' consists of expressions E and E' acting in parallel but not synchronizing.

Notice that interaction patterns do not contain recursion. The reason is that
they are intended to specify finite fragments of interaction as an abstract way
of representing component behaviour. In order to show the implications of this
choice, consider for instance a component **Reader** sequentially reading a file. File
items are received with an action **read?(x)** — the end-of-file condition being
represented by a special value **EOF**. Suppose that the component may decide
to break the transmission at any time by sending an action **break!()**. This
behaviour would be expressed in full (recursive) π-calculus as follows:

```
Reader = read?(x). ( [x!=EOF] Reader + [x=EOF] 0 ) + tau. break!(). 0
```

indicating the fact that the component will repeatedly present a **read?** action
until either an **EOF** is received or it decides (by performing a **tau** action) to break
the transmission. However, the (non recursive) interaction pattern representing
this particular component will simply read:

```
read?(x). 0 + tau. break!(). 0        // R1
```

in which some aspects of the behaviour —like recursion and the alternatives
after the **read?** operation— have been abstracted by *projecting* them over time,
and collapsing repeated actions into a single one.

Indeed, trying to describe all the aspects of the behaviour of a distributed
system in one shot unavoidably leads to complex formulations of low practical
usability. Instead, we focus on descriptions of the *finite* concurrent behaviours,
making the verification of properties more tractable. In some sense, the choice of
considering simple non-recursive interaction patterns resembles the use of types
in conventional programming languages. While type checking cannot in general
guarantee the correctness of a program, it does eliminate the vast majority of
programming errors [3]. Similarly, pattern compatibility guarantees *local* correctness, that informally reads as "a component, together with its environment,
is granted to succeed in its *current* step". For instance, the interaction between
an HTML client and a web-server via an HTML FORM may be verified by checking the compatibility of the finite protocols they follow, expressed as patterns.
This, obviously is not sufficient to guarantee the global success of the possibly
non-terminating client component running together with its open environment.

In fact, the framework we propose aims at defining a suitable model for open
systems, allowing for practical, possibly on-the-fly, verification. In this sense, the
finiteness of the approach aims both at dealing with the incompleteness inherent
in open systems, by limiting the analysis to what it is currently observable in
the system, and at providing computational tools that are not subject to an
unbound explosion of computational complexity.

A component may be represented by more than one role or pattern. Consider
now that our reader component copies to disk the received file, using actions
fwrite! and **fclose!**. Again, its behaviour in recursive π-calculus is:

```
Reader' = read?(x). ([x!=EOF] fwrite!(x). Reader' + [x=EOF] fclose!(). 0)
```

```
+ tau. break!(). fclose!(). 0
```

Now, instead of writing a single (but in fact, more complex) pattern for representing the component, we will partition its behaviour into two independent roles: one for describing how it reads the file (which is the pattern R1 previously defined), and the other describing its interaction with the file system, represented by the pattern:

```
tau. fwrite!(data). 0 + tau. fclose!(). 0     // R2
```

Thus, we allow for a modular representation and analysis of behaviour. Each role represents the reader from the point of view of the component to which the role is connected. Hence, while the decision of sending either a fwrite! or a fclose! action is motivated in the reader by the reception of data or end-of-file, the role R2 succeeds to express the point of view of the file system, for which the reader component seems to decide freely to send either action.

The special characteristics of mobility which are present in the π-calculus allow the creation and transmission of link names which can be later used for communication. This determines that the signature interface of a π-calculus interaction pattern is not fixed (like in other process algebras or in object-oriented environments), but instead they can be extended by link-passing.

As an example of these extensible interfaces, consider the pattern below, which specifies the behaviour of a component accepting queries in which a specific channel for returning the requested fact is indicated. The component is also able to raise an exception due to internal reasons (here represented by a tau action):

```
query?(return). return!(fact). 0 + tau. exception!(). 0
```

The pattern indicates that initially the component presents a signature interface consisting only of the actions query?(Link return) and exception!(). However, *after* performing the first of these actions, the interface is enlarged, and also return!(Data fact) must be considered part of it.

The notation we use for this purpose is the operator '>' (read as "before") which explicitly represents dependencies between link names in the interface. For instance, the interface of the component described above will be written as:

```
role QueryServer = {
    signature
        query?(Link return) > return!(Data fact);
        exception!();
    behaviour
        query?(return). return!(fact). 0 +
        tau. exception!(). 0 }
```

which indicates that the action return! will be performed through the link received in the previous query? action.

3   Adaptor Specification

Adaptation, in its generality, is a hard problem which involves a large amount of domain knowledge and may require complex reasoning. Hence, our approach aims at providing a methodology for specifying the required adaptation between two components in a general and abstract way. Moreover, the description of the necessary adaptation will be used to automatically construct a third component, that we call *adaptor*, which is in charge of mediating, when possible, the interaction of the two components so that they can successfully interoperate. In this section we will illustrate a simple and abstract language which permits us to describe the intended *mapping* among the functionalities of the two components to be adapted.

We first observe that adaptation does not simply amount to substituting link names. Consider for instance a component P that requests a file by means of an url, and a repository Q that first receives the url and then returns the corresponding file. Their behaviour interfaces are, respectively:

```
request!(url). reply?(page). 0      // P
query?(address). return!(file). 0   // Q
```

The connection between request! and query?, and between reply? and return! could be defined by the substitution:

```
σ = {t1/request, t1/query, t2/reply, t2/return}
```

that allows their interoperation. Notice that, after applying the substitution, the communication between Pσ and Qσ would be direct and unfiltered, since they will share link names. However this contrasts with encapsulation principles as, in general, one would like neither to modify the components nor to allow the sharing of names (methods or links) between different components. Moreover, it appears clear that this kind of adaptation can solve only renaming-based mismatchings of very similar behaviours. In general, one is interested in adapting more different situations where, for instance, reordering and remembering of messages may be necessary.

We represent an adaptor specification by a mapping that establishes a number of rules relating actions and data of two components. For instance, the mapping expressing the intended adaptation for the previous example is written as:

```
M = { request!(url) <> query?(url);
      reply?(file) <> return!(file); }
```

The intended meaning of the first rule of M is that every time P will perform a request! output action, Q must perform a corresponding query? input action. The use of parameters url and file in the mapping explicitly states the correspondence among data. Parameters have a global scope in the mapping, so that all the occurrences of the same name, even if in different rules, refer to the same parameter.

Intuitively speaking, a mapping provides a minimal specification of an adaptor that will play the role of a "component-in-the-middle" between two components P and Q. Such adaptor will be in charge of mediating the interaction between P and Q according to the mapping specification. It is important to observe that the adaptor specification defined by a mapping abstracts away from many details of the components behaviours. The burden of dealing with these details is put on the (automatic) adaptor construction process, that will be described in the next section. For instance, the behaviour interface of an adaptor satisfying the specification given by mapping M is:

```
request?(url). query!(url). return?(file). reply!(file). 0
```

Such adaptor will maintain the name spaces of P and Q separated and prevent the two from interacting each other without its mediation. Observe that the introduction of such an adaptor to connect P and Q has the effect of changing their communication from synchronous in asynchronous. Indeed, the task of the adaptor is precisely to *adapt* P and Q together, not to act as a transparent communication medium between them.

We conclude this section by sketching the syntax and usage of mappings for specifying different types of adaptation. (A full example of adaptation will be described in Sect.5.)

- *Multiple action correspondence.* While the previous example dealt with one-to-one correspondences between actions, adaptation may in general require relating groups of actions of different components. For instance, consider two components P and Q involved in an authentication procedure. Suppose that P authenticates itself by sending first its user name and then a password. Q instead is ready to accept both data in a single shot. Their behaviour interfaces and the mapping M specifying the required adaptation are:

```
user!(me). passwd!(pwd). 0     // P
login?(usr, word). 0           // Q

M = {user!(me), passwd!(pwd) <> login?(me,pwd);}
```

The mapping associates both output actions performed by P to the single input action performed by Q, indicating also the reordering of parameters to be performed by the adaptor.
- *Actions without a correspondent.* Adaptation must also deal with situations in which an action of a component does not have a correspondent in the other component. For instance, consider a component P that authenticates itself (actions usr! and passwd!), asks for the list of files which are present in a repository (dir! and getdir?), and then deletes a file (delete!). The repository server Q does not require a login phase, but it rather expects a password to be sent together with the invocation of each service it provides (ls? for listing files, and rm? for deleting a file):

```
user!(me). passwd!(pwd). dir!(). getdir?(list). delete!(file). 0   // P
ls?(password). return!(files). rm?(name, password). 0             // Q
```

From the viewpoint of Q, authentication concerns are spread over the whole interaction. Moreover, notice that the parameter me is not requested while pwd/passwd is used more times by Q.

In order to explicitly represent this conceptual asymmetry among the two components, and hence to facilitate the task of devising and reasoning about the high-level specification of a mapping, we have introduced the keyword none. The actions of a component which do not have a clear correspondent in the other component may be associated with none. Hence, the following mapping states that the login phase of P has not correspondence in Q and also that the parameter pwd must be recorded for subsequent uses.

```
M = { user!(me),passwd!(pwd) <> none;
      dir!() <> ls?(pwd);
      getdir?(files) <> return!(files);
      delete!(file) <> rm?(file, pwd); }
```

– *Nondeterministic associations between actions.* A difficult case for adaptation arises when the execution of a component action may correspond to different actions to be executed by the other component. Indeed, in general each component may perform local choices to decide what action to execute next. In such cases, adaptation should take care of dealing with many possible combinations of actions independently performed by the two components.
In order to feature a high-level style of the specification of the desired adaptation, we allow nondeterminism in the adaptor specification. For instance, suppose a component receiving a file by means of a single action read? while its counterpart may decide to send an action data!(x) or an end-of-file eof!(). The mapping will be specified by means of two separate rules:

```
read?(x) <> data?(x);
read?(EOF) <> eof!();
```

The adaptor derivation process will be then in charge of building an actual adaptor capable of dealing with all the possible specified situations. Once more, our goal is to allow the adaptor specification to abstract away from implementation details, and to leave the burden of dealing with these details to the (automatic) adaptor construction process. The use of nondeterministic associations will be illustrated further in the example of Sect.5.

4   Adaptor derivation

In this section we sketch how a concrete adaptor can be automatically generated, starting from two roles P and Q, and a mapping M. The adaptor derivation is implemented by (an extended version of) the algorithm we developed for checking the correctness of an open context of components [3]. The goal of the algorithm is to build a process A such that:

1. P|A|Q is successful (i.e. all traces lead to a successful state, where both P, Q and A have reduced to 0), and
2. A satisfies the given mapping M, that is, all the action correspondences and data dependencies specified by M are respected in any trace of P|A|Q.

The algorithm incrementally builds the adaptor A by trying to eliminate progressively all the possible deadlocks that may occur in the evolution of P|A|Q. Informally, while the derivation tree of P|A|Q contains a deadlock, the algorithm extends A with an action α that will trigger one of the deadlock states:

- Such action α is chosen so as to match a dual action $\overline{\alpha}$ on which P or Q are blocked. Notice that the adaptor is able to match only *some* of those actions. For instance, it cannot match an input action $\overline{\alpha}$ if it has not yet collected enough information to build a corresponding action α that satisfies the data dependencies specified in M.
- Since there may be more than one "triggerable" action $\overline{\alpha}$, at each step the algorithm non-deterministically chooses one of them to match, and spawns an instance of itself for each possible choice. If there is no triggerable action, then the algorithm (instance) fails.
- Each instance maintains a set $\mathcal{D}$ of data acquired by matching output actions, a set $\mathcal{F}$ of actions to be eventually matched so as to respect the correspondences stated by the rules of the mapping M, and a set $\mathcal{L}$ of link correspondences in order to guarantee the separation of name spaces between the two roles.
- Each algorithm instance terminates when the derivation tree of P|A|Q does not contains deadlocks. If the set $\mathcal{F}$ of actions to be matched is empty, then the algorithm instance successfully terminates and it returns the completed adaptor. It fails otherwise.

The overall algorithm fails if all its instances fail. Failure implies that the patterns P and Q can not be adapted according to the mapping M. If at least one of the instances returns an adaptor, the algorithm non-deterministically returns one of the adaptors found. This non-determinism is due to the non-determinism naturally present in concurrent systems. The definition of a representative of the class of the returned adaptors is currently under study: the general case presents some difficulties since the adaptors for the same patterns may be structurally much different. For the aims of this paper, it is important to remind that every returned adaptor makes P|A|Q successful.

For instance, considering again the third example of Sect.3 regarding the file repository server, the algorithm constructs the following adaptor A:

```
A = user?(me). passwd?(pwd). dir?(). ls!(pwd).
      return?(files). getdir!(files). delete?(file). rm!(file,pwd). 0
```

It is easy to verify that the composition P|A|Q is deadlock free, and that A satisfies the mapping, both in terms of action correspondence and data dependencies (e.g., A forwards pwd and file to Q only after receiving them from P.)

Moreover, in case of successful adaptor generation, the automatic construction phase also returns some information on the constructed adaptor. For instance, for the example above, the algorithm notifies that some data (viz., the value me) will be lost during the mediation, and that the adaptor will repeatedly send to Q the user password pwd though it is sent only once by P.

5   An Example of Adaptation

Consider a typical FTP transmission in which a file is sent by a server to a client. The example is simplified to show only the relevant details, while hopefully keeping its realistic flavour.

In order to make a modular specification of the problem, we will consider two different interactions between the client and the server, using two roles for describing their behavior. First, we will describe the behaviour of the client and the server regarding how to create and close an FTP session, and also how to request the typical put and get services for transmitting a file. Second, we will describe the details of file transmission using a separate pair of roles.

Hence, we will have two role-to-role connections, each one specified by a different mapping, from which the corresponding adaptors will be produced. Let us consider the first pair of roles. The roles IServer and IClient below describe the interface of the server and the client regarding the use of FTP commands.

```
role IServer = {
    interface open?(Link ctrl);
             user?(Data name, Data password, Link ctrl);
             put?(Data filename, Link ctrl);
             get?(Data filename, Link ctrl);
             close?(Link ctrl);

    behaviour open?(ctrl).
             user?(name,password,ctrl).
                  ( put?(filename,ctrl). close?(ctrl). 0
                  + get?(filename,ctrl). close?(ctrl). 0
                  + close?(ctrl) .0)  }
```

The role IServer above indicates how, for opening a session, a socket (represented by the link ctrl) must be provided. This socket will be used both for identifying the source of next commands (allowing thus multiple simultaneous sessions), and also for control communication between the client and the server. Once the connection is opened, the client must identify itself with a name and password. Then, put and get commands for file uploading and downloading can be issued to the server. Finally, the connection is ended with close.

```
role IClient = {
    interface login!(Data usr);
             pass!(Data pwd);
             getfile!(Data file);
             logout!();

    behaviour login!(usr).
             pass!(pwd).
             getfile!(file).
             logout!(). 0 }
```

On the other hand, suppose that the role IClient specifies that the client will connect with a login message by which it sends its identity, followed by a its password in a separate message (however no control socket is provided). Then, the client will ask for a certain file, and finally logs out.

It is worth observing that, in spite of the different behaviours of the two components, their adaptation can be simply specified by the mapping:

```
M = { login!(usr), pass!(pwd) <> open?(new ctrl), user?(usr,pwd,ctrl);
      getfile!(file) <> get?(file,ctrl);
      logout!() <> close?(ctrl); }
```

The first rule of M establishes the intended correspondence between two pairs of actions of the components. The mapping also exploits the use of action parameters to specify data dependencies among different actions of the components. In particular the ctrl parameter is employed in all the three rules to specify the needed adaptation due to the fact that the client does not specify the control socket in its protocol. The special keyword new in the first rule is used to specify the need for the adaptor to create a new name to match the server open? input action. As shown in Section 4, this mapping will produce the suitable adaptor:

```
A = login?(usr). pass?(pwd). (ctrl) open!(ctrl). user!(usr,pwd,ctrl).
    getfile?(file). get!(file,ctrl). logout?(). close!(crtl). 0
```

which allow both components to interact successfully. Let us consider now how a file is transmitted once a get command is issued by the client. Typically, the server will create a separate thread (daemon) for the transmission of the file. Accordingly, we will use another pair of roles, namely IGetDaemon and IGettingFile, for representing this facet of the interaction between client and server, respectively:

```
role IGettingFile = {
    interface read?(Data x);
            break!();

    behaviour read?(x). 0 + tau. break!(). 0 }

role IGetDaemon = {
    interface ctrl!(Link data, Link eof) >
                data!(Data x),
                eof!();

    behaviour (data,eof) ctrl!(data,eof).
                    ( tau. data!(x). 0 + tau. eof!(). 0 ) }
```

The differences between the two roles are the following:

- Server action ctrl! does not have a correspondent in the client, reflecting the fact that while the server creates specific links for each file transmission, the client uses fixed, predefined links for the same purpose. Hence, a suitable mapping rule for this situation is:

  ```
  none <> ctrl!(data,eof);
  ```

- The action for reading each piece of the file is called read? in the client, while the corresponding action in the server is data!. This mismatch can be easily solved with the mapping rule:

  ```
  read?(x) <> data!(x);
  ```

- The server may indicate at any moment the end of the file being transmitted by sending an eof!(), but the client does not have a corresponding message. This situation can be dealt with by using a special value in message read?, thus allowing the client protocol to end:

  ```
  read?(EOF) <> eof!();
  ```

– The client can autonomously decide (because of its local choice) to break the
transmission at any moment by sending a `break!()` message. This case is
more difficult to adapt, since the server and the adaptor might have already
engaged themselves in a pair of complementary `data` actions. This would
violate the one-to-one correspondence between actions `read?` and `data!` expressed by the second rule of the mapping (and no adaptor could be produced). We can solve this problem by stating also rules for mapping a client
`break!()` to the actions `read!` and `eof!` of the server. Hence, the whole
mapping would be:

```
M = { none <> ctrl!(data,eof);
      read?(x) <> data!(x);
      read?(EOF) <> eof!();
      break!() <> data!(y);
      break!() <> eof!(); }
```

Notice that the above mapping specifies action correspondences in a nondeterministic way. For instance, the last two rules state that the execution of the
`break!` action may correspond to either a `data!` action or to a `eof!` action on
the server side. Similarly, the second and fourth rule specify that the execution
of a `data!` output operation by the server may match either a `read?` or a `break!`
operation autonomously performed by the client.

It is important to observe that allowing nondeterministic correspondences in
the mapping features a high-level style of the specification of the desired adaptation. While the mapping simply lists a number of possible action correspondences
that may arise at run-time, the adaptor derivation process will be in charge of
devising the actual adaptor able to suitably deal with all the possible specified
situations. The adaptor produced from the above mapping is:

```
A = ctrl?(data,eof). ( data?(x). ( read!(x). 0 + break?(). 0 )
                     + eof?(). ( read!(EOF). 0 + break?(). 0 )
                     + break?(). ( data?(x). 0 + eof?(). 0 ) )
```

6   Concluding Remarks

Several authors have proposed to extend current IDLs in order to deal with
behavioural aspects of component interfaces. The use of FSMs to describe the
behaviour of software components is proposed for instance in [9,20,26,31]. The
main advantage of FSMs is that their simplicity supports a simple and efficient
verification of protocol compatibility. On the other hand, such a simplicity is a
severe expressiveness bound for modelling complex open distributed systems.

Process algebras feature more expressive descriptions of protocols, enable
more sophisticated analysis of concurrent systems [1,24,25], and support system
simulation and formal derivation of safety and liveness properties. In particular,
the π-calculus, differently from FSMs and other algebras like CCS, can model
some relevant features for component-based open systems, like dynamic creation
of new processes, dynamic reorganization of network topology (mobility), and
local and global choices. The usefulness of π-calculus has been illustrated for

describing component models like COM [13] and CORBA [16], and architecture description languages like Darwin [19] and LEDA [6].

However, the main drawback of using process algebras for software specification is related to the inherent complexity of the analysis. In order to manage this complexity, the previous work of the authors has described the use of modular and partial specifications, by projecting behaviour both over space (roles) [7] and over time (finite interaction patterns) [3]. The calculus presented in this paper preserves most of the above mentioned features.

A general discussion of the issues of component interconnection, mismatch and adaptation is reported in [2,12,14], while formal approaches to detecting interaction mismatches are presented for instance in [1,7,11]. The problem of software adaptation was specifically addressed by the work of Yellin and Strom [31], which constitutes the starting point for our work. They use finite state grammars to specify interaction protocols between components, to define a relation of compatibility, and to address the task of (semi)automatic adaptor generation. Some significant limitations of their approach are related with the expressiveness of the notation used. For instance, there is no possibility of representing local choices, parallel composition of behaviours, or the creation of new processes. Furthermore, the architecture of the systems being described is static, and they do not deal with issues such as reorganizing the communication topology of systems, a possibility which immediately becomes available when using the π-calculus. In addition, the asymmetric meaning they give to input and output actions makes it necessary the use of *ex machina* arbitrators for controlling system evolution.

Another closely related work is that of Reussner [28], who proposes the extension of interfaces with FSMs in order to check correct composition and also to adapt non-compatible components. Protocols are divided into two views: the services the component offers, and those it requires from its environment. One limitation of the work is that these two views must be orthogonal, i.e. each time a service is invoked in a component it results the same sequence of external invocations, while this usually depends on the internal state of the component. It should be also noticed that in Reussner's protocols there is no indication of action signs, and only method invocation is represented, while our approach involves a more general setting in which any dialogue or protocol between components can be specified. Finally, adaptation is considered in this work only as *restriction* of behaviour; if the environment does not offer all the resources required, the component is restricted to offer a subset of its services, but no other forms of adaptation (like name translation, or treatment of protocol mismatch) is considered.

The main aim of this paper is to contribute to the definition of a methodology for the automatic development of adaptors capable of solving behavioural mismatches between heterogeneous interacting components.

Our work falls in the research stream that advocates the application of formal methods, in particular of process algebras, to describe the interactive behaviour of software systems. As shown for instance in [3,7], the adoption of π-calculus to extend component interfaces paves the way for the automatic verification of properties of interacting systems, such as the compatibility of the protocols followed by the components of the system.

While the proposed methodology lays a foundation for the automatic development of adaptors, we foresee several interesting further developments. The first we intend to address is the formal verification of properties of the generated adaptor, such as security properties, as suggested in [20,31]. In practice, such a verification would allow an application to check that its security policy will not be spoiled by the inclusion of a new (adapted) component.

References

1. R. Allen and D. Garlan. A formal basis for architectural connection. *ACM Trans. on Software Engineering and Methodology*, 6(3):213–49, 1997.
2. J. Bosch. Adapting object-oriented components. In *2nd. International Workshop on Component-Oriented Programming (WCOP'97)*, pages 13–22. Turku Centre for Computer Science, September 1997.
3. A. Bracciali, A. Brogi, and F. Turini. Coordinating interaction patterns. In *ACM Symposium on Applied Computing (SAC'2001)*. ACM Press, 2001.
4. A.W. Brown and H.C. Wallnau. The current state of CBSE. *IEEE Software*, 1998.
5. G. H. Campbell. Adaptable components. In *ICSE 1999*, pages 685 – 686. IEEE Press, 1999.
6. C. Canal, E. Pimentel, and J. M. Troya. Specification and refinement of dynamic software architectures. In *Software Architecture*, pages 107–126. Kluwer, 1999.
7. C. Canal, E. Pimentel, and J. M. Troya. Compatibility and inheritance in software architectures. *Science of Computer Programming*, 41:105–138, 2001.
8. D. Chappell. *Understanding ActiveX and OLE*. Microsoft Press, 1996.
9. I. Cho, J. McGregor, and L. Krause. A protocol-based approach to specifying interoperability between objects. In *Proceedings of TOOLS'26*, pages 84–96. IEEE Press, 1998.
10. E. Clarke, O. Grumberg, and D. Long. Verification tools for finite-state concurrent systems. In *A Decade of concurrency–Reflections and Perspectives*, Lecture Notes in Computer Science, 803. Springer, 1994.
11. D. Compare, P. Inverardi, and A. L. Wolf. Uncovering architectural mismatch in component behavior. *Science of Computer Programming*, 33(2):101–131, 1999.
12. S. Ducasse and T. Richner. Executable connectors: Towards reusable design elements. In *ACM Foundations of Software Engineering (ESEC/FSE'97)*, number 1301 in LNCS. Springer, 1997.
13. L.M.G. Feijs. Modelling Microsof COM using π-calculus. In *Formal Methods'99*, number 1709 in LNCS, pages 1343–1363. Springer, 1999.
14. D. Garlan, R. Allen, and J. Ockerbloom. Architectural mismatch: Why reuse is so hard. *IEEE Software*, 12(6):17–26, 1995.
15. D. Garlan and B. Schmerl. Component-based software engineering in pervasive computing environments. In *4th ICSE Workshop on Component-Based Software Engineering*, 2001.
16. M. Gaspari and G. Zavattaro. A process algebraic specification of the new asynchronous CORBA messaging service. In *Proceedings of ECOOP'99*, number 1628 in LNCS, pages 495–518. Springer, 1999.
17. George T. Heineman. An evaluation of component adaptation techniques. In *2nd ICSE Workshop on Component-Based Software Engineering*, 1999.

18. S. Hissam K. Wallnau and R. Seacord. *Building Systems from Commercial Components.* The SEI Series in Software Engineering, 2001.
19. J. Magee, S. Eisenbach, and J. Kramer. Modeling darwin in the π-calculus. In *Theory and Practice in Distributed Systems*, number 938 in LNCS, pages 133–152. Springer, 1995.
20. J. Magee, J. Kramer, and D. Giannakopoulou. Behaviour analysis of software architectures. In *Software Architecture*, pages 35–49. Kluwer, 1999.
21. Microsoft Corporation. .NET Programming the Web. http://msdn.microsoft.com.
22. R. Milner. The polyadic π-calculus: a tutorial. Technical report, University of Edinburgh, Octubre 1991.
23. R. Milner, J. Parrow, and D. Walker. A calculus of mobile processes. *Journal of Information and Computation*, 100:1–77, 1992.
24. A. P. Moore, J. E. Klinker, and D. M. Mihelcic. How to construct formal arguments that persuade certifiers. In *Industrial-Strength Formal Methods in Practice.* Springer, 1999.
25. E. Najm, A. Nimour, and JB. Stefani. Infinite types for distributed objects interfaces. In *Proceedings of the third IFIP conference on Formal Methods for Open Object-based Distributed Systems - FMOODS'99.* Kluwer, 1999.
26. O. Nierstrasz. Regular types for active objects. In O. Nierstrasz and D. Tsichritzis, editors, *Object-Oriented Software Composition.* Prentice Hall, 1995.
27. OMG. *The Common Object Request Broker: Architecture and Specification.* Object Management Group. http://www.omg.org.
28. R. H. Reussner. Enhanced component interfaces to support dynamic adaption and extension. In *34th Hawaiin International Conference on System Sciences.* IEEE Press, 2001.
29. Sun Microsystems. JavaBeans API specification. http://java.sun.com.
30. A. Vallecillo, J. Hernández, and J. M. Troya. New issues in object interoperability. In *Object-Oriented Technology: ECOOP 2000 Workshop Reader*, number 1964 in LNCS, pages 256–269. Springer, 2000.
31. D. M. Yellin and R. E. Strom. Protocol specifications and components adaptors. *ACM Trans. on Programming Languages and Systems*, 19(2):292–333, 1997.

A Component Model for Field Devices[*]

Oscar Nierstrasz[1], Gabriela Arévalo[1], Stéphane Ducasse[1],
Roel Wuyts[1], Andrew P. Black[2,**], Peter O. Müller[3],
Christian Zeidler[3], Thomas Genssler[4], and Reinier van den Born[5]

[1] Software Composition Group, Institut für Informatik und Angewandte Mathematik,
University of Bern, Switzerland,
{oscar,ducasse,wuyts}@iam.unibe.ch, www.iam.unibe.ch/~scg/
[2] Department of Computer Science & Engineering, Oregon Health & Science University,
black@cse.ogi.edu, www.cse.ogi.edu/~black/
[3] ABB Research Center, Germany,
{peter.o.mueller,christian.zeidler}@de.abb.com, www.abb.com
[4] FZI Research Center for Information Technologies, Germany,
genssler@fzi.de, www.fzi.de
[5] OTI, The Netherlands,
Reinier_van_den_Born@oti.com, www.oti.com

Abstract. Component-based software development is becoming mainstream for conventional applications. However, components can be difficult to deploy in embedded systems because of non-functional requirements. PECOS is a collaborative project between industrial and research partners that seeks to enable component-based technology for a class of embedded systems known as "field devices". In this paper we introduce a component model for field devices that captures a range of non-functional properties and constraints.

1 Introduction

Software for embedded systems is typically monolithic and platform-dependent. These systems are hard to maintain, upgrade and customize, and they are almost impossible to port to other platforms. Component-based software engineering would bring a number of advantages to the embedded systems world such as faster development times, the reuse of existing components, and the ability for domain experts to interactively compose and adapt sophisticated embedded systems software. In order to apply CBSD to embedded systems, however, the following questions remain to be answered:

- *Component models:* What kind of component models are needed to support CBSD for embedded systems software?

- *Non-functional requirements:* How can we reason about non-functional constraints of systems based on properties of their constituent components?

- *Tools:* What tools are need to specify, compose, validate and compile embedded systems applications built from components?

The PECOS project[***] aims to enable component-based software development for embedded systems. In order to achieve concrete results within a limited frame, PECOS is driven by a case study in the domain of *field devices*, which are field deployable con-

---

[*] An extended version of this paper is available from: www.iam.unibe.ch/~scg/.
[**] Visiting SCG.

J. Bishop (Ed.): CD 2002, LNCS 2370, pp. 200–209, 2002.

trol devices briefly described in section 2. Section 3 presents a running example, and section 4 introduces the PECOS field device component model, focusing on the structural aspects. In section 5 we present the execution semantics of the component model, by translation to Petri nets. By extending this interpretation to time Petri nets [12], we intend to reason about real-time constraints and automatically generate real-time schedules. Finally, in section 6, we summarize the current state of the project, which is still in progress.

2   PECOS

ABB's Instruments business unit develops a large number of different *field devices*, such as temperature, pressure, and flow sensors, actuators, and positioners. As field devices turn into commodities, the software increasingly determines the competitiveness of the devices. As the market demands new functionality in shorter time cycles, software begins to dominate the development and maintenance costs of field devices.

2.1   Field devices

A *field device* is a reactive, embedded system. Field devices make use of sensors to continuously gather data, such as temperature, pressure or rate of flow. They analyse this data, and react by controlling actuators, valves or motors. To minimize cost, field devices are implemented using the cheapest available hardware that is up to the task. A typical field device may contain a 16-bit microprocessor with only 256kB of ROM and 40kB of RAM.

The software for a typical field device, such as the TZID pneumatic positioner shown in figure 1, is monolithic, and is separately developed for each kind of field device.

Figure 1   Pneumatic positioner TZID

2.2   PECOS goals

The goal of PECOS is to enable CBSD for embedded systems by providing an environment that supports the specification, composition, configuration checking, and deployment of embedded systems built from software components.

By focusing on the field device case study, PECOS intends to deliver a demonstrator that validates CBSD for embedded systems. Specifically, PECOS intends to deliver both a *component model* suitable for characterizing software components for field devices, and a *composition environment* for expressing, validating and compiling compositions of components conforming to the model.

***Funded by the European Commission as project IST-1999-20398 and by the Swiss government as BBW 00.0170. The partners are Asea Brown Boveri AG (ABB, Germany), Forschungzentrum Informatik an der Universität Karlsruhe (FZI, Germany), Object Technology International AG (OTI Netherlands), Institut für Informatik und Angewandte Mathematik, University of Bern (UNIBE, Switzerland).

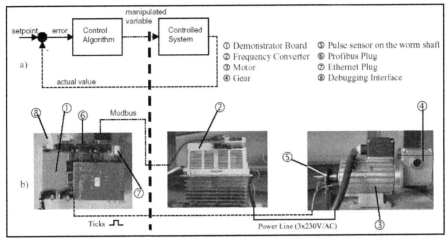

Figure 2   Pecos demonstrator field device

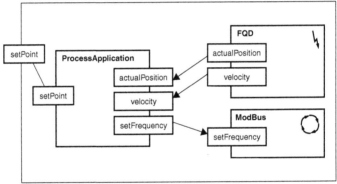

Figure 3   FQD Control loop example

3   PECOS Case Study

In order to validate CBSD for embedded systems, the PECOS project is developing the hardware and software for a demonstration field device. The task of the PECOS field device is to control a three-phase motor connected to a valve (see figure 2). The motor is driven by a frequency converter which can be controlled over *Modbus* from the field device. The motor can be coupled to a valve either directly via a worm shaft or using additional gearing (4). A pulse sensor on the shaft (5) detects its speed and the direction of rotation. The PECOS board (1) is equipped with a web-based control panel (7) with some basic elements for local operation and display. The demonstrator can be integrated in a control system via the fieldbus communication protocol *Profibus PA* (6). The device is compliant to the profibus specification for Actuators [4][5].

3.1   Running Example

We will use the following example to illustrate the PECOS component model and composition language.

Part of the PECOS case study is concerned with setting a valve at a specific position between *open* and *closed*. Figure 3 illustrates three connected PECOS components that collaborate to set the valve position; the desired position is determined by other components not shown here. In order to set and keep the valve at a certain position, a control loop is used to continuously monitor and adjust the valve.

- The ModBus component is responsible for interfacing to a piece of hardware called the *frequency converter*, which determines the speed of the motor. The frequency to which the motor should be set is obtained from the ProcessApplication component. ModBus outputs this value over a serial line to the frequency converter using the ModBus protocol (hence its name). The ModBus component runs in its own thread, because it blocks waiting for a (slow) response from the frequency converter.

- The FQD (Fast Quadrature Decoder [8]) component is responsible for capturing events from the motor. This component abstracts from a micro-controller module that does FQD in hardware. It provides the ProcessApplication with both the velocity and the position of the valve.

- The component ProcessApplication obtains the desired position of the valve (setPoint) and reads the current state of the valve from the FQD component. This information is then used to compute a frequency for the motor. Once the motor has opened the valve sufficiently, ascertained by the next reading from the FQD, the motor must be slowed or stopped. This repeated adjustment and monitoring constituted the control loop.

This example illustrates several key points concerning the field device domain.

- *Cyclic behaviour:* each component is responsible for a single task, which is repeatedly executed.

- *Information flow through ports:* components communicate by means of shared data. The interface of a component consists of a set of shared data ports.

- *Threading:* some components are passive, while others have their own thread of control.

- *Separate scheduler:* control flow is separately specified by a scheduler for the composite component.

4 A Component Model for Field Devices

The component model presented here has been especially tailored to the domain of field devices. Although it may have broader implications for other classes of embedded systems, we do not make that claim here.

The PECOS field device component model has been defined to reflect an *architectural style* for field devices [9]. As such, we define a vocabulary of *components*, *ports* and *connectors* and the *rules* governing their composition. As in related approaches, components may only be connected if their provided and required ports are compatible [11].

Components. A *component* is a computational element with a *name*, a number of *property bundles* and *ports*, and a *behaviour*. The *ports* of a component represent data that may be shared

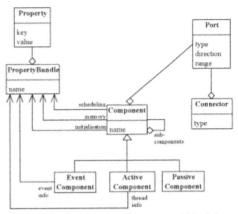

Figure 4   The PECOS Component Model

with other components. The *behaviour* of a component consists of a procedure that reads and writes data available at its ports, and may produce effects in the physical world.

A *leaf component* is a "black-box" not further defined by model, but instead directly implemented in the host programming language. It has an interface consisting of a set of ports, and properties specified by its property bundles.

A *composite component* contains a number of connected subcomponents, the ports of which form the *internal ports* of the composite. A composite component also has *external ports,* which are the only ones that are externally visible. The external ports are *connected* to appropriate internal ports. The subcomponents are not visible outside the composite that contains them.

The field device domain requires three kinds of components.

- **Passive Components** do not have their own thread of control. A passive component is explicitly scheduled by the active component that is its nearest ancestor in the component hierarchy (its active ancestor). Passive components are typically used to encapsulate a piece of behaviour that executes synchronously and completes in a short time-cycle.

- **Active Components** do have their own thread of control; they are used to model ongoing or longer-lived activities that do not complete in a short time-cycle.

- **Event Components** are those whose behaviour is triggered by an event. They are used to model pieces of hardware that frequently emit events, such as motors that give their rotation speed, or timers that emit a timing event when a certain deadline has passed. Whenever the event fires, the behaviour is executed immediately.

Ports. A *port* is a shared variable that allows a component to communicate with other components; *connected* ports represent the *same* shared variable. A port specifies:

- a *name*, which has to be unique within the component;
- a *type*, characterizing the data that it holds;

- a *range* of values (defined by a minimum and maximum value) that can be passed on this port; and

- a *direction* ("in", "out" or "inout") indicating whether the component reads, writes, or reads and writes the data. An inout port behaves exactly like a pair uni-directional ports, one in, and the other out.

Ports of *peer components* can only be connected if they have the same type and their direction is *complementary*, *i.e.*, an in port can only be connected to an out port. *Internal* ports of a composite component can only be connected to the *external* ports if they have the same type and their direction is *compatible*, *e.g.*, an internal in port can be connected to an external in port. Internal ports may be left unconnected, so it is allowed to connect an internal inout port to an external out port.

Connectors. A *connector* specifies a data-sharing relationship between ports. It has a *name*, a *type*, and a list of *ports* it connects. (Here we consider only binary connectors.)

Properties. A *property* is a tagged value. The tag is an identifier, and the value is typed. Properties characterise components.

Property bundles. A *property bundle* is a named group of properties. Property bundles are used to characterize aspects of components, such as timing or memory usage.

4.1   Example revisited

Returning to the example of figure 3, we see that FQD is an event component, ProcessApplication is a passive component and ModBus is an active component. The composition will be modelled as a composite component.

FQD has "out" ports actualPosition and velocity, connected to "in" ports of the same name belonging to ProcessApplication. The in port setPoint belonging to ProcessApplication is shared with the composite component that encapsulates this composition. It is not yet connected to a compatible "out" port. Finally, the "out" port setFrequency is connected to the "in" port of the same name belonging to ModBus.

5   Synchronization and Timing

Two issues must be addressed to complete the model: first, how read/write and write/write conflicts are avoided on the (shared) external ports, and second, how components are scheduled to meet deadlines.

We will do this using a Petri net interpretation of valid compositions. Using plain Petri nets we can model concurrent activities of component compositions, scheduling of components, and synchronization of shared ports. This part of the model is reasonably well-understood. Using time Petri nets we hope to reason about timing constraints, and generate real-time schedules; this topic is still under investigation.

5.1   Synchronization

Our Petri net procedures of the field device component model makes use of three different kinds of places and tokens. (i) *Data places* model ports; each data place has a single token representing the shared data available at that port. (ii) *Control places* are used to schedule components. Each active component has its own independent control subnet to model its schedule; there is exactly one token in each control subnet. (iii) *Event places* model the generation of an event.

A component is modelled as a Petri net fragment with a single control place that can be used to *start* it, and a single *end* place to signal that it has terminated (figure 5). When components are composed, a *schedule* must be generated that somehow moves the token from the *end* place of a component to the *start* place of the next one to be scheduled.

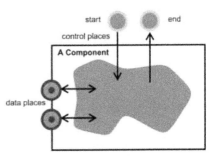

Figure 5   Components as nets

The *behaviour* of the component is a subnet that has read and write access to its data ports. The nature of these subnets depends on the kind of component.

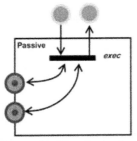

Figure 6   Passive leaf components

Passive leaf components are particularly simple to model. Their behaviour consists of a single *exec* transition that reads or write the data places (figure 6).

Because two passive components that share a port must be serialized, synchronization problems can arise only when active components are connected to other components. Active components compete for their external data ports with their surrounding environment. To address this problem, we *split* the external ports of active components into two parts: an *outer port*, to which the outside world has free access, and an *inner port*, to which the active component has access.

These two ports are synchronized by copying the data from one to the other (depending on the direction of the port) in a special *synchronization method* (or "sync method"). This method may be generated or specially tailored. We model this by a *sync* transition that reads and writes the inner and outer ports and is triggered by the *start* control place.

It is important to realize that the *inner* ports are actually the *shared resources*, since they are the only ones exposed to concurrent accesses (*i.e.*, from the *sync* transition and from the internal behaviour of the active components).

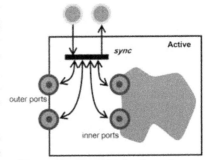

Figure 7   Synchronization of inner and outer ports

The *outer* ports are never exposed to concurrent accesses, because they are only accessible from the transitions of the outer control net, which contains only a single token.

The behaviour of an active leaf component is modelled as a separate control subnet consisting of a *critical section*, which may access the inner ports, and a non-critical section. The control subnet of an active component is a loop containing a single control token.

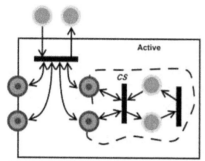

Figure 8   Active schedule with critical section

An event component is similar to an active component, except that its control subnet does not cycle, but is triggered by an external event.

To model *composite components*, we simply coalesce all the connected data places, and we connect the start and end control places of the subcomponents according to the required schedule.

Data ports may be connected to represent data *flow*, or to represent the fact that a port of a composite component is exported from one of its constituent components. For the Petri net procedures, there is no distinction — in both cases, the connected ports represent the *same* shared variable and are therefore modelled by the same, coalesced data place.

We can see this in figure 9. Connected outer ports of all the components are each represented by a single, shared data place. This holds not only for the dataflow of velocity and actualPosition from FQD to ProcessApplication but also for the setPoint port which is visible from the outside. Inner and outer ports of active and event components, on the other hand, are *not* coalesced, since they must be explicitly synchronized.

The figure also illustrates how composite components schedule their parts. The schedule, which is triggered by the *start* place of the composite, first fires FQD, then ProcessApplication, and finally ModBus. Since FQD and ModBus have independent behaviour (*i.e.*, triggered by an event or running in a separate thread), the schedule is responsible only for synchronizing the data ports.

The constructed net is clearly deadlock-free: the only conflicts between simultaneously enabled transitions occur where sync transitions compete with critical sections of active components. Since each of these transitions lock all the required data ports simultaneously, no *waits-for* cycles are possible, and hence no deadlock can arise.

5.2   Timing

To construct a schedule for a composition of components, certain scheduling information must be associated with each subcomponent; this includes the worst-case execution time of the subcomponent and the desired cycle time. For an active subcomponent, this information must be provided separately for the *sync* and *exec* methods. It is also be necessary to specify a (partial) ordering for the execution of the subcomponents in a composition.

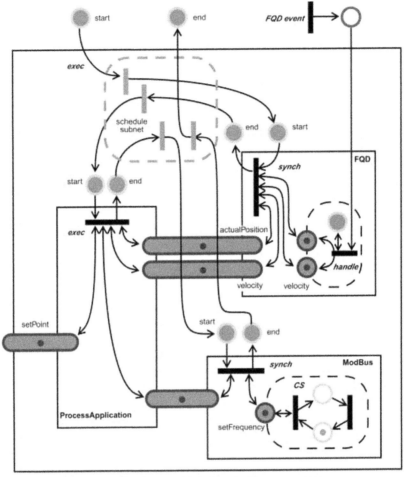

Figure 9   Petri net model of control loop example

The simplest form of schedule is a cyclic executive, in which components are wired together directly, such that each passes control to the next. Such schedules are very efficient, but are feasible only for the very simplest of compositions. Such a schedule can be represented in the Petri net model by inserting transitions between the end place of one component and the start place of the next.

So long as the schedule can be computed entirely statically, there is no need to explicitly represent the scheduling information for the components: it is represented implicitly in the schedule itself, but that schedule can be calculated off-line. However, it may still be desirable to verify the scheduler produced in this way. We have been investigating the use of time Petri nets [13] to represent the schedulers, and various Petri net tools such as Poses++ [3] and TPTPN [10] to assist in their analysis. We have also been investigating the use of hierarchical constraint solvers (such as Cassowary [1]), to capture the timing requirements and partial ordering of components and check the feasibility of schedules, or even to generate them when this is possible.

6   Status and Future Work

In this paper we have presented some intermediate results of the PECOS project. The component model developed for PECOS addresses the requirements identified for the case study outlined above. Ongoing activities include: (i) formalization of the component model, (ii) investigation of various techniques, such as time Petri nets and hierarchical constraint solvers, to generate real-time schedules, (iii) implementation of components to support the PECOS case study demonstrator, (iv) implementation of the language mapping to generate executable code from specifications of component compositions.

7   References

[1]   Greg J. Badros and Alan Borning, "The Cassowary Linear Arithmetic Constraint Solving Algorithm: Interface and Implementation," Technical Report, no. UW Technical Report 98-06-04, University of Washington, 1998.

[2]   Embedded C++ home page, www.caravan.net/ec2plus

[3]   Gesellschaft für Prozeßautomation & Consulting bH home page, www.gpc.de.

[4]   PROFIBUS International, PA General Requirements, Version 3.0 (www.profibus.org)

[5]   PROFIBUS International, Device Data Sheet for Actuators, Version 3.0

[6]   Bastiaan Schönhage, "Model mapping to C++ or Java-based ultra-light environment", Pecos Deliverable D2.2.9-1, www.pecos-project.org

[7]   Benedikt Schulz, Thomas Genssler, Alexander Christoph, Michael Winter, "Requirements for the Composition Environment", Pecos Deliverable D3.1, www.pecos-project.org

[8]   Semiconductor Motorola Programming Note, Fast Quadrature Decode TPU Function (FQD), TPUPN02/D.

[9]   Mary Shaw and David Garlan, *Software Architecture: Perspectives on an Emerging Discipline*, Prentice-Hall, 1996.

[10]   TPTPN home page, www.diit.unict.it/users/scava/tptpn.html.

[11]   Rob van Ommering, Jeff Kramer, Jeff Magee, "The Koala Component Model for Consumer Electronics Software", IEEE Computer, March 2000, Vol. 33, No. 3, pp. 78-85.

[12]   Jiacun Wang, *Timed Petri Nets*, Kluwer Academic Publishers, 1998.

[13]   B. Berthomieu and M. Diaz. Modeling and verification of time dependent systems using time Petri nets. IEEE Transactions on Software Engineering, 17(3), pp. 259–273, 1991.

A Translation System for Enabling Flexible and Efficient Deployment of QoS-Aware Applications in Ubiquitous Environments*

Duangdao Wichadakul and Klara Nahrstedt

Department of Computer Science, University of Illinois at Urbana-Champaign,
{wichadak, klara}@cs.uiuc.edu

Abstract. Ubiquitous Quality of Service(QoS)-aware applications, such as e-business or multimedia delivery are becoming available anywhere anytime. In the past decade, also QoS-oriented middleware services, assisting QoS-aware applications with different aspects of QoS provisions, have been proposed. Assuming the availability of these middleware services, in this paper, we present the *application to middleware service translation* system. This system helps an application developer to develop a QoS-aware application which can be deployed flexibly and efficiently in ubiquitous environments with different available middleware services. We introduce the middleware abstraction layer (MAL) between the application view of middleware and the specific middleware implementations. The translation system assists the QoS-aware application in two phases: (1) environment-independent translation, and (2) environment-dependent translation. The first phase maps the QoS-aware application to configurations of middleware services without indication of specific implementations, to satisfy the qualitative QoS requirements. Its result is the portable MAL representation. The second phase helps the application developer to customize the MAL representation within a specific deployment environment. It deals with (a) mapping of MAL representation into configurations of specific middleware implementations, and (b) mapping of application quantitative QoS requirements into specific middleware implementation's expected parameters. Our translation system facilitates the rapid growth of QoS-aware applications in the ubiquitous environments.

1 Introduction

The QoS-aware applications such as e-business, audio/video streaming, world wide web, and health care system are becoming ubiquitous. Users can instantiate and access these applications anytime, anywhere and use any computing devices.

* This work was supported by the National Science Foundation under contract number 9870736, the Air Force Grant under contract number F30602-97-2-0121, NSF CISE Infrastructure grant under contract numbers NSF EIA 99-72884EQ and NSF CCR-9988199, and NASA grant under contract number NASA NAG 2-1250.

In the past decade, several QoS-oriented middleware services dealing with system resource management [1,2,3], different types of adaptations [4,5], or different types of communications [6,7,8], have been proposed to assist in QoS provision for different applications. Assuming the availability of these QoS-oriented middleware services in different ubiquitous computing environments, the challenging question is: *"How to develop a QoS-aware application which can be deployed flexibly and efficiently in different environments, with different available middleware services, and satisfy acceptable quality of service(QoS)?"*

Developing a QoS-aware application like this is not straight forward due to the following limitations. First, available middleware services are platform-specific, and implemented in different languages, with specific semantics and expected parameters. Second, they are designed only to run for specific classes of applications (e.g., multimedia), or to handle particular aspects of QoS provisions (e.g., real-time streaming, real-time messaging, reliable messaging, adaptability, security), with different levels of QoS provisions (e.g, hard, soft, best effort).

Due to these limitations, the problems of developing and deploying such a QoS-aware application are: (1) the application developer can only *statically* decide and deploy a specific configuration of middleware implementations; (2) the application developer needs to well understand characteristics of each selected underlying middleware implementation, and knows how to appropriately map application QoS requirements into its specific semantics, and expected parameters; and (3) the QoS-aware application is bound to deployment environment where the selected middleware implementation exists, for which the application was developed.

Our approach to the problems is to investigate an *application to middleware service translation system* which will map and bind application service components in a component-based application to appropriate middleware services in a configurable and portable fashion. We introduce *middleware abstraction layer (MAL)* between application view of middleware and the specific middleware implementations. MAL abstracts from individual middleware implementations, and represents a high-level functional view to the application. The translation system performs the mappings between application and middleware services in three main steps (see Fig. 1): (1) mapping of application service components to configurations of generic middleware services (e.g. CPU scheduling service), resulting in MAL representation; (2) mapping of each configuration of generic middleware services in MAL representation to possible configurations of specific middleware implementations (e.g., DSRT [2] for CPU scheduling service) available in specific deployment environment; and (3) mapping of application service components' quantitative QoS parameters (e.g., frame rate, frame size) to specific semantics, and expected parameters of specific middleware implementation (e.g., expected cycle time, and computation time of DSRT). The application to middleware service translation system is a core subsystem of our overall QoS compilation framework (Q-Compiler)[9].

The rest of the paper is organized as follows. In Sect. 2, we give the overview of our QoS compilation system (Q-Compiler) to place in context the application

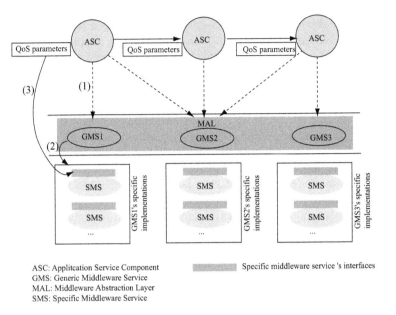

ASC: Applitcation Service Component
GMS: Generic Middleware Service
MAL: Middleware Abstraction Layer
SMS: Specific Middleware Service

Specific middleware service 's interfaces

Fig. 1. Mapping Steps in Application to Middleware Service Translation System

to middleware service translation system. In Sect. 3, we present the architecture of the application to middleware service translation, its main entities which enable the flexible and efficient deployment of QoS-aware application in different deployment environments. In Sect. 4, we discuss the related work. Finally, we draw conclusions in Sect. 5.

2   Q-Compiler Overview

Q-Compiler is a meta-level compilation system, which takes QoS specifications of a distributed component-based QoS-aware application as input. Then, assisted by a run-time middleware such as $2K^{Q1}$, it translates QoS specifications in multiple phases into end-to-end system/resource configurations. We will briefly discuss the QoS specifications as well as individual compilation phases to provide sufficient background information for discussing our application-to-middleware service translation.

2.1   QoS Specifications

QoS specifications (Fig. 2) are the *"source code"* of the Q-Compiler. An application developer implements a QoS-aware application by customizing these

---

[1] Run-time $2K^Q$ middleware [9] comprises of a group of QoS-related management services forming the execution environment for instantiating and managing a distributed component-based QoS-aware application.

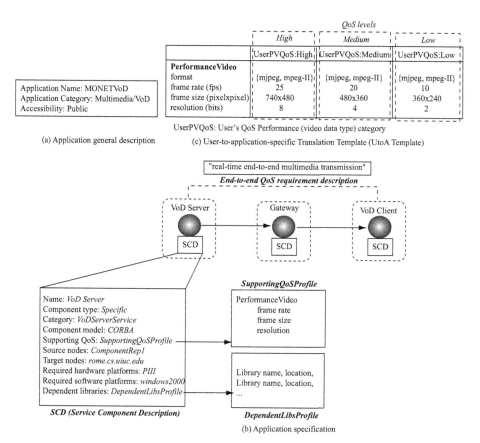

(a) Application general description

(c) User-to-application-specific Translation Template (UtoA Template)

(b) Application specification

Fig. 2. QoS Specifications for a Video-on-Demand Application (Example)

specifications. QoS specifications include: (a) *application general description*, (b) *application specification*, and (c) *user-to-application-specific translation template (UtoA template)*.

Application general description allows the application developer to specify the general information about the application, such as application name, application category, and its accessibility.

Application specification includes the *application functional dependency graph*, which is labeled with an *end-to-end QoS-requirement description*, and composes of different *application service components (ASCs)*. The functional dependency graph allows the application developer to express an application via the composition of specific, generic, or composite application service components, flexibly. The graph is *fully-defined* if all its application service components are specific. Otherwise, it is *partially-defined*. The *end-to-end QoS-requirement description* allows the application developer to label the application functional dependency graph or sub-graphs with different specific *end-to-end qualitative* QoS requirements. Each *application service component* is associated with a *service component description* which allows the application developer to specify detailed component information (e.g., name, hardware/system software requirements, resource requirements). Each service component description is associated with the *supporting QoS profile*, and the *dependent libraries profile*. The supporting QoS profile consists of QoS categories and their *quantitative* QoS dimensions the application service component supports. The dependent libraries profile consists of a list of application service component's dependent libraries, and their locations or pointers to their locations.

User-to-application-specific translation template (UtoA template) defines the mapping between different user QoS levels and corresponding application specific QoS categories and their dimensions[2].

2.2   Q-Compiler Model

Q-Compiler (see Fig. 3) consists of three phases: (Phase I) *symbolic configuration translation*; (Phase II) *application to middleware service translation*; and (Phase III) *distributed multi-resource translation*.

(Phase I) takes QoS specifications and compiles the partially-defined application functional dependency graph into **symbolic QoS configurations** where each configuration is a fully-defined functional graph of application components with consistent end-to-end QoS. This phase, modeled as a constraint satisfaction problem [11], generates possible delivery forms for the application to be executable in ubiquitous environments. (Phase II) consists of two sub phases: (Phase II.a) compiles symbolic QoS configurations into **MAL representation**. MAL representation represents the associations between each symbolic QoS configuration and possible configurations of generic middleware services. (Phase II.b) compiles each association in MAL representation into **application-middleware association**, representing associations between each symbolic QoS configuration and possible specific middleware implementations available in the deployment environment. (Phase III) maps each association in the application-middleware association into distributed multi-resources requirements representing a **system QoS configuration**.

Phase I and Phase II.a are *environment-independent* because they perform translations logically without concerning about physical environment constraints. Phase II.b and Phase III are *environment-dependent* because they perform translations corresponding to physically available middleware implementations in specific deployment environment. The environment-independent translations help developing a generic, portable QoS-aware application. The environment-depend-

---

[2] *QoS category* and *QoS dimension* are part of *QoS specifications* to characterize nonfunctional properties of an application. A *QoS dimension* defines a qualitative or quantitative attribute for a *QoS category* [10]. For example, QoS dimensions "format", "frame rate", "frame size" and "resolution" are attributes of QoS category "PerformanceVideo". Note that in our compilation framework, we limit a QoS dimension to a *quantitative* attribute.

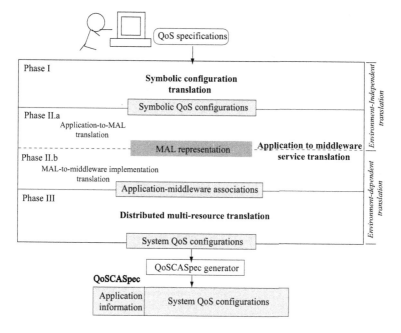

Fig. 3. Q-Compiler Model

ent translations help customizing the QoS-aware application with specific deployment environment.

The compiled result of the Q-Compiler, in a specific deployment environment, is *QoS-aware Component-based Application Specification (QoSCASpec)*. QoSCASpec includes (1) application description, and (2) a set of system QoS configurations. QoSCASpec is QoS-enabled meta information which can be utilized flexibly by a run-time middleware such as $2K^Q$, during the application instantiation, and adaptation (reconfiguration) in a specific deployment environment. As discussed in Sect. 1, in this paper, we mainly focus on the mapping problems in the Q-Compiler Phase II.

3   Application to Middleware Service Translation

Application-to-middleware service translation deals with the following problems: (1) "how to develop a QoS-aware application which is independent from specific deployment environment and specific middleware implementations?", (2) "how to flexibly and efficiently deploy this QoS-aware application into different environments with different available specific middleware implementations and satisfy acceptable quality of service (QoS)?" To solve these problems we present the architecture of the application-to-middleware service translation (see Fig. 4), which consists of two main processes: (1) *application-to-MAL translation*, and (2) *MAL-to-middleware implementation translation*. We describe these two processes in details, in the following section.

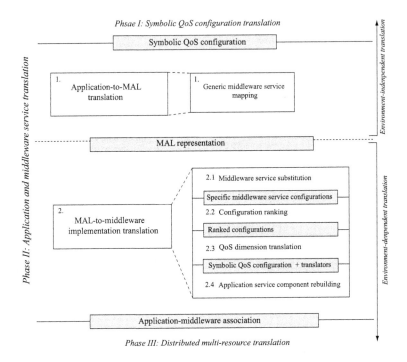

Fig. 4. Application to Middleware Service Translation Architecture

3.1 Application-to-MAL Translation

Application-to-MAL translation, corresponding to mapping (1) in Fig. 1, helps an application developer to associate a QoS-aware application with generic middleware services, independent of specific deployment environment and specific middleware implementations. The core of the application-to-MAL translation is the labeling decision engine. The *Labeling decision engine* is based on *mapping rules*, as shown in Fig. 5. The mapping rules are pre-defined and relate end-to-end QoS requirements to generic middleware services. QoS requirements are predicates, and operations are suggestions of possible configuration(s) of generic middleware services, their placements, and their association to application service components in the symbolic QoS configuration.

The result of application-to-MAL translation is MAL representation, as shown in Fig. 6, for the Video-on-Demand (VoD) application (shown in Fig. 2). MAL representation consists of (i) symbolic QoS configurations and their associations with generic middleware services[3], (ii) application service components' descriptions, and (iii) ranking policies.

---

[3] In our current system, we classify the available middleware implementations into categories (e.g., CPU scheduling service, bandwidth broker service, fuzzy-control

> if subgraph is labeled with "real-time end-to-end multimedia
> transmission"
>   then (1) all application service components in the subgraph need
>   local CPU broker service;
>   (2) all application service components dealing with transmission
>   among distributed machines need bandwidth broker service.
> ...

Fig. 5. Generic Middleware Service Mapping Rules

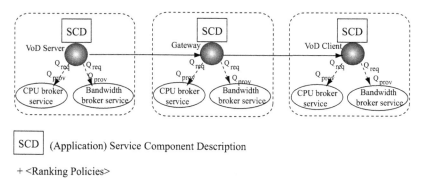

SCD   (Application) Service Component Description

+ <Ranking Policies>

Fig. 6. MAL representation for VoD's Symbolic QoS Configuration (Example)

3.2   MAL-to-Middleware Implementation Translation

MAL-to-middleware implementation translation helps an application developer to customize and deploy a QoS-aware application, represented as MAL presentation, into different deployment environments, flexibly and efficiently. The translation is based on the following steps. **Middleware Service Substitution**, corresponding to mapping (2) in Fig. 1, determines all possible configurations of specific middleware implementations[4], in the considered deployment environment, for each generic middleware service configuration in MAL representation. The substitution process is modeled as a constraint satisfaction problem[11], described as follows. Considering MAL representation in Fig. 6, each generic middleware service is considered as a symbolic variable. Each variable will be substituted by a set of specific middleware implementations satisfying specific requirements (e.g., hardware/system software requirements). An edge between an application service component and a generic middleware service in the graph represents the compatibility constraint between their QoS requirements (Q_{req}) and QoS provisions (Q_{prov}). Q_{req} is the vector of application-specific QoS categories and their dimensions. Q_{prov} is the vector of service quality that the

---

  adaptation-based middleware service, real-time messaging service) corresponding to
  their functionality. The generic middleware service represents a specific category of
  the implementations.
[4] We assume that a specific middleware implementation advertises itself with detailed
  descriptions, in a directory service, available in specific deployment environment.

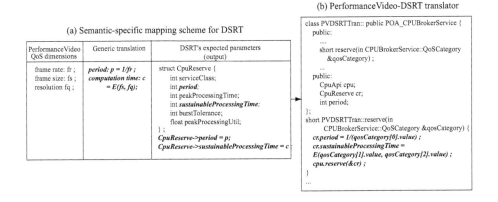

Fig. 7. Semantic-Specific Mapping Scheme for DSRT and PerformanceVideo-to-DSRT Translator

specific middleware implementation can provide. Q_{req} and Q_{prov} are compatible if Q_{prov} satisfies Q_{req}. Note that the satisfiability check needs the translation between Q_{req}'s and Q_{prov}'s semantics. This translation deploys a semantic-specific mapping scheme, as shown in Figure 7.(a).

Configuration Ranking ranks among specific configurations for each generic middleware service configuration. The ranking algorithm weights each specific middleware implementation[5] in a configuration using constraints[5] such as its requirement of system resources (e.g., memory footprint, CPU processing time), its supporting levels of QoS provisions (e.g., soft, hard, best effort), and its instantiation overhead (e.g., dynamic downloading) if unavailable in a specific location. Note that we can vary weights among constraints, corresponding to different major concerns, and generate multiple ranked specific configurations for each generic middleware service configuration.

QoS Dimension Translation, corresponding to mapping (3) in Fig. 1, bridges the gap between application-specific *quantitative QoS requirements* (specified via QoS category and its dimensions), and a specific middleware implementation's semantics, and expected parameters. QoS dimension translation determines a proper translator for each pair of application-specific QoS dimensions and specific middleware implementation. A proper translator can be built by a tool of the Q-Compiler, or manually built by an application developer. A specific translator (see Fig. 7.(b)) wraps up a specific middleware implementation's interfaces with a *semantic-specific translation scheme* (see Fig. 7.(a)). A semantic-specific mapping scheme represents an analytical translation or a mapping from application-specific QoS dimensions into specific middleware implementation's semantics and expected parameters.

---

[5] We assume that these information can be queried from the directory service available in the deployment environment.

Application Service Component Rebuilding process helps instrumenting and rebuilding application service component's code with specific translator's interfaces. The rebuilding process performs only if the application service component's rebuilt version with the instrumented translators' interfaces is unavailable in the *Rebuilt Application Service Component Repository*[6]. This repository helps to reduce the overhead in the code instrumentation, and rebuilding processes.

The results of the MAL-to-middleware implementation translation are *application-middleware associations* which will be passed to the third phase of the Q-Compiler for distributed resource translation. The application-middleware associations with their resource requirements compose *system QoS configurations* and are represented as the *QoS-aware Component-based Application Specification (QoSCASpec)*. During the application instantiation and execution, the underlying run-time middleware such as $2K^Q$, will select the best system QoS configuration from the application's QoSCASpec, for application setup and adaptation (reconfiguration), corresponding to the current deployment environment, and resource availability.

4   Related Work

Besides the related work in the area of QoS-oriented middleware services discussed in Sect. 1, MAL representation, introduced in this paper, shares the same ideas as of the EJB's deployment descriptor [12], and CCM's descriptors [13](e.g, CORBA software, CORBA component, and component assembly descriptors), and shares the similar idea as of COM+'s attributed-based or declarative programming [14]. In the area of QoS mapping and QoS translation, QoS translations, based on analytical functions, are proposed. For example, in our group, in [15] Nahrstedt et al. propose a translation from a multimedia application's QoS parameters into transport subsystem's QoS parameters, in [16] Kim et al. propose a translation from MPEG video parameters into CPU requirements, and in [3], Viswanathan proposes the analytical translations from MPEG video parameters into CPU requirements required by the transportation task for video transmission, and into network bandwidth requirements. In [17], Dasilva presents a framework for predicting end-to-end QoS at the application layer based on mapping of QoS guarantees across layers in the protocol stack. Our translation system utilizes some of these translations as semantic-specific mapping schemes.

5   Conclusion

Emerging ubiquitous QoS-aware applications call for a new developing tool which can help an application developer to develop a QoS-aware application which can be deployed efficiently and flexibly in the ubiquitous environments with the satisfactory QoS. Assuming the availability of QoS-oriented middleware services,

---

[6] *Rebuilt Application Service Component Repository* collects the version(s) of the application service components built with specific translators.

in this paper, we present a translation system between the application and middleware services as an enabling tool. Key features of our translation system are: (1) helping an application developer to develop a component-based QoS-aware application with the broader aspects (e.g., real-time, reliability, availability, security, or their combination) of service quality; and (2) dealing mainly with the configurability of different generic middleware services and their specific implementations, which can provide the service quality according to the qualitative and quantitative QoS requirements for the application in different ubiquitous environments. We believe that the availability of the architecture like our translation system will facilitate the rapid growth of QoS-aware applications in ubiquitous environments.

We are prototyping the application-to-middleware service translation, as the enhancement of the implemented Q-Compiler, described in [9]. Experimental preliminary results of the Q-Compiler and the run-time $2K^Q$ middleware can be found in [9]. We plan to evaluate the effectiveness of this approach, as part of the active space project [18].

References

1. R. Rajkumar, C. Lee, J. Lehoczky, and D. Siewiorek. A resource allocation model for qos management. *In Proceedings of the IEEE Real-Time Systems Symposium*, pages 298–307, December 1997.
2. H. Chu and K. Nahrstedt. Cpu service classes for multimedia applications. *In Proceedings IEEE International Conference on Multimedia Computing and Systems*, pages 296–301, June 1999.
3. A. K. Viswanathan. *Design and Evaluation of a CPU-aware Communication Broker for RSVP-based Networks*. Master thesis, University of Illinois at Urbana-Champaign, Department of Computer Science, 2000.
4. B. Li and K. Nahrstedt. A control-based middleware framework for quality of service adaptations. *IEEE Journal of Selected Areas in Communications, Special Issue on Service Enabling Platforms*, 17(9):1632–1650, September 1999.
5. R. Vanegas, J.A. Zinky, J.P. Loyall, D.A. Karr, R.E. Schantz, and D.E. Bakken. Quo's runtime support for quality of service in distributed objects. *In Proc. of IFIP International Conference on Distributed Systems Platforms and Open Distributed Processing (Middleware 1998)*, pages 207–222, September 1998.
6. D. Schmidt, D.Levine, and C. Cleeland. *Advances in Computers, Marvin Zelkowitz (editor)*, chapter Architectures and Patterns for High-performance, Real-time ORB Endsystems. Academic Press, 1999.
7. Object Management Group Inc. Corba 2.5 - chapter 22 - corba messaging. *online documentation at http://www.omg.org/cgi-bin/doc?formal/01-09-26*, September 2001.
8. Object Management Group Inc. Corba 2.5 - chapter 24 - real-time corba. *online documentation at http://www.omg.org/cgi-bin/doc?formal/01-09-28*, September 2001.
9. D. Wichadakul, K. Nahrstedt, X. Gu, and D. Xu. 2kq+: An integrated approach of qos compilation and component-based, run-time middleware for the unified qos management framework. *In Proc. of IFIP/ACM International Conference on Distributed Systems Platforms*, November 2001.

10. S. Frolund and J. Koistinen. Quality of service specification in distributed object systems design. *In Proceedings of the Fourth USENIX Conference on Object-Oriented Technologies and Systems*, pages 1–18, 1998.
11. E. Tsang. *Foundations of Constraint Satisfaction*, chapter Introduction. Academic Press, 1993.
12. Sun Microsystems. Enterprise javabeans tm specification, version 2.0. *online documentation at http://java.sun.com/Download5*, August 2001.
13. Object Management Group Inc. Corba 3.0 new components chapters. *online documentation at ftp://ftp.omg.org/pub/docs/ptc/01-11-03.pdf*, November 2001.
14. Mary Kirtland. The com+ programming model makes it easy to write components in any language. *Microsoft System Journals, online documentation at http://www.microsoft.com/com/wpaper/default.asp*, December 1997.
15. K. Nahrstedt and J. Smith. Design, implementation and experiences with the omega end-point architecture. *IEEE Journal on Selected Areas in Communication*, 14(7):1263–1279, September 1996.
16. K. Kim and K. Nahrstedt. *Building QoS into Distributed Systems, Andrew Campbell, Klara Nahrstedt (editors)*, chapter QoS Translation and Admission Control for MPEG Video, pages 359–362. Chapman and Hall, November 1997.
17. L. A. DaSilva. Qos mapping along the protocol stack: Discussion and preliminary results. *In Proceedings of IEEE International Conference on Communications*, pages 713–717, June 2000.
18. Manuel Romn, Christopher K. Hess, Anand Ranganathan, Pradeep Madhavarapu, Bhaskar Borthakur, Prashant Viswanathan, Renato Cerqueira, Roy H. Campbell, and M. Dennis Mickunas. Gaiaos: An infrastructure for active spaces. *Technical Report UIUCDCS-R-2001-2224 UILU-ENG-2001-1731, Universiy of Illinois at Urbana-Champaign.*

An Infrastructure
for CORBA Component Replication[*]

Vania Marangozova and Daniel Hagimont

SARDES Project, INRIA Rhône-Alpes ZIRST,
655 av. de l'Europe, Montbonnot 38334 St Ismier cedex, France,
Vania.Marangozova@inria.fr,Daniel.Hagimont@inria.fr

Abstract. Traditionally applied to availability problems in various distributed computing domains (caching, fault-tolerance, disconnections), replication solutions remain difficult to implement and challenging to reuse. In this paper we propose a component-oriented approach in which replication is treated as a part of the configuration/reconfiguration aspect of an application. The approach allows an easy reuse of replication solutions and their integration through adaptation in existing distributed component-based services. We apply the approach to an implementation of the CORBA component model: OpenCCM.

1   Introduction

Traditionally applied to availability and performance problems in the areas of fault tolerance, caching and disconnection management, replication gains considerable importance with recent developments in global and mobile computing. However, the emerging highly-dynamic environments ask for new replication solutions. The problems of rapid and easy conception, reuse and adaptation of existing replication solutions are more topical than ever.

Due to their lack of generality, current replication solutions do not respond to the needs of reuse and adaptation. In fact, they apply to specific computing domains (databases, web management, etc.) and depend strongly on the underlying system architecture. As a result, even if identical replication principles apply to different contexts, replication solutions' reuse remains a real challenge.

Component-based architectures are a promising approach in the quest of a generic replication environment. In fact, replication solutions' domain-specificity limitation can be dealt with using the component encapsulation principle. Furthermore, the need of reuse and adaptation of replication solutions integrates well in the logic of the fundamental software(component) reuse principle.

In this article we investigate on an adequate infrastructure support for replication integration in component-based systems. We describe a deployment/reconfiguration approach to replication and show the facility with which different protocols can be attached to components without modifying their core business

---

[*] This research is partially funded by the RNTL project ARCAD.

J. Bishop (Ed.): CD 2002, LNCS 2370, pp. 222–232, 2002.

code. Our work is based on the OpenCCM [11] platform: an implementation of the CORBA Component Model (CCM) [12].

The article is organized as follows. Section 2 details replication issues in component-based systems. Section 3 describes the used OpenCCM platform. Our infrastructure for replication configuration, as well as its application to two replication scenarios, is presented in Section 4. Sections 5, 6 and 7 discuss respectively the lessons learned, related work and future perspectives.

2   Replication in Component Systems

Contrary to the object-based platforms centered on distributed application development, the component paradigm considers the entire application life cycle. Paying a particular attention to applications' administration, the paradigm promotes the separation between the components' business logic implementations and the system services they use. In component-based middleware like Enterprise Java Beans [14], this principle is reified by *container* servers hosting component instances and managing component-associated system services in a separate way. Components are thus reused, without modifications of their business code, in the context of different applications with different system management requirements.

A component-based replication infrastructure, aiming at component reuse in different replication contexts as well as at replication solution reuse in different application contexts, should provide adequate solutions to two major points. The first point concerns the choice and the mechanisms for creating and placing copies on different network nodes (*replication*) while the second considers the relations established between these copies (*consistency*).

Replication configuration should be a main characteristic of a flexible replication management solution. It should be possible to configure the set of replicable entities (*what*), to define the most appropriate moment for replication (*when*) and to control optimal copy placement (*where*). This is a rather ambitious objective given that standard distributed systems use either no replication (remote procedure calls) or fixed replication schemes with predefined and systematically used replicated entities. Java RMI [15] or the new CORBA3 standard do allow the co-existence of replicable and remotely accessible objects but do not allow the switch between the two without functional code modification. A *non intrusive* replication management in a component-based system should prevent functional modifications and allow for a future integration of the corresponding treatments in a container. Replication will thus be naturally considered as a part of the component's configuration and administration.

Consistency configuration and adaptation is a major objective for a target infrastructure intended to allow reuse of components with different replication scenarios. This conclusion has emerged after a considerable research on consistency showing the inexistence of a universal protocol [2], the insufficiency of application specific solutions [3] and the encouraging results on consistency adaptation [13]. Consistency should be therefore managed in the same way as replication: it should be part of the component's configuration and administration.

Before describing the principles of our infrastructure for flexible component replication, we present the platform used for our work: OpenCCM.

3   The OpenCCM Platform

In order to address deployment and administration issues in distributed applications' life cycles, the CORBA standard proposes the CORBA Component Model (CCM) [12]. The model defines a server side component framework integrating component interface specification, component implementation, application deployment and execution. Implemented at the University of Lille I, OpenCCM [11] is an available open source, Java-based, CORBA-compliant, partial implementation of CCM.

3.1   OpenCCM Components

OpenCCM component types are explicitly declared in terms of components' used and provided interfaces (*ports*). Fig.1 gives the IDL declaration for an agenda application in which users can connect to an agenda server and register, edit or remove rendezvous from their plannings. The corresponding `ManageReservations` interface is *provided* by the `Server` component and *used* by the `Client` component.

OpenCCM component instances, as well as their corresponding ports, are represented by standard CORBA objects that we call respectively component objects and port objects. A component object references the corresponding component implementation and all component's ports objects. This structure is the basis of the OpenCCM introspection facilities. During deployment, introspection is used to acquire port references and to establish component interconnections. At runtime, introspection allows to explore these interconnections and to access the corresponding port references needed for component method invocations.

```
struct Reservation{...};     typedef sequence<Reservation> listReservations;

interface ManageReservations {                     //Business interface
    void addReservation(in Reservation res);
    void RemoveReservation(in string resId);
    listReservations getReservations();

component Client {                                 //The client component
    uses ManageReservations to_S;}                 //Used interface

component Server {                                 //The server component
    attribute name;                               //Configuration attribute
    provides ManageReservations for_C;}            //Provided interface
```

Fig. 1. A component description of a simple application

3.2   OpenCCM Containers

OpenCCM does not implement a separate container entity but integrates container functions in component implementations using specialization of the component generation process. The component inheritance tree is actually enriched in order to include specific OpenCCM classes defining introspection and port interconnection operations. The resulting component implements a standard CORBA IDL interface (obtained through a mapping from the initial description) containing both the business interfaces and the additional introspection and port management interfaces. In the case of the agenda example, the mapping produces the `Client` and `Server` interfaces shown in Fig.2.

The predefined `CCMObject` interface is responsible for providing all generic introspection operations. The `Client`'s get_connection_to_server and the `Server`'s provide_for_clients methods are introspection operations returning the references to the respective `ManageReservations` ports (corresponding to the used and provided interfaces). A `Client` instance uses the obtained reference to invoke a `Server` component. The other operations are used for connection management and are discussed in the next section.

```
interface Client : CCMObject { ...Fig.1. business code     //Component Client
    void connect_to_S(in ManageReservations cnctn);        //Port management
    ManageReservations disconnect_to_S();                  //Port management
    ManageReservations get_connection_to_S();}             //Introspection

interface Server : CCMObject {...Fig.1. business code      //Component Server
    ManageReservations provide_for_C(); }                  //Introspection
```

Fig. 2. Component-oriented standard IDL description of the agenda

3.3   OpenCCM Deployment

OpenCCM deployment is done by a deployment program which includes statements for component archives installation, for component instance creation, for component configuration and interconnection, and for application launching. Component interconnection is done using the port management interface. In the case of our agenda application, the `Client`'s port management interface contains the connect_to_server and disconnect_to_server operations through which the client is connected and disconnected to the server (Fig.2).

OpenCCM defines a basic deployment environment manipulated through a simple API. The way it is used in a schematic deployment program for our agenda application is given in Fig.3. The basic steps include the choice of the deployment hosts (1), the installation of components' implementations (2), the creation of component instances (3), their configuration (4), the component interconnection (5) and finally, the application launching (6).

```
//(1) Obtain the deployment servers
// ns is the CORBA's NamingService
ComponnentServer cs1 = ns.resolve("CS1");

//(2) Install component archives
//inst is the cs1's installation factory
inst.install("agenda","agenda.jar");

//(3) Create components
//sh/ch are components' instance managers
Server s = sh.create();
Client c1 = ch.create();
```

```
//(4) Configure components
// s.name("Server");

//(5) Connect client and server
// Get ports using introspection
ManageReservations for_C=
        s.provide_for_C();

// Establish connection
c1.connect_to_S(for_C);

//(6) Launching
s.configuration_complete();
```

Fig. 3. OpenCCM deployment of the agenda

4   Replication Management in OpenCCM

We discuss the design choices for an adaptable replication management infrastructure in the first part of this section. In the second part we describe our experience in which we apply the proposed principles to two replication scenarios for the agenda application.

4.1   Principle

Non intrusive replication management (cf. section 2) requires mechanisms configuration of both the replication and consistency aspects.

We integrate **replication configuration** at the deployment level (Open-CCM's deployment programs). In fact, copy creation and placement spell well in terms of application architecture configuration which is itself defined during deployment. CCM deployment actually describes *what* and *where* components are to be deployed, how these components are to be connected and is meant (even if it is not the case yet) to specify architectural reconfigurations (*when*). The replication aspect adds the specification of the set of replicable components (*what*), the best copy placement (*where*), the consistency management (*how*) and the most appropriate moment for replication (*when*).

We base **consistency configuration** on interception objects, consistency links and component-specific state management. *Interception objects* allow to integrate consistency management without modification of the components' business code. They intercept copy invocations and trigger consistency actions. The latter take the form of pre and post treatments for the intercepted method calls which continue to be delegated to the initial component implementations.

Consistency protocols define consistency relations between copies and provide treatments to maintain these relations valid. Logically, these treatments require the existence of copy interconnections to propagate consistency actions. We call these connections *consistency links*.

Most consistency protocols access component internal data. In our prototype we preserve the component encapsulation principle but take advantage of a component-specific state management by leaving the state access primitives implementation to the component developer. Consistency protocols can thus use these primitives and ignore component implementation details.

The concrete interception objects' and consistency links' implementations depend on the specific consistency protocol chosen for a given application. The next section describes the way these entities are generated in order to provide replication-aware deployment in the OpenCCM platform.

4.2   Implementation

As discussed in the previous section, our component replication management is based on interception objects used to catch component invocations and to execute consistency treatments, on consistency links used to interconnect replicas and on component accessor functions used to manipulate internal data.

An **interception object** in our prototype is a component object implementing the same interfaces as the corresponding component but whose code contains the consistency protocol implementation. The functional code of a component is managed in a separate object and is referenced by the interception object for invocation propagation. Notice that this design is equivalent to the interposition object used to manage containers in the EJB component model.

The **consistency link implementation** requires that a consistency protocol expert (who is also responsible of the implementation of the consistency actions) define the nature of the interfaces between the component copies. The interfaces have to be IDL-described and are used to generate the final replicable component.

As mentioned in the previous section, the **component state manipulation** treatments are provided by a developer who is aware of the component's semantics. For Java components, we provide a default implementation based on Java Serialization.

Generation of replication management code i.e. the definition of the consistency link interfaces, the integration of the consistency protocol implementations and finally the adaptations to the applications deployment programs is currently done by hand. Tools for automation of the pretty systematic replicable component generation process are under development.

In Fig.4, both the component to be replicated and the consistency protocol to be applied are represented by their IDL definitions and their implementations. The consistency protocol's definition declares the consistency links interfaces involved in the component copies' coordination. The protocol implements these interfaces as well as the component's business interfaces in order to intercept the corresponding invocations. The resulting replicable component implements the interfaces and includes the implementations of both the initial component and the chosen consistency protocol.

The procedure for integrating a replication scenario in a given component-based application involves the following actions. First, a developer is to provide the **component business-logic implementations**. If a component is to be replicated, he will need to provide primitives for state capture and restoration. In order to integrate a **consistency protocol implementation**, a replication

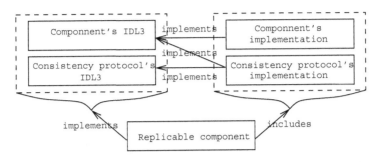

Fig. 4.

expert has to implement the corresponding protocol and to provide its IDL interfaces. The **generation of the replicable components** is based on the former actions: the component and consistency IDL definitions are merged and associated with the corresponding implementations to generate the resulting replicable component. Finally, the **replicated architecture deployment** may take place. Components and their copies, as well as component interconnections including the needed consistency links are explicitly created in the deployment program.

4.3   Experience

We have applied the above infrastructure principle to two replication scenarios for the agenda application. The first one implements a simple disconnection scenario while the second implements a caching system.

Disconnection protocol. In the agenda's disconnection scenario we keep the same component business implementations (The IDL descriptions are those of Fig.1 and Fig.3). We just make the `Server` component `Serializable` and benefit from a default state management procedure including the two primitives `State captureState()` and `void restoreState(State state)` granting access to the component's internal data (of type `State`).

The consistency protocol (Fig.5 shows the IDL definition) distinguishes between master and slave server copies (`role` attribute). A slave server is a disconnected copy of a master server. When a disconnection process is launched, the slave server is created on the machine getting disconnected and initialized with

```
component Server {                 interface DiscPtcl {
    attribute Role role;               void make_copy();
    provides DiscPtcl for_disc;        void reconcile();
    uses DiscPtcl to_disc; }           State get_state();
                                       void push_log(in Log log); }
```

Fig. 5.

```
public ServerImpl() {
  if (role.isMaster())
    realObj = new ServerActualImpl();
  else log = new SimpleLog(); }

public void
addReservation(Reservation res) {
  realObj.addReservation(res);
  if (role.isSlave()) log.put(res);}
```

```
public void reconcile() {
  to_disc.push_log(log)};

public State get_state() {
  return realObj.captureState();}

public void push_log(Log log) {
  realObj.restoreState(state);}

public void make_copy() {
  realObj = to_disc.get_state();}
```

Fig. 6.

```
//(1) Create components
srv = SFactHost2.create();
srv.role("Master");
clnt = CFactHost1.create();

//(2) Connect client and server
ManageReservations for_C =
srv.provide_for_C();
clnt.connect_to_S(for_C);

//(3) DISCONNECTION
//Create a copy
copy = SFactHost1.create();
copy.role("Slave");
```

```
//(4) Update copy before disconnection
copy.makeCopy();

//(5) Update connections
clnt.disconnect_to_S();
for_C= copy.provide_for_C();
clnt.connect_to_S(for_C);
DiscPrtcl = srv.provide_for_disc();
copy.connect_to_disc(for_disc);

//(6) RECONNECTION
copy.reconcile();
clnt.disconnect_to_S();
clnt.connect_to_S(srv.provide_for_C());
```

Fig. 7.

the state of the master. At reconnection, the possibly diverged slave and master states are reconciled. Reconciliation is based on a simple redo protocol using a log of disconnected operations.

The consistency protocol implementation is shown in Fig.6. The interception object holds a reference to the component's actual implementation and forwards invocations e.g. addReservation. If the current component is a slave copy, the interception treatment logs the operation for further reconciliation.

Fig.7 shows the deployment program for the disconnectable application architecture. After creation of the server and client components (1), they are interconnected (2). Upon disconnection (3), a slave server copy is created. Its internal state is synchronized (4) and the connections are updated (5) in order to connect the client to the created copy. Upon reconnection (6), the two copies of the agenda are reconciled and the client is reconnected to the master server.

Caching protocol. For the agenda's caching scenario we have implemented a version of the entry consistency protocol (multiple-readers/single-writer). Inspired by the Javanaise system [6], the protocol associates a locking policy (read/write) to each method of the agenda server and ensures the consistency of cached copies before forwarding an invocation.

The sites where caching should be applied are specified in the deployment program. A master site stores the persistent version of the server component and a client may address either the remote master copy or a local replica. The

```
//consistency link server to client          //consistency link client to server
interface Server2Client {                     interface Client2Server {
  State reduce_lock();                           State lock_read();
  void invalidate_reader();                       State lock_write();
  void State invalidate_writer();}               void State reduce_lock();
                                                void augment_lock();}
```

Fig. 8.

consistency links between replicas (Fig.8) use operations for fetching (in read or write mode) an up-to-date component copy and for copy invalidation.

5 Lessons Learned

We have shown that it is possible to manage replication as an adaptable non functional property in a component-based system. Furthermore, we have identified deployment configuration and component interface implementation as the two conceptual places for non functional replication integration. Deployment is used for replication scheme definition in applications' architecture configuration. Interface interception is used for consistency management and is to be part of an adaptable container architecture (a major EJB as well as CCM research issue).

We believe that, in addition to the explicit deployment phase, introspection and port management are OpenCCM's most interesting features for non functional replication management. The explicit reference manipulation helps reference integrity preservation upon reconfiguration. At the moment of writing, EJB does not provide a similar functionality.

6 Related Work

Configurable replication is a major issue in works on distributed shared memory providing multiple consistency protocols [2] or in mobile databases projects introducing optimistic consistency and application-specific reconciliation[5]. CORBA-centered research is also very present with works on flexible caching. The CASCADE [4] project for example is based on the CORBA interceptor mechanism while Flex [10] uses object subclassing and object-personalized state capture. The cited projects do certainly consider replication configuration and in some solutions are rather close to the mechanisms used in our experiment. However, they remain domain-specific while our work aims at overcoming this limitation and reconciles issues coming from different domains.

Adaptation in general is a major objective in language platforms interested in easy source code modification [9], in frameworks considering middleware architectures [1,7] and in operating system reconfiguration projects [8]. However, the existing works do not address the most difficult issue in replication adaptation: the analysis of the way replication can be defined as a separate aspect and the appropriate application of adaptation mechanisms.

Adaptation in component-based middleware is a very recent issue and existing adaptation efforts typically focus on non functional management of well specified properties like transactions, security and persistence but not replication. The presented work is one of the rare efforts on replication adaptation. In fact, most works treating replication in a component-based environment are EJB-oriented and apply fixed replication solutions based on replication of the underlying relational databases. In our knowledge, this is the first experiment with (non-functional) replication adaptation in the CORBA component model.

7   Conclusion and Future Work

We have investigated the integration of replication management in a component-based platform. We have proposed and implemented an infrastructure allowing to configure replication aspects in a non functional way. We have successfully integrated the proposed principles in the first Java-based implementation of the CORBA component model, OpenCCM, by preserving its CORBA compliancy. Our design is based on interception objects (to be comprised in the future OpenCCM's adaptable containers) and on deployment configuration extended to include replication policy description. We have defined the procedures for using this infrastructure and have shown its application in two scenario cases: a caching entry consistency system and a simple disconnection management.

An immediate perspective of this work is to provide the tools for automatic generation of the replicable components. Even if we have described the procedure, most of the replication integration work is done manually and can be automated. A tool for deployment program transformation (in order to integrate a specified replication policy) could also be provided.

Another interesting perspective of this work is the investigation of the way this infrastructure can be applied to other component models. Candidates are notably Microsoft's COM and EJB but also more abstract models like the standard ODP.

Finally, replication is only one system aspect and CCM one particular component model. The work presented in this paper takes part in a broader project aiming at the implementation of a generic and reflexive component-based middleware allowing encapsulation of different component types (EJB, CCM ...) and adaptation for transparent integration of non-functional system aspects (persistence, security, replication ...).

References

1. G. Blair, G. Coulson, P. Robin et M. Papathomas, An architecture for next generation middleware. In Proc. of Middleware'98. 191-206, Sept. 1998.
2. J.Carter. Design of the Munin Distributed Shared Memory System. Journal of Parallel and Distributed Computing, 29(2):219-27, 1995.
3. P. Dechamboux, D. Hagimont, J. Mossiere, and X. R. de Pina. The Arias Distributed Shared Memory: an Overview. In 23rd Intl Winter School on Current Trends in Theory and Practice of Informatics, LNCS 1175, 1996

4. G. Chockler, D. Dolev, R. Friedman, and R. Vitenberg. Implementing a Caching Service for Distributed CORBA Objects. In Proc. of Middleware'00,1-23, April 2000.
5. A. Demers, K. Petersen, M. Spreitzer, D. Terry, M. Theimer, and B. Welch. The Bayou Architecture: Support for Data Sharing Among Mobile Users. In Proc. of the IEEE Workshop on Mobile Computing Systems and Applications, 2-7, Dec. 1994.
6. D. Hagimont, F. Boyer. A Configurable RMI Mechanism for Sharing Distributed Java Objects. IEEE Internet Computing, 5(1): 36-44, Jan.-Feb. 2001
7. R. Hayton, A. Herbert, et D. Donaldson. Flexinet: a flexible, component oriented middleware System. SIGOPS'98, Portugal, Sept. 1998
8. J. Helander and A. Forin, MMLite: A Highly Componentized System Architecture. Eight ACM SIGOPS European Workshop, Portugal, Sept. 1998.
9. G. Kiczales, E. Hilsdale, J. Hugonin, M. Kersten, J. Palm, and W. G. Griswold. An Overview of AspectJ. In J. L. Knudsen, editor, ECOOP 2001, Object-Oriented Programming, LNCS 2072. Springer-Verlag, June 2001.
10. R. Kordale and M. Ahamad. Object caching in a CORBA compliant system. USENIX Computing Systems, 9(4):377-404, Fall 1996.
11. R. Marvie, P. Merle, J-M. Geib, M. Vadet, OpenCCM : une plate-forme ouverte pour composants CORBA, CFSE'2, France, April 2001.
12. Object Management Group. CORBA Components: Joint Revised Submission. Aug. 1999. OMG TC Document ptc/01-10-26 (Components FTF interim report)
13. M. van Steen, P. Homburg, and A.S. Tanenbaum. Globe: A Wide-Area Distributed System. IEEE Concurrency, Jan.-March, 1999
14. Sun Microsystems. Enterprise Java Beans Specification Version: 2.0. 2000.
15. Sun Microsystems. Java Remote Method Invocation Specification. 1998.

Architectures of Enterprise Systems: Modelling Transactional Contexts

Iman Poernomo[1], Ralf Reussner[1], and Heinz Schmidt[2]

[1] DSTC Pty Ltd, Monash University, Caulfield East, Victoria, Australia 3145,
{imanp,reussner}@dstc.com
[2] School of Computer Science and Software Engineering, Monash University,
Caulfield East, Victoria, Australia 3145,
hws@csse.monash.edu.au

Abstract. Software architectural description languages (ADLs) are used to specify a high-level, compositional view of a software application, defining how a system is to be composed from coarse-grain components. ADLs usually come equipped with a rigourous state-transition style semantics, enabling formal understanding of distributed and event-based systems [6]. However, additional expressive power is required for the description and understanding of enterprise-scale software architectures – in particular, those built upon newer middleware, such as implementations of Java's EJB specification [2] or Microsoft's COM+/.NET [8]. Such middleware provides additional functionality to a configuration of components, by means of a context-based interception model [12]. We explore an ADL that can define architectures built upon such middleware. In this paper, we focus on modelling transactional architectures built on COM+ middleware.

1 Introduction

Over the past decade, middleware has undergone considerable evolution to meet the needs of the enterprise. The enterprise requires software solutions which are business-oriented, mission-critical, maintainable, flexible and distributed. It is now common to deliver such solutions by utilizing a component-based middleware, such as Java's EJB specification [2] or Microsoft's COM+/.NET [8]. A key feature of such middleware is the provision of infrastructure to support integration of cross-component functionality at the configuration level. For example, the COM+ architect may specify security or transactional settings over groups of interoperating components through Component Services. Such specification results in the addition of pre-programmed functionality to components, enabling the developer to focus on business-oriented design and programming.

In COM+, this kind of cross-component functionality is provided through context-based model of call interception. Here, deployed components are conceived as residing within a context that potentially intercepts and manipulates each call that crosses the context boundary. The advantage of this approach is that the middleware provides the ability for contexts to manage the interaction

J. Bishop (Ed.): CD 2002, LNCS 2370, pp. 233–243, 2002.
© Springer-Verlag Berlin Heidelberg 2002

between components, without the need for the programmer to write management code. In EJB implementations, a similar result is achieved through the container-server model. The ubiquity of this kind of computation has resulted in the need for the enterprise system architect to design systems that involve both components and contexts. In this paper, we outline an approach to modelling architectures that use contexts. Here, we consider software architecture to be a compositional view of how coarse-grain system elements (such as COM+ components and contexts) are assembled to form a piece of software. We extend architectural description language (ADL) approaches to meet our goal [6,5].

We focus on transactional contexts. These contexts add transactional functionality to components, without the need for the programmer to write transactional code. Transactional contexts make the job of the programmer easier, eliminating the need to write management code. However, without the use of a formal architectural approach to contexts, the architect runs the risk of error. Currently, many designers use an informal architectural style to define context-component relationships in a system. Our work is novel, as it presents the first formal architectural description language that includes such relationships in its system descriptions. While our approach focuses on modelling COM+ transactional contexts, a similar approach can be taken for EJB implementations.

Our approach is as follows. In Section 2, we define an architectural description language (ADL) for middleware-based architectures in terms of components and contexts. In Section 3, we give a semantics for our architectural descriptions, modelling component and transactional context use via finite state machines.

2   Architectural Description

The TrustME ADL is fully described in [9]. Like other ADLs, it provides a means of defining compositions of component-based systems [5,6]. In this paper, we outline the subset of TrustME relevant to describing transactional contexts for COM+ middleware-based architectures, the grammar of which is given in Fig. 1.

In modelling middleware-based systems, we decompose a system into hierarchies of contexts, each containing components, linked to each other by connections between their services:

- *Components* are self-contained, coarse-grain computational entities, potentially hierarchically composed from other components. Our ADL's components are intended to directly represent COM+ components of an implementation.
- *Services* represent an abstraction of the type of messages that may be sent between components. A service may be either provided or required by a component.
- *Contexts* are used to model transactional contexts of COM+ (and can be extended to model container/servers of EJB implmentations).

Components and services are analogous to components and interfaces in Darwin, to components and ports respectively in C2 and ACME, or to processes and ports

Grammar for component declarations, $ComDec$
    component $ComType$ $\{$
                     $(Comp : ComType)^*$
                     $(\mathbf{bind}(Comp.Service, Comp.Service))^*$
                     $\mathbf{map}(Comp.Service, Service)$
                     $\mathbf{provides} : (Service)^*$ $\mathbf{requires} : (Service)^*$ $\}$

Grammar for transactional context declarations, $ContextDec$
    context $ContextType$ $\{$
                     $((Context : ContextType)|(Comp : ComType))^*$
                     $\mathbf{bind}(Context|Comp.Service, Context|Comp.Service)$

Grammar for architectures
    architecture $\{$
                     $(ComDec|ContextDec)^*$
                     $((Context : ContextType)|(Comp : ComType))^*$
                     $\mathbf{bind}(Comp.Service, Comp.Service)^*$
                     $\mathbf{map}(Context|Comp.Service, Service)^*$ $\}$

Fig. 1. The grammar for components, contexts and architectures. $ComType$, $ContextType$ and $Service$ range over a sets of names.

in MetaH [5,6]. However, our ADL differs from these other languages, in that it enables representation of transactional contexts as first class entities. This for modelling middleware-based systems.

Our ADL is a typed, class-based metamodel: contexts and component types are defined via class declarations, and may be instantiated to be reused within other contexts, components or architecture definitions. To instantiate a component C of type T, we write $C : T$. We define the subcomponents of a component or context $C : T$ to consists of all components contained in the declaration of T, together with their subcomponents. We write $subcomponents_C$ for this set. The set of subcontexts $subcontext_C$ of a context $C : T$ is similarly defined, consisting of all contexts contained in the declaration of T, together with their subcontexts.

A service s of a component A may be referred to within a larger component, context or an architecture by a C++/Java style qualification: $A.s$. Also, a provided service s of a component A that is defined within a context C may be referred to, outside the context, by a further qualification $C.A.s$. This reflects the fact that, in implementation, the provided services of a component within a transactional context may be called by a component outside of the context. Within a compound component, architecture or context, the required service of a subcomponent may use the provided service of another component. This is defined via a **bind** declaration. A compound component exposes provided services which may delegate calls to provided services subcomponents. The same may be said of required services. This is defined via a **map** declaration.

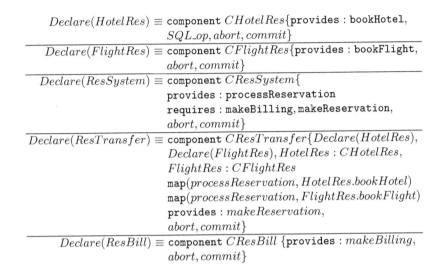

Fig. 2. Five COM+ components, specified as ADL component declarations. We abbreviate these declarations by $Declare(CResSystem)$, $Declare(CResTransfer)$ and $Declare(CResBill)$ in the rest of the paper.

Example 1. Our example architecture involves a simple hotel reservation system, built from three COM+ components – $ResSystem$, $ResTransfer$, $ResBill$. These components are instances of class types $CResSystem$, $CResTransfer$, $CResBill$. The component $ResTransfer$ uses subcomponents $FlightRes$ (of type $CFlightRes$) and $HotelRes$ (of type $CHotelRes$). Upon recieving an event notification from the first component that a hotel reservation is to be made by a user, the second component performs B2B operations with the Hotel and the airliner for which the reservation is made. Upon receiving the same type of event notification, the third component performs billing operations against the user's credit card. When the event is sent out, $ResTransfer$ and $ResBill$ will execute concurrently. However, we require transaction support over both these components: if one fails, then calls to either component must be rolled back. This will prevent a user being billed if the hotel they wish to book at is full, and will prevent the hotel from accepting a guest if their credit is bad. We require separate transaction support for calls to $FlightRes$ and $HotelRes$ from within $ResTransfer$, to prevent a flight being reserved if the hotel is full. Fig. 2 defines the components of our example in the syntax of TrustME.

2.1   Architectures

In implementation, the designer defines transactional contexts by assigning transaction settings to component deployments. We reflect this by considering transactional contexts as first class entities in our ADL.

There are five possible transaction settings in COM+ (there are similar settings for EJB implementations). *1. Disabled.* This setting means that a component is not transactional, and therefore should not make calls to any managed resources, or to componenents which managed resources. *2. Not supported.* This setting indicates that the component will not run within a transaction. If the component is called from within a transaction's activity, COM+ creates the component in a context running outside of the current activity. *3. Supported.* This indicates that the component will run in a transaction, but does not require one. *4. Required.* This indicates that the component requires a transaction to run. If the component is not currently in a transaction, COM+ will start a new transaction. *5. Requires new.* This indicates that the component requires a new transaction. If the component is called from within a transaction, COM+ will start a new transaction activity for this component. Use of this setting ensures that this component's transaction is unaffected by the success or failure of others.

A transactional COM+ architecture is implemented by assigning these settings to a group of COM+ components. We model such implementations by means of contexts.

Example 2. Our architecture will consist of all components contained within the same transactional context, and with *ResBill* (and thus its subcomponents) contained within a subcontext. Our architecture is depicted in Fig. 3. The required services of *ResSystem*, *makeReservation* and *makeBilling*, are bound to the provided services *makeReservation* and *makeBilling* of *ResTransfer* and *ResBill* respectively. This specifies that when *ResSystem* requests that the reservation be made and billed, *ResTransfer* and and *ResBill* will respectively handle these functions. To meet our transactional requirements, the three COM+ components *ResSystem*, *ResTransfer* and *ResBill* have settings of *required, supported* and *supported* respectively. A transactional context intercepts calls made to and from *ResBill*. This is represented by declaring a context type *CResBillContext* and context instance *ResBillContext* that uses *ResBill*. The the required services of other components are bound to the provided services of *ResBill* inside this context.

```
architecture {
  Declare(CResSystem), Declare(CResTransfer), Declare(CResBill)
  context CResSystemContext {
    ResSystem : CResSystem, ResTransfer : CResTransfer, ResBill : CResBill
    bind(ResSystem.makeReservation, ResTransfer.makeReservation),
    bind(ResSystem.makeBilling, ResBill.makeBilling)                        }
  ResSysContext : CResSystem, ResTransfer : CResTransfer, ResBill : CResBill
  bind(ResSystem.makeReservation, ResTransfer.makeReservation),
  bind(ResSystem.makeBilling, ResBillContext.makeBilling)                   }
}
```

Fig. 3. An architecture in which the three components are in a transactional context, with *ResTransfer* (and its subcomponents) in a separate, nested transaction.

Note that non-transactional systems can still be defined, using components and connections without contexts. The form of these architectures are similar those that are definable in other ADLs, involving a collection of components, together with binding connections between their provided and required services.

3   Semantics

The language of our ADL depicts the static structure of a system. To understand the dynamic behaviour of a system, we define a semantics for the elements of our language.

3.1   Semantics of Basic Components

We do not try to give a comprehensive description of a component's sematics. Since components themselves are able to perform arbitrary universal computations, a comprehensive description of their semantics also would require a model of universal computational power. Unfortunately, universal models are hard to analyse and many interesting properties are undecidable.

Hence, we restrict our semantics to describe the aspect of input-output behaviour. We model this aspect with finite-state machines (FSMs), for which efficient algorithms exist for testing equivalence and inclusion and performing liveness and safety analysis.

Definition 1 (Finite State Machine). *A Deterministic Finite State Machine (FSM) D is a tuple $D = (E, A, Z, \delta, F, z_0)$. E is called event alphabet, A is the event alphabet, Z denotes the set of states, $F \subseteq Z$ is the set of accepting (final) states. $z_0 \in Z$ is a designated* start-state. *$\delta : Z \times E \times A \to Z$ is a total* function.

We often denote the transition function as a set of transitions, where we write each transition as a tuple $(fromState, event, action, toState)$, meaning that $\delta(fromState, event, action) = toState$ and that the action $action$ is associated with that state transition.

A basic component has a semantics given by a FSM, whose event-alphabet consists of the component's provided services and whose action-alphabet consists out of the component's required services. Our semantics assumes that every basic component $C : T$ has a so called *component-FSM* (CFSM) describing its input-output behaviour.

Definition 2 (Component-FSM). *For a given component C, the component-FSM (CFSM) $C\text{-}FSM_C = (E_C, A_C, Z_C, \delta_C, F_C, z_{0_C})$ is defined as follows:*

- *for each service $m \in provides_C \cup internal_C$ two distinct events m_{start} and m_{end} exist in the event alphabet E_C. m_{start} denotes the call of service m, m_{end} its return.*
- *the action alphabet A_C consists of the component's required services.*

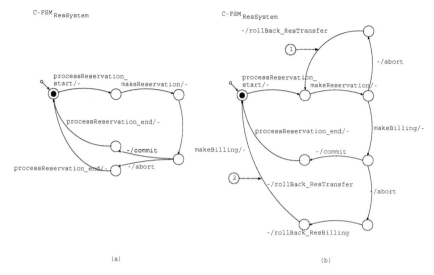

Fig. 4. (a): C-FSM of the *ResSystem* component. (b): Transactional C-FSM of the *ResSystem* component.

The C-FSM of a component provides a mapping from called provided services to resulting call made to external components via required services. The transition function δ for a component defines the possible changes to the the state of the component that occur when it receives events through its provided services, or when it sends events through its required services. Each transition is annotated with either an event or an action.

Example 3. In Fig. 4(a) we present the C-FSM of the *ResSystem* component.

3.2 Semantics of Compound Components and Nontransactional Architectures

The semantics of a compound component is given by a C-FSM, which is derived from the semantics of the compound component's subcomponents. The idea is to examine the bindings between provided and required services of the components and provided and required services of subcomponents respectively. This information can be used to define FSMs that model an entire sequence of actions and events that result from calling provided services. We refer to these FSMs as service FSMs. Then, we examine the mappings from the provided and required services of C to provided and required services of subcomponents. We combine this information with service FSMs to model the event and action sequences that can result from calling the component's provided services. This results in the component's C-FSM. See [11,10] for details.

An architecture that consists solely of hierarchically composed components (without transactional contexts) has a semantics defined in a similar way to that

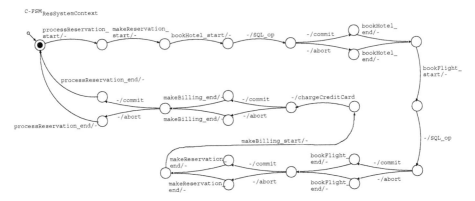

Fig. 5. C-FSM of the nontransactional architecture obtained by removing transactional contexts from Fig. 3.

of compound components. As an example one can consider Fig. 5, the C-FSM for the architecture described in Fig. 3 with transactional contexts removed.

3.3   Architectures with Transactional Contexts

Transactional contexts change the way contained components interoperate. This is mirrored through changes to the overall behavioural semantics for an architecture. We model transactional contexts. Just as a middleware can add transactional cross-component functionality, the presence of contexts in an architecture adds additional behaviour to the semantics of contained components.

Definition 3. *For a given FSM $A = (E_A, A_A, Z_A, \delta_A, F_A, z_{0_A})$ and component C, the mapping $\Phi : Z_A \to \mathbf{P}(subcomponents_C)$ assigns for each state $s \in Z_A$ a set of components $D \subseteq Z_A$, where $d \in D$ is true if (and only if) on a path from the start state z_{0_A} to the state s a service p with $\zeta(p) = d$ has been called.*

Definition 4 (Rollback-Automata). *For a given set of states $D \subseteq Z_A, D = \{d_1 \cdots d_n\}$ of a given FSM A we define the* rollback-automata *as a FSM $r_A(D) = (E_r, A_r, Z_r, \delta_r, F_r, z_{0_r})$, where $Z_r := l_0 \cdots l_n$, $z_{0_r} := l_0$, $F_r := \{l_n\}$ and $\delta_r(l_{i-1}, d_i) := l_i$, for $i \in [1..n]$*

Algorithm 1 (Translation of CR-FSM into transactional CR-FSM)

Input: non-transactional CR-FSM $A = (E_A, A_A, Z_A, \delta_A, F_A, z_{0_A})$
Output: transactional CR-FSM $B = (E_{tr(A)}, A_{tr(A)}, Z_{tr(A)}, \delta_{tr(A)}, F_{tr(A)}, z_{0_{tr(A)}})$

Build mapping $\Phi : Z \to \mathbf{P}(subcomponents_C)$;
⟨e.g., by dataflow algorithms.⟩
B=A.clone();

for each set $s \in dom(\Phi)$ **do**
    add rollback-automata $r_A(s)$ to B;
    add transition $(\Phi^{-1}(s), abort, z_{0_r})$ to B;
    state $f := l.l \in F_r$;
    identify states z_{0_A} and f;
⟨do not make z_{0_A} a final state, unless it allready has been one.⟩
od

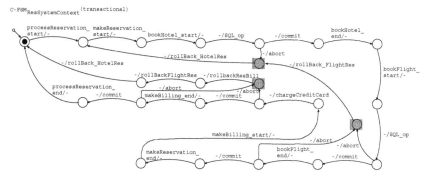

Fig. 6. Transactional C-FSM for the architecture of Fig. 3.

Example 4. Applying this algorithm to the non-transactional C-FSM of *ResSystem* results in the transactional C-FSM given in Fig. 4(b).

Nested transactional contexts can be treated by applying algorithm 1 to the innermost transactional contexts, then recursively to outer contexts. Thus, the C-FSM of the overall context has to be constructed. The sub-FSMs of the inner transactional contexts can be identified by the start states of their services. The part of the overall C-FSM which already has been processed as inner contexts, must be marked and excluded from further processing of the outer contexts. In the example of figure 4(b), the rollback-transition marked as 1 leads to the beginning of the inner transactional context for the component *ResTransfer* because its triggering *abort*-transition occurs within the inner transactional context. The rollback-transition marked as 2 leads to the outer transactional context, since it results from an *abort* transition of the outer transactional context.

In Fig. 6 we show the result of applying algorithm 1 on the C-FSM of the the architecture of Fig. 3. Since some rollback automata are combined, we marked the start states of rollback automata as shaded states.

4   Related Work and Conclusions

In this paper we examine extensions to ADLs that facilitate modelling of architectures involving transactional contexts. Our main contributions are: 1. We define a simple ADL for textually defining industrial middleware architectures, 2. we provide a compositional finite state machine based semantics for compositional component architectures, 3. we extend this semantics to incorporate architectures that involve transactional contexts.

Our basic approach to syntax and semantics is similar to that of other ADLs . Some form of semantics is used to define models of basic components' behaviour. For example, Darwin [5] uses the π-calculus [7], Rapide [4] uses partially order event sets and Wright [1] can use a form of CSP [3]. The language of the ADL is used primarily to impose structure on over a system's behavior, expressing its composition from components. Semantically, the composition-forming constructs are associated with semantic functions, which describe how a composite component's behavioural semantics is formed from subcomponents' behavioural semantics.

However, to the best of our knowledge, no work has been done previously on the syntax and semantics of architectures of middleware-based systems with transactional contexts. The advantage of finite state machines when modelling component-architectures is the availability of efficient checks for interoperability and substitutability. However, further work needs to be done to adapt our approach to more expressive forms of semantics, such as the π-calculus. Also, here we have only modelled transactional contexts: we are currently extending our system to model other middleware contexts.

Acknowledgements

The authors would like to thank the anonymous reviewers for their useful suggestions and Wolfgang Blass for his fruitful help.

References

1. Robert J. Allen. *A Formal Approach to Software Architecture*. Ph.D. thesis, School of Computer Science, Carnegie Mellon University, Pittsburgh, PE, USA, May 1997.
2. Sun Microsystems Corp., The Enterprise Java Beans homepage. http://java.sun.com/products/ejb/.
3. C. A. R. Hoare. *Communicating Sequential Processes*. Prentice/Hall, 1985.
4. D.C. Luckham, J.J. Kenney, L.M. Augustin, J. Vera, D. Bryan, and W. Mann. Specification and analysis of system architecture using rapide. *IEEE Transactions on Software Engineering*, 21(4):336–355, Apr 1995.
5. J. Magee, N. Dulay, S. Eisenbach, and J. Kramer. Specifying distributed software architectures. *Lecture Notes in Computer Science*, 989:137–155, 1995.
6. Nenad Medvidovic and Richard N. Taylor. A classification and comparison framework for software architecture description languages. *IEEE Transactions on Software Engineering*, 26(1):70–93, Janurary 2000.
7. Robin Milner. Concurrency and compositionality, 1991. Workshop at Goslar.
8. Microsoft Corp., The .net homepage. http://www.microsoft.com/net/default.asp.
9. Iman Poernomo, Heinz Schmidt, and Ralf Reussner. The TrustME language site. Web site, DSTC, 2001. Available at http://www.csse.monash.edu.au/dsse/trustme.

10. Ralf H. Reussner. *Parametrisierte Verträge zur Protokolladaption bei Software-Komponenten.* Logos Verlag, Berlin, 2001.
11. Heinz W. Schmidt and Ralf H. Reussner. Automatic Component Adaptation By Concurrent State Machine Retrofitting. Technical Report 25/2000, Fakultät für Informatik, Universität Karlsruhe (TH), Am Fasanengarten 5, D-76128 Karlsruhe, Germany, 2000.
12. Clemens Szyperski. Components and architecture. *Software Development,* 8(5), October 2000.

Software, Component, and Service Deployment in Computational Grids

Gregor von Laszewski[1], Eric Blau[1], Michael Bletzinger[2], Jarek Gawor[1], Peter Lane[1], Stuart Martin[1], and Michael Russell[1]

[1] Argonne National Laboratory, 9700 S. Cass Ave., Argonne, IL 60439
[2] National Center for Supercomputing Applications, Champaign, IL 61821,
gregor@mcs.anl.gov

Abstract. Grids comprise an infrastructure that enables scientists to use a diverse set of distributed remote services and resources as part of complex scientific problem-solving processes. We analyze some of the challenges involved in deploying software and components transparently in Grids. We report on three practical solutions used by the Globus Project. Lessons learned from this experience lead us to believe that it is necessary to support a variety of software and component deployment strategies. These strategies are based on the hosting environment.

1 Introduction

Grids comprise an infrastructure enabling scientists to use a diverse set of distributed software, services, and components that access a variety of dispersed resources as part of complex scientific problem-solving. This infrastructure includes the use of compute resources such as personal computers, workstations, and supercomputers; access to information resources such as directory services and large-scale data bases; and access to knowledge resources such as collaboration with colleagues. A central role in defining Grids is the creation of virtual organizations that define sharing and trust relations between the diversified set of resources. Deployment of software, components, and services must be governed by the appropriate definition of rules and policies. Such sharing rules may be rather simple, as demonstrated by the SETI@home project [10] to allow the creation of commodity compute resources pools. The resources are contributed by a large number of individuals. It is important to recognize that providing an easy deployment strategy with easy-to-understand rules of engagement results in integration of resources that can be provided by nonexperts. More complex rules are defined as part of virtual organizations spanning resources among traditional compute centers. They enable access to high-end resources (such as supercomputers) and advanced instruments (such as a particle collider). Examples are the DOE Science Grid [2], the NASA Information Power Grid (IPG), and the Alliance Virtual Machine Room (VMR) [14,1]. Sharing rules govern the privileged use of resources contributed by the centers. The deployment of software, services, and components in such production Grids is performed by experts and well-trained administrative staff following guidelines set within and between such compute centers. In each case it is important to develop proper deployment strategies as part of every Grid-enabled infrastructure.

In the rest of the paper we first present a simple example that introduces several issues that must be addressed while deploying software, components, and services in Grids. Based on our requirements analysis, we have identified three scenarios that allow us to deploy components in a Grid-based infrastructure. We compare these scenarios and present our conclusions.

2   Example

We present a simple example illustrating a small set of requirements that we must deal with. In Figure 1 a group of scientists needs to deploy a problem-solving environment on various resources in the Grid to conduct a large matrix factorization as part of the structure determination of a molecule in three-dimensional space.

Initially, we need to identify a set of suitable resources to perform our task. Often we will identify resources that have the potential to perform a given task but may not have the necessary software deployed on them. We can proceed in

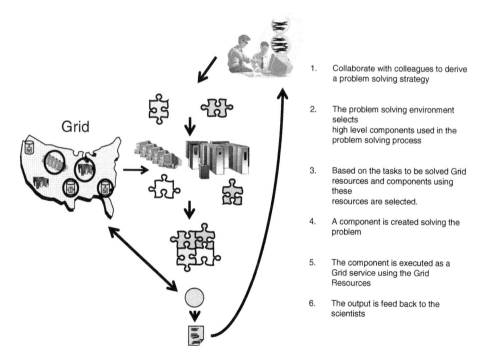

Fig. 1. Component deployment and assembly to support the scientific problem-solving process in Grids.

one of two ways: eliminating the resource because its software environment is insufficient for the task, or installing the appropriate software to provide the appropriate functionality. Once our environment is present, we access a set of Grid services allowing the composition of a Grid-enabled application based on Grid services and components. For the resources of choice we determine appropriate components suitable for performing our requested task. These components are assembled and executed in order to deliver feedback to the scientists. We emphasize that the scientists do not have to know the algorithmic details of the solving process, as they are hidden in the components. These details include on which Grid resources the factorization is performed or which algorithm is used. Thus, the Grid is used as a utility that returns the information requested as part of the complex problem solving process.

To make such a Grid-enabled environment possible, we must integrate several locally maintained code repositories into a virtual code repository. From it we must discover, select, and assemble the components best suited for the task. The selection of components is determined by the functional properties, performance, licensing issues, and cost. We must address the issue of whether the components can be trusted to be executed on a resource. We must ensure that the interfaces between components provide functional compatibility and,in some cases, version compatibility in order to engage in the creation of reproducible results. Version control must be strictly enforced not only on the delivery of components but also potentially while using statically or dynamically linked libraries. A discovery process must be designed in such a way that only authenticated users may know the existence or the properties of the components. Moreover, prior to the use of the component, the user must be able to judge its functionality and approve it for inclusion within other components. Smart components acting in behalf of users themselves must be able to perform similar component assembly strategies. This may mean that the same query and assembly of a component for user A could result in a completely different implementation for user B, who may have different access rights to resources within the Grid.

3   Deployment Cycle

As part of our previous example we identified three basic user communities that must be integral part of every deployment strategy: *programmers and designers* that are developing software, components, and services in a collaborative fashion to be deployed in the Grid; *administrators* that deploy them; and *application users* that access deployed software, component, and services. Thus, in order to address the complex issues related to deployment, the software engineering cycle must reflect dealing with this issue in each stage, while at the same time forcing and supporting interactions between designers, administrators, and users.

A blueprint for managing deployment of Grid software, services, and components is depicted in Figure 2. It supports the packaging, deployment, and iterative process of improving the infrastructure. The goal of this rigorous software process is to reduce the effort to deploy and maintain the infrastructure that

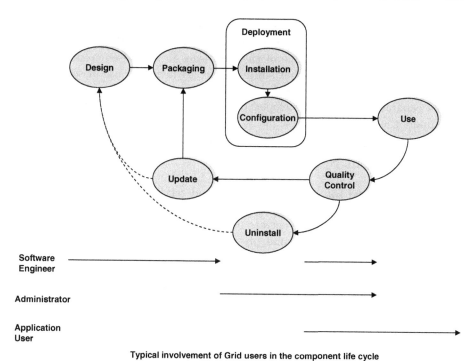

Fig. 2. Deploying and maintaining software, components, and services in Grids is a resource-intensive task that requires an iterative interaction between designers, administrators, and users

enables the effective use of the complex environment by the application users or scientists, and also by other Grid architects developing new Grid services.

So far we have not distinguished between what we understand under software, components, and services because we believe that our observations are applicable to each one of these categories. In order to deploy components and services in Grids, we need to prepare what the Grid community sometimes calls a hosting environment. Such hosting environments provide the necessary software infrastructure for executing Grid-related services and components. The the Java Virtual machine, J2EE, .NET, a prepackaged Grid hosting environment [1], or simply a particular version of an operating system are examples. In order to prepare such a hosting environment, we can obviously benefit from software engineering practices that deal with software deployment as it "defines the assembly and maintenance of the resources necessary to use a version of a system at a particular site" [15]. Once we have established a hosting environments, we can develop services [9] that are based on the hosting environment and components that uses the services as part of a component framework. The problems associated with deployment are manifold and not unique to Grids. Nevertheless, common commercial distributed environments such as CORBA [13] provide insufficient support for the deployment in Grids: whereas these technologies usually target a single administrative domain, Grids encompass multiple domains while keeping them autonomous. One of the key issues in a Grid environment must be a security infrastructure that simplifies deployment and use of services and components. A convenient Grid Security Infrastructure (GSI) including single-signon capability has been developed by the Globus Project, which we can use to support the deployment cycle [3].

4   Deployment Scenarios

Deployment of Grid software, components, and services imposes numerous requirements. Hence we cannot assume that a single strategy fulfills all of these requirements. Instead, we concentrate on three common scenarios that we have identified within our example and provide a deployment strategy solution for each of them. We have termed them thick, thin, and slender in analogy to terminology used in the Internet community.

Thick Deployment: A Grid designer develops software enabling services that are installed locally on a computer by an administrator. Such component and services are typically written in C and may be run with root access on the machine. They usually are tightly integrated with an operating system.

Thin Deployment: A scientist is using a Web browser to access Grid Services in a transparent fashion. The communication is performed only through a browser interface and does not allow installation of any software on the client machine on which the browser runs. A thin Grid service may allow the scientist to interface with a thick Grid service.

Slender Deployment: A slender client allows a platform-neutral deployment under the assumption that an appropriate hosting environment is already present (through, for example, the use of a thick service). A good example of such a slender deployment service is the use of Webstart within a JVM hosting environment. It allows the browser to cache components locally, as well as integrate specialized local available applications within the Web interface.

In the next sections, we describe a deployment strategy for each of the scenarios in the Grid.

5   Thick Deployment

Discussed in [4] is a subset of deployment issues for Grid services and components based on traditional programming languages such as C and FORTRAN and applied to the Globus Toolkit. As an initial solution, the Globus Project, together with NCSA, has developed a Grid Packaging Tool (GPT) that simplifies creation and the deployment of precompiled software. The code is prepared with auto configuration tools and is also available as source code. The GPT separates machine architecture probing from the tests done for a single site or machine deployment. This approach allows a component to be precompiled for a certain architecture and then deployed during installation by means of a setup script.

Hence, the only probing needed is a dependency check that makes sure the required dependent packages are available.

Issues that are intended to be addressed with this tool are as follows:

- An intercomponent dependency checker that can track dependencies at compile, link, and runtime.
- A versioning system that identifies compatibility between different versions of components based on a variation of the libtool versioning.
- Distribution of binaries with compile time flavors, such as the numerical resolution.
- Distribution of relocatable binaries that are independent of any absolute path within the distribution.
- Integration of dependencies to external programs and libraries not distributed with the current component.
- Support for runtime configuration files that allows the custom configuration of components that are installed with statically based runtime managers, for example, the modification of runtime parameters after the package has been installed in the destination path.
- Support for source code distribution of the components.
- Inclusion of metainformation in the description of the components to assist in the preservation of the components.
- A packaging manager that helps during the installation, upgrade, and uninstallation of components that is compatible to existing packaging managers such as RedHat packing manager (RPM).

The packaging toolkit has been tested on the 2.0 beta version of the Globus Toolkit. As part of this test, various packages have been released that are targeted toward different platforms but also include various sets of components. In future versions it is expected that administrators may choose a particular set of components and the platform and may get a custom-assembled package in return. The automatic generation of metadata related to this package is integrated into the Grid Information Infrastructure that is implemented as part of MDS. Thus, it will be possible to query for installations of the Globus Toolkit and the supported features on various domains. The benefit of using a native C implementation of Grid components is based on their speed.

6   Thin Deployment

Although the packaging mechanism for the Globus Toolkit allows software architects to develop software, services, and components that can be installed and configured by system administrators and Grid component designers, it is still quite complex because of the requirement to support sharing, persistence, and updates. To simplify the task of deployment on a client side, many projects suggest developing thin clients that expose the scientific problem-solving process through convenient Web-based interfaces. A good example for such a Grid-based application is the astrophysical computing portal (see Figure 3) [19] allowing

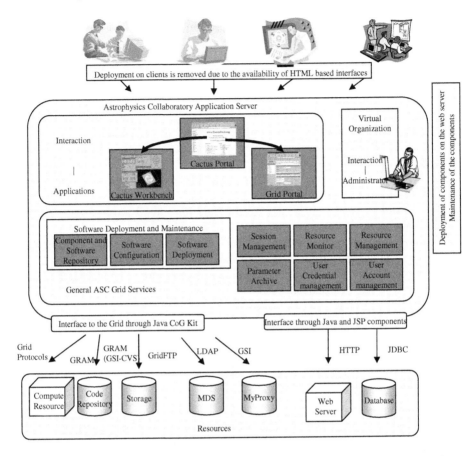

Fig. 3. Structure of the ASC application server showing the various components.

scientists to access supercomputing resources and interact as required by the astrophysical community.

This application contains two different aspects making it interesting for the deployment of components in computational Grids. First, the thin clients enable application users to easily interact with the system without updating their local software, as all communication is performed through a Web-based portal using HTML and DHTML technologies. If state-of-the-art Web browsers are available on the application users' clients, no additional installation task is required. Naturally, the designer of the software must put special care into fulfilling the application users' needs and must provide sufficient guidance for administrators to install such a portal. Customization for users is provided by saving the state of the last interaction with the portal. Second, the portal is used to develop reusable components as part of the Cactus framework.

The portal provides access to familiar tools such as a GSI-enhanced CVS. Other users are able to access components from a shared component repository.

The Globus Toolkit provides the necessary security infrastructure. Additional administrative overhead is needed to maintain such a portal and to determine policies for access to the software repository, for the software configuration, and for automatic software deployment.

7   Slender Deployment

Practical experience with slender Grid services has shown that the user interface provided by the current generation of browsers is too limited or requires in many cases unreasonably long startup cost. At SC2001 in Denver we demonstrated how the use of slender services and components can support component development and deployment in computational Grids (see Figure 4). Slender clients are developed in an advanced programming language and can be installed through a Web-based portal on the local client. This approach allows the creation of advanced portals and the integration of locally available executables as part of the problem-solving process. Furthermore, it enables the integration of sophisticated collaborative tools provided by a third party.

Although the creation of slender clients can be performed in any programming language, we have chosen in our prototype to use the Java programming language. We rely on the Java CoG Kit [17] for the interface to Grid resources

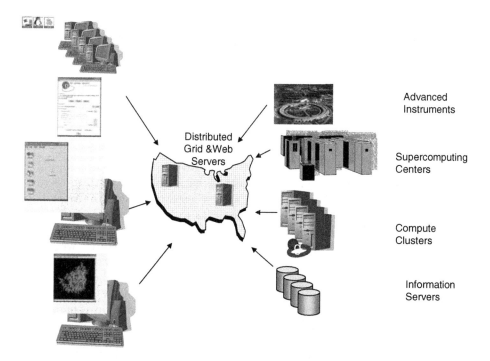

Advanced
Instruments

Distributed
Grid &Web
Servers

Supercomputing
Centers

Compute
Clusters

Information
Servers

Fig. 4. The slender client environment allowing to significantly simplifying the deployment and maintenance of clients accessing Grid functionality.

that can be accessed through the slender clients. For our demonstration we developed two popularly used components and deployed them through the Java Web Start technology. Java Web Start provides a deployment framework that allows client users with access to a local resource to install Java components that can be accessed from the cache of the local browsers. Thus it reduces the installation time if the component is used more than once. Additionally, it provides an automatic framework for updating the component if a new one is placed on the Web server. Using the protocols defined by the Globus Project, we achieved interoperability between the Globus Toolkit and our Web-enabled slender clients. Tests confirmed the usability of our approach as part of the deployment strategy for Grid computing. Indeed, users not familiar with the Web Start technology were able to deploy the components in just two minutes on their clients. This is in dramatic contrast to other similar Grid software that is sufficiently complex so that users typically must attend a training session to learn about the installation process. Although the packaging toolkit described earlier is aimed to improve this situation, the developers must maintain a significant variety of binary releases that are to be installed with an installshield-like capability on Linux/Unix and Windows platforms. While using Java for this task, we cover a significant portion of the target machines and are even able to support the Macintosh platform, so far not explored by the packaging effort. During SC2001, we also demonstrated the integration of programs natively installed on the client in a Grid components framework. Specifically, we obtained data via a secure connection to a Globus Toolkit-enabled information resource and displayed it with the help of a natively compiled molecular viewer (rasmol). This easy deployment methodology enables the inclusion of new resources and services within the computational Grids. Furthermore, we are able to integrate certificates in components that can be used to guarantee authenticity and portability between deployed components.

8   Comparison of the Scenarios

Experiments with the various deployment scenarios in Grid settings revealed a number of advantages and disadvantages of each approach. In Table 1 we summarize our results. Each of the approaches can access native components in C or FORTRAN, with relatively low overhead. Nevertheless, using a native compiler will have performance advantages while accessing libraries written in C and Fortran. Such advantages, however, come at a price, since no uniformly accepted component framework exists. In contrast, significant benefits can be achieved by using Java as the component integration language [8]. The benefits include implicit integration of documentation and metainformation as part of the Java packaging. These packages can be signed with the standard Java keytool to generate signatures for improving the authenticity of the packages before download. Component repositories can thus be implemented as part of existing Web services, enabling others to share their components with the community easily. Moreover, as pointed out before, the Java Web Start technology provides

Table 1. Comparison between the various scenarios

Feature	Thick	Slender	Thin
1 Primary interface to C/FORTRAN	native	JNI	Third tier
	fast	medium	slow
2 Primary language	C/Fortran, Java	Java	HTML
3 Possible Java programs	application	applets	applets
		applications	
4 Component versioning	libtool	tag	N/A
5 Component interoperability through signature	no	yes	N/A
6 Component metainformation	libtool, rpm	certificates	HTML tag
7 Component repository	Web-server, cvs	Web-server	Gsi-cvs
8 Source repository	Web-server, cvs	Web-server	N/A
9 Portable GUI	Tcl/Tk, Qt	Swing	HTML
10 Sophistication of the GUI	high	high	low
11 Interactivity not limited to browser [20]	yes	yes	no
12 Speed of interface interaction	high	high	low
13 First-time activation cost	high	low	none
14 Cost for subsequent use	low	low	high
15 Support for power users	yes	yes	no
16 Incremental component update	difficult	easy	N/A
17 Integration of client-side programs	yes	yes	no
18 Access restriction to client by sophisticated policies	no	yes	no
19 Standard Component Framework	no	Beans/EJB [16]	none
20 Sandboxing	difficult	yes	no
21 Desktop integration	no	yes	no
22 Offline operation	yes	yes	no
23 Automatic installation of supporting components	no	yes	no
24 Deployment in Grids	distributed	distributed	replicated
25 Deployment protocol	To be defined	JNLP	none

a usable mechanism for installing such signed components on local clients. Other advantages are the availability of a sophisticated user interface development environment that interfaces with the desktop and can so far not be replicated with HTML/XML technologies.

Java does, however, have potential disadvantages. In the slender scenario, portability is defined by the availability of a JVM for the targeted Grid resource. Since some Grid resources lack sufficient support for Java, these resources must be interfaced through native libraries. Another disadvantage may be the restrictions in the address space or the speed numerical calculations are performed (though studies show that the Java performance can be dramatically improved [12]). In our experience many application users and designers are initially pleased with an HTML-based interface but quickly experience frustration because the Interface does not provide for enough flexibility and speed during a continuous period of use. An example of such an application is given by the use of our Java-based MDS browser [18], which has thousands of users (in contrast to its original CGI counterpart, which was simply too slow in continuous use). The ability to sandbox client-side applications is a further advantage of the slender client and enables one to create sophisticated high-throughput compute resources similar in spirit to SETI@home [10], Condor.

9   Related Work in the Grid Community

Work on component assembly and deployment was being performed in Grid-related activities even before the term Grid was coined [16]. More recently, the Globus Project has defined a schema for a metacomputing directory service [6] that allows one to store metainformation about components that are installed on remote resources. Moreover, with the input of the Globus Project team, University of Tennessee researchers have completed a schema proposal to the Grid Forum [11]. Such developments will be carefully watched by new efforts such as the European GridLab project and the DOE Science Grid projects, which will need to address the deployment issue of Grid components and services. The research conducted in this paper will be beneficial for this work. Other relevant efforts are, for example, [7,5]

10   Summary

In this paper we have outlined three scenarios that significantly affect the deployment strategy of components within Grids. Although none of the deployment strategies is all encompassing, together they solve many aspects of component deployment in Grids. We found the strategy of signed slender clients to be significantly superior to the thin-client approach supported by other communities. In fact, we found that often artificial requirements were put in place to prevent developers from considering slender client deployment strategies, even when such strategies allow integrating previously written client software. Additionally, we have shown that with the availability of Java we were able to deploy components with ease on Java-enabled platforms including Solaris, Linux, Windows, and Macintosh. We view our continuing research in this field as essential for the acceptance and the success of Grids.

Acknowledgments

This work was supported by the Mathematical, Information, and Computational Science Division subprogram of the Office of Advanced Scientific Computing Research, U.S. Department of Energy, under Contract W-31-109-Eng-38. DARPA, DOE, and NSF support Globus Project research and development. We thank Ian Foster and Brian Toonen for valuable contributions in this ongoing research. This work would not have been possible without the help of the Globus Project team. Globus Toolkit and Globus Project are trademarks held by the University of Chicago.

References

1. Ncsa in the box packages. http://www.ncsa.uiuc.edu/TechFocus/Deployment/, 2001.
2. The DOE Science Grid, 2001. http://www-itg.lbl.gov/Grid/.
3. The Globus Security Web pages, Dec. 2001. http://www.globus.org/security.
4. Bill Allcock, Eric Blau, and Michael Bletzinger. The Globus Packaging Desing Document, 2001. http://www-unix.globus.org/packaging/rfc.html.
5. D. C. Arnold and J. Dongarra. The netsolve environment: Progressing towards the seamless grid. In *Proc. International Workshop on Parallel Processing*, 2000.
6. K. Czajkowski, S. Fitzgerald, I. Foster, and C. Kesselman. Grid Information Services for Distributed Resource Sharing. In *Proc. 10th IEEE International Symposium on High Performance Dis-tributed Computing*, 2001. http://www.globus.org.
7. J. Frey, T. Tannenbaum, I. Foster, M. Livny, and S. Tuecke. Condor-g: A computation management agent for multi-institutional grids. pages 55–66, 2001.
8. Vladimir Getov, Gregor von Laszewski, Michael Philippsen, and Ian Foster. Multi-Paradigm Communications in Java for Grid Computing. *Communications of ACM*, 44(10):119–125, 2001. http://www.globus.org/cog/documentataion/papers/.
9. Steve Graham, Simeon Simeonov, Toufic Boubez, Glen Daniels, Doug Davis, Yuichi Nakamura, and Ryo Neyama. *Building Web Services with Java: Making Sense of XML, SOAP, WSDL and UDDI*. SAMS, December 2001.
10. W. T. Sullivan III, D. Werthimer, S. Bowyer, J. Cobb, D. Gedye, and D. Anderson. A new major SETI project based on Project Serendip data and 100,000 personal computers. In *Proc. of the Fifth Intl. Conf. on Bioastronomy.*, Astronomical and Biochemical Origins and the Search for Life in the Uni-verse., 1997. http://setiathome.ssl.berkeley.edu/woody_paper.html.
11. Jeremy Miller. Grid Software Object Specification, 2001. http://www-unix.mcs.anl.gov/gridforum/gis/reports/software/software.pdf.
12. José E. Moreira, Samuel P. Midkiff, Manish Gupta, Pedro V. Artigas, Peng Wu, and George Almasi. The NINJA Project. *Communications of ACM*, 44(10):102 – 109, 2001.
13. OMG. CORBA: Common Object Request Broker Architecture, 2001. http://www.omg.org.
14. John Towns. The Alliance Virtual Machine Room, 2001. http://archive.ncsa.uiuc.edu/SCD/Alliance/VMR/.
15. Andre van der Hoek, Richard S. Hall, Antonio Carzaniga, Dennis Heimbigner, and Alexander L. Wolf. Software deployment: Extending configuration management support into the field. *Crosstalk, The Journal of Defense Software Engineering*, 11(2), February 1998.
http://www.cs.colorado.edu/serl/cm/Papers.html#CROSSTALK98,
http://www.stsc.hill.af.mil/crosstalk/1998/feb/deployment.asp.
16. Gregor von Laszewski. An Interactive Parallel Programming Environment applied in atmospheric Science. In N. Kreitz, editor, *Making its Mark, Proceedings of the 6th Workshop of The use of Parallel Processors in Meteorology*, pages 311–325. World Scientific European Centre for Medium Weather Forecast, Reading, UK, 1996.
17. Gregor von Laszewski, Ian Foster, Jarek Gawor, and Peter Lane. A Java Commodity Grid Kit. *Concurrency and Computation: Practice and Experience*, 13(8-9):643–662, 2001. http://www.globus.org/cog/documentation/papers/cog-cpe-final.pdf.

18. Gregor von Laszewski and Jarek Gawor. Copyright of the LDAP Browser/Editor, August 1999.
19. Gregor von Laszewski, Michael Russell, Ian Foster, John Shalf, Gabrielle Allen, Greg Daues, Jason Novotny, and Edward Seidel. Community Software Development with the Astrophysics Simulation Col-laboratory. *Concurency and Computation*, to be published, 2002. http://www.globus.org/cog.

Model, Notation, and Tools for Verification of Protocol-Based Components Assembly

Pascal Rapicault[1,2], Jean-Paul Rigault[1], and Luc Bourlier[1]

[1] RAINBOW and SPORTS Projects, I3S Laboratory,
University of Nice Sophia Antipolis and CNRS (UMR 6070),
F-06902 Sophia Antipolis Cedex, France
[2] Object Technology International, Inc. (OTI),
firstname.lastname@essi.fr

Abstract. Assembly of blackbox components is made difficult by the lack of precise information on the way components interact. What is needed is a behavioral model of the component, at the input and output interface levels. This paper introduces the notion of behavioral points of view and an associated graphical notation, SyncClass, to represent such a model. The underlying semantics of SyncClass makes it possible to automatically verify component assembly, either for individual components or for a whole system.

1 Introduction

We are currently working on the definition and the implementation of a CASE environment, named Co2[1], which provides notations and tools to specify, develop, and use components.

This communication focuses on the notations and tools devoted to the *user* of components, that is the person who assembles existing components to build an application. More specifically it addresses the problem of verifying components assembly, either for individual components or for a whole system.

The ideal way of assembling components should rely on the sole knowledge of the component interfaces (*blackbox reuse* [19]). However the reality is different, and the developers often require knowledge about component internals (*glassbox reuse* [19]). Indeed the user is generally provided with a static description of the interface (a simple list of operations) whereas information about the valid sequences of operation calls would be needed. The latter information is what we call the component *protocol of use*.

The situation is even worse when components are organized into a component framework [19]. In order to respect a given component protocol, the user cannot just consider his/her own calls to the component but also the calls originating from other components and targeted to the component under study. Thus the user has to guess the part of the protocol to which he/she must comply.

---

[1] Co2 stands for *Components and Composition*

J. Bishop (Ed.): CD 2002, LNCS 2370, pp. 257–268, 2002.

This reveals that to use a component framework the knowledge of individual component protocols is not sufficient and that describing the messages exchanged among components is also required. Thus we need to accompany the input interface with the description of an *output interface*. In the same way as the input interface comes with a protocol of use, the output interface should sport a *protocol of composition*.

In order to describe these protocols without showing too much of the inner behavior, we propose a protocol model and a lightweight notation that can be used from analysis to reuse time. This graphical notation, called SyncClass, and the associated tools to verify the assembly of components constitute the major topics of this paper. SyncClass diagrams are used to represent both the input and the output protocols of components; they are to be embedded into the components. Since our main objective is to make the verification automatic, SyncClass has to rely on formal semantics. Because of our cultural background as well as for the many tools it proposes, we chose the so-called Synchronous Model [10,4].

This paper is organized as follows: section 2 describes existing techniques used to represent protocols, including the synchronous model itself. Section 3 describes the model and the language of SyncClass, and an example of this notation is used in section 4. Section 5 briefly presents the relationship between the synchronous model and our component model, and section 6 details static and dynamic verification.

2   Models for Components Protocols

In the following, we only mention the most common techniques for representing protocols. To get further information on emerging works in the domain (and even broader) one may refer to the workshop on "Specification and Verification of Component-based Systems" at OOPSLA'01 [1].

Automata-Based Models. A popular choice for representing protocols (of any kind) is finite state machines and their derivatives (e.g., regular expressions, path expressions [7]...). However, it is not suitable to describe complex behavior because automata lack readability when the number of states and/or transitions becomes large.

The work on "regular types" [15] follows the same line. It aims at checking type substitutability [12] and uses automata to specify the protocol of a type. However, regular types do not describe the effect of method calls; thus they are not appropriate to express interactions between components.

Architectural Description Languages. ADLs generally represent the architecture of a system as a combination of two kinds of entities: components and glue [2]. A component is a unit of computation, a connector describes a connection protocol. This model is flexible in that it permits to reuse components or connectors independently. However, even if the component/connector distinction can be twisted to represent components and frameworks [18], we do not think that ADLs are appropriate for blackbox components. Indeed, ADL components have no context dependencies and thus they need connectors to establish links with other components. In the blackbox reuse model, a component is aware of the components to which it connects.

UML-Based Models. UML component diagrams are purely structural and do not depict dynamic information like operation calls and protocols. Sequence diagrams, collaboration diagrams and statecharts specify the dynamic aspects of a system. However, the first two ones are meant to represent only one execution of the system and many diagrams are necessary to cover (even partially) the all the possibilities; the third ones are used to detail the inner states of objects and can also describe protocols [16, p. 2-175]. However, because Statecharts semantics is not satisfactory to build a proof system, most works interested in proof systems have to introduce their own ad hoc formalism[2].

Synchronous Model. In order to represent protocols, we chose the synchronous model [9,4]. It is a specialization of the theory of automata. The reasons for this choice are multiple: the model relies on formal semantics allowing automated proofs [6], and comes with a complete development platform which provides model checkers and simulators. There exists several textual or graphical languages supporting it (Esterel [5], Lustre [10], Argos [13], SyncCharts [3]), and there is a research and commercial support for the tools.

To the best of our knowledge, synchronous languages have never been applied to software component specification, despite their proof capabilities. The description of the synchronous model is out of the scope of this paper; we shall just introduce the concepts we use in section 5.

3   A Model and a Language for the Protocol

3.1   What Do We Mean by a Component?

Our definition of a component includes the following characterisitics: it is a unit of composition, it is encapsulated (it promotes black box reuse), it provides an input interface (a set of operations described by their signatures), it provides an output interface (a set of called operations together with the external components which sport them). These four first items are closed to Szyperski's component definition where "a component is a unit of composition with contractually specified interfaces and explicit context dependencies" [19].

The following three characteristics are related to the execution model that we consider. A component constitutes an unit of execution, acting as a reactive entity, it contains one thread of execution (there might be several but method reentry is not authorized), its methods run to completion. This may appear as

---

[2] To get convinced, one just has to look at the session(s) on Statecharts semantics in the yearly UML Conference.

limitations. Indeed, our work cannot presently support the general concurrency issues. Thus we restrict to a pure sequential use of components, an approach which is still useful in many applications (see for instance [14]).

Finally a component embeds its own documentation. This last characteristics is essential for our work. We claim that a component is not only a piece of code, but that it must contain the documentation for using it. Embedding the documentation constitutes the last step of component development, just before final releasing.

In our view, this documentation must be usable by automatic verification tools and still be readable by human beings. Thus it should externally describe the protocol of the component, without displaying internal details. Moreover, writing this documentation should not constitute extra work ; it should be derivable from the analysis and design models.

3.2   Behavioral Points of View

We introduce the notion of behavioral points of view to describe the protocol of a component from a given perspective. For each component, we identify two such perspectives: the *client point of view* expresses how the component should be used, the *composition points of view* describe how the component uses other components.

To illustrate these points of view, we consider the hypothetical system made of three components presented on figure 1.

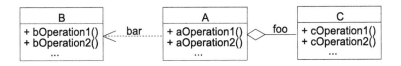

Fig. 1. A system made of three components.

The Client Point of View. The client point of view describes the protocol of use of a component. It is the dynamic counterpart of the static interface: it specifies in which order the component operations can be called. Thanks to this view, a user knows when an operation can be called or when it must not be.

There is one client point of view per component. Thus, in the three components example, there are three client points of view. For instance the client view of A describes the valid order of calls to aOperation1, aOperation2...

Composition Points of View. Whereas the client point of view focuses on the protocol of one component, composition points of view abstract the protocol with which one component uses an other one. Thus, a given component has one composition point of view for each other component to which it is associated.

The composition point of view of component A with respect to component B specifies both the operations of B used by A and the order of the corresponding calls. Thus it constitutes a part of the dynamic specification of the output interface.

For the given example, we have one composition point of view describing how A uses B. It gives the protocol used by A to communicate with B. It represents a relation order over B's operations. A second composition point of view does the same for components A and C. Two more composition points of view are needed to reflect the reverse associations (i.e., B w.r.t. A, and C w.r.t. A).

Relation between Client and Composition Points of View. These two kinds of points of view are not independent. Indeed, the composition point of view of A with respect to B depends on the list of operations called by A and on the order of the corresponding calls. Since these B operations are called from A, it also depends on the order with which A operations are called (that is the client point of view of A).

The corresponding descriptions should not be duplicated; instead, they should be consolidated into a unique (graphical) representation. This representation extends the client point of view of a component A by adding to any operation of A the operations it calls on other components. This synthetic representation, that we call the *component protocol*, not only describes the input interface behavior but also completely specify the dynamics of the output interface. As a consequence, it makes it possible to know the overall communication protocol among components.

The composition points of view are just restrictions of the component protocol. In the example, the composition point of view of A w.r.t. B corresponds to the set of operations that are called by component A and that are defined in B's protocol. The composition points of view can be automatically built from the component protocol. It is important to note that, dualy, the composition point of view of A w.r.t. B is also a restriction of the client point of view of B.

Of course, the number of views increases quickly. However, in a real system, all the views are not required for every component. The component developers will only provide the views for those components for which there is an interest in precise documentation or verification.

Those views are provided with the component they describe. In our three components example, the client point of view of A comes with component A, as does the composition point of view of A w.r.t. B and the one of A w.r.t. C.

3.3 SyncClass: A Graphical Language for Behavioral Points of View

In order to represent those views, we chose to introduce a graphical language, close to what is already known by designers, so it can easily be used and understood. It is named SyncClass[3]. SyncClass inherits from SyncCharts [3], a synchronous extension of Harel's StateCharts [11].

---

[3] We write SyncClass to describe the model, and syncClass to describe an instance of it.

Graphically SyncClass is an automata-based representation, made of states and transitions, as represented on figure 2. Macrostates make it possible to encapsulate a subautomaton and provide a hierarchical decomposition feature. Note that a transition cannot cross the border of a macrostate. The concurrency, expressed in SyncClass by dashed lines splitting a macrostate into several parts, does not represent true runtime concurrency. It indicates that the operations contained in the subparts are not depending on each other. Such a macrostate is said to be *composite*. The notation defines four kinds of transitions. An *initial transition* starts with a black circle; its target is the initial state. A *regular transi-*

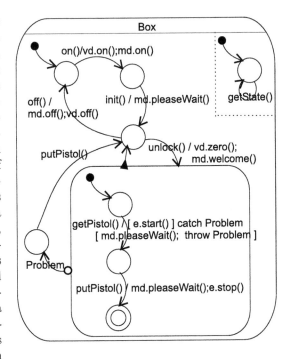

Fig. 2. Example of a SyncClass.

tion is represented by a simple arrow and corresponds to an operation call. An *exception transition* is represented by an arrow starting with a circle and corresponds to an exception raised by the component itself; it means that the component protocol enters some exception mode and it will be the responsibility of the user to catch the exception and to ensure a valid continuation. Finally a *normal termination* transition starts with a triangle; it is automatically triggered when a macrostate reaches a final state (a final state is represented by a double circle).

Only exception transitions and regular transitions can and must be labeled. For regular transitions, the label is divided into two parts separated by a slash. The left part represents the signature of the operation that will *trigger* the transition, and the right part (also called the *action* part) is an abstraction of the operation behavior: it uses a small language to describe the control flow of the operation designated in the left part. This language offers optionality[4] (indicated by a # prefix), iteration (a list of instructions enclosed within braces), exception catching ([...] catch *exception* [...]) and raising (operator throw), and operation call (using the dot notation to specify the target component). Semicolons separate instructions and indicate sequentiality. The label of exception transi-

---

[4] The condition expression itself is not represented: the inner state is not shown and thus encapsulation is not broken.

tions is only made of a left part representing the exception that causes this transition to be triggered.

Thus a syncClass represents the overall protocol of a component: the left part of transitions corresponds to the client point of view whereas the right part corresponds to the composition ones.

The operational semantics of SyncClass is the following: the initialization of a syncClass is done by activating all top level macrostates, which is equivalent to triggering their initial transition, that is to activate their initial state. This is done recursively. After the initialization has been done and all along the syncClass "execution", several states may be active. Regular and exception transitions are triggered when their origin state is active and the corresponding operation [resp. exception] is called [resp. raised]. When a transition leaving an active macrostate[5] is triggered, the macrostate is no longer active. When an active simple macrostate reaches its final state, its normal termination transition (if any) is triggered. The end of a composite macrostate is reached when every subpart reaches its end. When an unexpected trigger occurs, it is considered as an error.

When a transition is triggered, the associated action part is executed which causes its messages to be sent. If an instruction is marked as optional, this indicates the possibility of several exclusive execution paths.

4   An Example: A Petrol Pump

This section gives an example of syncClass to represent the behavioral points of view of a petrol pump system. The petrol pump is made of five components: a box, a pistol, an engine, a volume display, and a message display. The class diagram on figure 3 describes the associations among the components. The role names on the associations will be used to denote target components when sending messages.

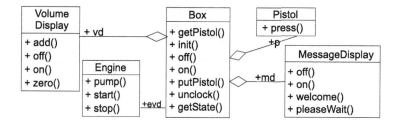

Fig. 3. Class diagram of the petrol pump.

---

[5] A macrostate is said to be active if it contains an active (macro)state.

In fact, figure 2 presents the component protocol of the Box. The Box is considered as the "main" component since it switches the others on. The client point of view indicates that operation on needs to be called first. One can also see that operation on of the box calls operations on of the volume and message displays. Only once the on operation of the box has been executed, can the operation init be called. The action part on the getPistol transition, shows an example of exception catching.

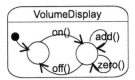

Fig. 4. Component protocol of the volume display.

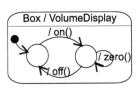

Fig. 5. Composition view of the box with respect to the volume display component.

The component protocol of the volume display presents the sequence of authorized operations (figure 4). The absence of action on the transitions in the protocol indicates that this component can be used alone.

The composition point of view of the box w.r.t. the volume display (figure 5) specifies the order in which the operations of VolumeDisplay are called by the Box. It is a restriction of the protocol of Box. By comparing this composition point of view to the client point of view of VolumeDisplay (figure 4), one can deduce that VolumeDisplay is probably used by something else than Box. Indeed the box only uses a subset of VolumeDisplay operations (operation add is not called). Facing such a situation, the user needs to determine whether the missing operations are called by other components or whether he/she is required to call them.

5   SyncClass and the Synchronous Model

As indicated in section 2, we use the synchronous model as a formal basis. This model allows us to use its model checkers, its simulators, and its languages either textual like Esterel [5] or its graphical equivalent, the SyncCharts [3]. We could not use the usual synchronous notation since our model differs from the synchronous one on the following points: an operation call cannot be considered as instantaneous (we need to distinguish beginning and end of methods); we do not need a general broadcast ; we have to make our SyncClass model deterministic, even though the application is not. Thus we have an automatic translation of SyncClass to SyncCharts. However we are short of space to describe the translations.

6   Verification of Components Assembly

6.1   Static Verification

The mapping to a semantically sound model allows to use model checkers for static verification. We support two kinds of static verification. One checks the compatibility of one component with respect to another one and the other checks a complete system of components.

For both kinds of verification we use model checking [6,9]. Indeed, it provides automatic tools to prove properties on automata. These properties are classically represented by observers, which are also synchronous (SyncCharts), composed in parallel with the system to prove. The proof relies on the exploration of the overall state space (system and observers).

Checking the Compatibility of One Component with an Other One. Here the objective is to check whether a given component, say A, correctly uses an other component, say B, with which it is associated. In our model this means to verify the compatibility between the composition view of A w.r.t. B and the client view of B. In the example of the petrol pump, one could check whether the box correctly uses the volume display. To do so, we consider the composition point of view of the box w.r.t. the volume display (figure 5), and the client point of view of the volume display (figure 4).

We associate an observer to each operation. Its role is to check that each call is correctly received. For this the operation is instrumented, so that it sends an acknowledge signal (ack) when it starts. Owing to synchronous signals broadcast, the observer has just to check that the call and the acknowledge match each other. Figure 6 presents the observer for operation on of component Box: if the operation is called and no acknowledge is received, an error signal is emitted (KO). The observers as well as the needed instrumentation are automatically generated.

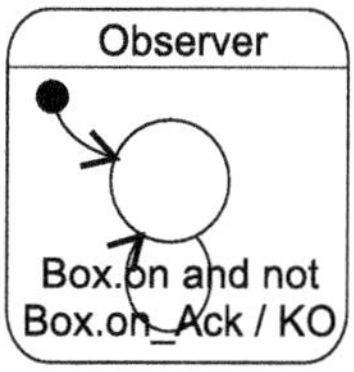

Fig. 6.   SyncCharts of the observer used for static verifications.

Then the client point of view of the box and one of the composition point of view are composed in parallel together with the observers for all the operations involved in the composition point of view. The result is fed into the model checker which is then asked to find whether the KO message can possibly be emitted.

System Checking. The goal of this second kind of static verification is to check whether an assembly of components can cooperate so that each component respects the others protocol. For example, one can check whether the five components constituting the petrol pump can work together.

This verification requires a specification of the (overall) protocols of all the components. They contain all the information required: the protocol, and the interaction of a component with the others. The verification also requires an observer which listens to all operation calls and check that they are all correctly received. This observer is thus a parallel composition of simple observers such as the one in figure 6.

It is necessary to constrain the exploration order of the model checker, so that call sequences that are known to be erroneous are not considered–otherwise the checker will automatically fail since unexpected operation will be called. Such sequences can be automatically computed from component protocols. If an error occurs (KO gets emitted) the model checker is able to display a sequence of operation calls causing the problem. If no error appears, then it is sure that the system under test will behave correctly provided that it is used correctly.

Instead of being computed from component protocols, the input sequences can be produced by the user. An interesting case is when they are derived from the user glue code. The check will then indicate whether or not the system fails when used by the glue. This can be seen as a kind of integration test.

Another benefit is to verify component replacement. If we substitute a component with another one in a validated system, the same verification techniques apply to check whether this substitution is correct.

Both kinds of static verification have been implemented and the petrol pump has been checked. The verification of the whole system took approximately 26 seconds on a Pentium III 1Ghz.

6.2   Run-Time Verification

The goal of run-time verification is to detect operation calls which do not respect component protocols. For this, we use the syncClass embedded within the component. Each operation call is dynamically checked against this syncClass.

To avoid two versions of each component, one for debug and one for the final release, we have to trap operation calls: we use meta-programming techniques when applicable. We successfully implemented dynamic verification [17], first for simple classes using Javassist [8], then for JavaBeans components using their built-in meta-facilities. For these examples, the documentation has been embedded into the component most suitable format. For JavaBeans, we enhanced the meta information associated with the beans so that it may contain the protocol. For the classes, we added the documentation in the user attribute zone of the classfile.

7   Conclusion

This paper introduces a graphical notation, named SyncClass, to describe component protocols of use. This protocol is composed of two kinds of behavioral points of view: the client view describes the valid sequences of operations that can be applied to the component; the composition view specifies the way one component uses another one. In this approach, the documentation is fully integrated into each component and SyncClass constitute an essential part of it.

SyncClass relies on the Synchronous Model, which permits to take advantage of synchronous platforms and tools. In particular we show how model checkers can use the embedded syncClasses to automatically verify components assembly, at the individual component level as well as at system level. The same documentation may also be used at run-time to dynamically check proper component usage.

The Co2 environment, the context of this work, provides tools to ensure the consistency between component implementation and their protocol documentation. This is even more true when the syncClasses can be derived from the design documents. Most of the Co2 tools (SyncClas editor and generator, code generator, interface with model checker...) have been implemented, only a test generator is missing. Co2 addresses not only the component developer's task but also the component user's one. The embedded documentation (especially SyncClass) bridges the gap between the two activities.

Some features of SyncClass were not presented here. The most important one is callback specification, which is part of the composite view. Another is the possibility to handle a restricted form of concurrency instead of assuming a pure sequential usage of components.

Other features would be desirable, such as supporting a general model of concurrency. An other important issue is related to the graphical representation of component interfaces (both input and output) and component interconnections. A third improvement would be to handle component inheritance and substitutability. These features will constitute the topic of future work.

In a near future we shall also experiment our notation and tools on bigger examples, such as the framework BLOCKS [14] in order to demonstrate the applicability of our approach to real life systems.

References

1. Specification and verification of component-based systems workshop at OOPSLA 2001. Workshop ISU TR 01-09a, Department of Computer Science, 2001.
2. Robert Allen and David Garlan. A formal basis for architectural connection. *ACM Transactions on Software Engineering and Methodology*, 6(3):213–249, July 1997.
3. Charles André. Representation and analysis of reactive behaviors : a synchronous approach. In *CESA*, pages 19–29, july 1996.
4. Gérard Berry. *Proof, Language and Interaction: Essays in Honour of Robin Milner*, chapter The foundations of Esterel. MIT Press, 2000.
5. Gérard Berry and Georges Gonthier. The ESTEREL synchronous programming language: design, semantics, implementation. *Science of Computer Programming*, 19(2):87–152, 1992.
6. Amard Bouali. Xeve: An esterel verification environment (version v1.3). Technical Report RT-214, INRIA, October 1997.
7. R. Campbell and N. Habermann. The specification of process synchronization by path expressions. In *Proc. Int. Symp. on Operating Systems*, LNCS 16, pages 89–102. Springer-Verlag, 1974.
8. Shigeru Chiba. Load-time structural reflection in Java. In *ECOOP 2000, Sophia Antipolis and Cannes, France*, LNCS 1850, pages 313–336. Springer-Verlag.
9. Edmund M. Clarke, Orna Grumberg, and Doron A. Peled. *Model Checking*. The MIT Press, Cambridge, Massachusetts, 1999.
10. Nicolas Halbwachs. *Synchronous Programming of Reactive Systems*. Kluwer Academic, 1993.
11. David Harel. Statecharts: A visual formalism for complex system. *Science of Computer Programming*, 8(3):231–274, 1987.
12. Barbara Liskov and Jeannette M. Wing. A new definition of the subtype relation. In *ECOOP '93, Kaiserslautern, Germany*, LNCS 707, pages 118–141. Springer-Verlag.

13. Florence Maraninchi. Operational and compositional semantics of synchronous automaton compositions. In *CONCUR '92*, LNCS 630, pages 550–564. Springer-Verlag, 24–27 1992.
14. Sabine Moisan, Annie Ressouche, and Jean-Paul Rigault. BLOCKS, a Component Framework with Checking Facilities for Knowledge-Based Systems. *Informatica*, 25(4), 2001.
15. Oscar Nierstrasz. Regular types for active objects. In Oscar Nierstrasz and Dennis Tsichritzis, editors, *Object-Oriented Software Composition*, pages 99–121. Prentice Hall, 1995.
16. Object Management Group (OMG). OMG Unified Modeling Language Specification. URL: http://www.omg.org/, February 2001. version 1.4 (draft).
17. Pascal Rapicault and Frédéric Mallet. Behavioral specification of Java components using SyncCharts. In *Workshop on pervasive component systems*, June 2000.
18. Joãn Pedro Sousa and David Garlan. Formal modeling of the enterprise JavaBeans component integration framework. In *FM'99*, LNCS 1709, pages 1281–. Springer Verlag, September 1999.
19. Clemens Szyperski. *Component Software: Beyond Object-Oriented Programming*. ACM Press and Addison-Wesley, New York, NY, 1998.

Author Index

Lecture Notes in Computer Science

For information about Vols. 1–2287
please contact your bookseller or Springer-Verlag